# Summary of Contents

# Build Your Own AJAX Web Applications

by Matthew Eernisse

# Build Your Own AJAX Web Applications

by Matthew Eernisse

Copyright © 2006 SitePoint Pty. Ltd.

**Expert Reviewer**: Stuart Langridge **Editor**: Georgina Laidlaw
**Managing Editor**: Simon Mackie **Index Editor**: Bill Johncocks
**Technical Editor**: Craig Anderson **Cover Design**: Jess Bentley
**Technical Director**: Kevin Yank **Cover Layout**: Alex Walker
**Printing History**:
 First Edition: June 2006

Published by SitePoint Pty. Ltd.

424 Smith Street Collingwood
VIC Australia 3066.
Web: www.sitepoint.com
Email: business@sitepoint.com

ISBN 0–9758419–4–7
Printed and bound in the United States of America

## About the Author

Matthew lives in Houston, Texas, USA, and works for the Open Source Applications Foundation building the web UIs for Scooby, a next-generation web-based calendar client, and Cosmo, a calendar server. In his abundant free time, he writes about AJAX, JavaScript, Ruby, and PHP at Fleegix.org, and operates EpiphanyRadio, a webcast radio station. Matthew plays drums and speaks fluent Japanese.

## About the Expert Reviewer

Stuart Langridge has been playing with the Web since 1994, and is quite possibly the only person in the world to have a BSc in Computer Science and Philosophy. He invented the term "unobtrusive DHTML" and has been a leader in the quest to popularize this new approach to scripting. When not working on the Web, he's a keen Linux user and part of the team at open-source radio show LUGRadio, and likes drinking decent beers, studying stone circles and other ancient phenomena, and trying to learn the piano.

## About the Technical Director

As Technical Director for SitePoint, Kevin Yank oversees all of its technical publications—books, articles, newsletters, and blogs. He has written over 50 articles for SitePoint, but is best known for his book, *Build Your Own Database Driven Website Using PHP & MySQL*. Kevin lives in Melbourne, Australia, and enjoys performing improvised comedy theatre and flying light aircraft.

## About SitePoint

SitePoint specializes in publishing fun, practical, and easy-to-understand content for web professionals. Visit http://www.sitepoint.com/ to access our books, newsletters, articles, and community forums.

*To my wife, Masako, and my three little boys—Hiromasa, Akira, and Yoshiki—for all their love, patience, and support.*

# Table of Contents

# Preface

In the ten years or so since I made my first static web page, it's been amazing to see the evolution of the Web as a platform—first for the exchange of information, and then for actual applications, running right in the browser. And now the AJAX explosion is taking web development to the next level. Using the power of AJAX-style development, you can create applications that rival desktop apps in their power and responsiveness and, best of all, you don't have to rely on ugly hacks and kludges to get there.

What is AJAX? The acronym originally stood for "Asynchronous JavaScript and XML"—quite a mouthful—but it has since come to refer to a style of development that uses web technologies like XML, DOM, CSS, and JavaScript to create uber-interactive web documents that behave like full-blown applications. None of these AJAX technologies are actually all that new (even the AJAX "secret sauce," XMLHttpRequest, has been around for years), but not a lot of people really knew how to use them to the fullest. Now, with the proliferation of "Web 2.0" applications that push the web-app envelope, and its cool, easy-to-remember name, the AJAX style of development is really starting to take off.

In the early days, web apps used server-side scripting like CGI, as well as simple web forms and image rollovers in the browser. Now we're seeing developers take major steps forward to enhance the user experience with the ability to update the UI in pieces, instead of requiring a single, enormous redraw, and client-side functionality like drag-and-drop and edit-in-place. Today's web applications are more interconnected as well, and are sometimes made up of data from multiple services or sources. A browser-based AJAX app is a fantastic platform for providing this kind of super-interactive, networked app experience to users. And the best part is that the AJAX revolution is still just getting started, so now's a great time to jump in.

This book gives me a chance to show some cool ways in which you can use AJAX techniques to add real power and responsiveness to your web applications while supporting accessibility and backward compatibility. The beauty of AJAX is that it lets you do all this using straightforward, standards-based code, so you won't be seeing weird hacks or browser-specific code in this book. So, roll up your sleeves—I hope you're ready to get your hands dirty in some AJAX code!

# Who Should Read this Book?

This book is aimed primarily at web application developers who are already familiar with basic client-side web technologies like CSS and JavaScript.

If that's not you, don't be put off: this book will suit you if you're willing to do some learning as you go. JavaScript syntax is pretty straightforward, and we're using plain, vanilla code that's pretty much free of browser-specific workarounds. We also provide links to valuable resources that you can use to learn more about the technologies used in AJAX development.

Some traditional applications programmers may also find this book of interest for seeing how they can create a real desktop-app-style user interface that runs in a browser. More and more of these guys will be looking to dip their toes into the AJAX pool as "web application development" and plain "application development" continue to converge.

# What's In this Book?

This book contains eight chapters. Each chapter builds on the concepts and techniques introduced in the previous ones, so if you're still fairly new to web development, you're probably better off to take the chapters step by step, in order. If you're a battle-hardened veteran, it might make more sense for you to jump around among the topics that interest you.

### Chapter 1: AJAX: The Overview
This chapter takes you through a quick overview of AJAX and the technological building blocks that work together to make an AJAX web application. It also looks back briefly on the ugly coding gymnastics that web developers had to use back in the Bad Old Days before AJAX, to help explain why AJAX is such a massive step forward. If you're not an old hand at web development, this chapter will provide an introduction to the basic technologies you'll need in order to embark upon modern client-side web development with AJAX.

### Chapter 2: Basic XMLHttpRequest
XMLHttpRequest is the heart and soul of AJAX. It makes AJAX web development possible by allowing browsers to make HTTP requests to a server without reloading the page. This chapter takes you through the process of putting together a very simple AJAX JavaScript library; it will give you a good grounding in how XMLHttpRequest makes requests, and an understanding of the different ways you can access the results returned from the server.

With the under-the-hood knowledge of XMLHttpRequest you'll get from this chapter, you'll be able to work with almost any JavaScript XMLHttpRequest library, and confidently diagnose and debug issues with XMLHttpRequest in your web application.

### Chapter 3: The "A" in AJAX

A is for "asynchronous." Asynchronicity is what makes AJAX so cool: XMLHttpRequest gives you the power to pull content from the server any time you want, without reloading the entire web page. In this chapter, you'll build your first real AJAX app—a web app monitor that uses XMLHttpRequest to poll a server with basic HTTP GET requests, and reports the time it takes to get a response. This app demonstrates some of the complexity we must deal with in a browser-based AJAX app, including the timing of events, timeouts, and keeping users continuously informed about what the application is doing with the help of animations and status messages.

### Chapter 4: AJAX and POST Requests

We move to the grown-ups' table in this chapter, which focuses on AJAX HTTP POST requests. POST is the bread-and-butter of web forms, and the process of sending packages of data back to the server. Combining it with some tasty AJAX can make your app a lot more palatable to users. The demonstration code in this chapter shows off one of the optimal uses for AJAX: it's a web app login that uses XMLHttpRequest to pass user authentication data back to the server, and displays status messages inline on the page. You'll also learn how to create this kind of AJAX-y UI without breaking the app's accessibility or backwards compatibility.

### Chapter 5: Broader AJAX with Edit-in-place

When non-developer types talk about AJAX web applications, they usually mean more than just XMLHttpRequest. In this chapter, we'll demonstrate a little of what those people are talking about as we discuss edit-in-place. The demo code for this chapter creates a basic blog page that lets you edit the entries right on the page, instead of having to go to a separate web form. It displays a nice, fading color animation effect to let users know when the application is busy processing their edits.

### Chapter 6: Web Services and Slide-and-hide

This chapter moves us into the interconnected Web 2.0 world with a basic overview of web services and a demonstration that shows how you can wire up your AJAX web app to them. The application we'll work with in this chapter plugs into Amazon's ECS (E-Commerce Service) web service with some simple REST-style HTTP requests to perform book searches. Unlike a boring old web form submission that loads the results in a new page, this app pulls down the XML results, formats them nicely, then uses a cool slide-and-hide effect to insert them right into the page.

### Chapter 7: More Web Services and a **Back** Button

There's more to web services than REST. This chapter goes into more depth on the topic of web services, providing example code for an accessible AJAX search application that talks to the Google Web APIs, Del.icio.us, and the EBay platform using more sophisticated methods such as SOAP and XML-RPC. We also discuss two separate ways to fix the classic AJAX Back Button Problem—one that builds navigation for the search history into the application, and a hack that forces the browser's real Back button to behave properly.

### Chapter 8: Drag and Drop with AJAX Chess

This final chapter uses an in-the-browser game of AJAX Chess to demonstrate a sophisticated drag-and-drop interface in which absolute-positioned UI elements are placed relative to the window size, drag constraints are used, and drop functionality triggers XMLHttpRequest requests to the server to save each move in the game. The complex interactivity of this app is managed through a global event listener setup that routes all user input through a single point, but gives you the flexibility to process events the way you want. The AJAX Chess game also shows a basic way to synchronize the application state between browsers with polling, and how to abort and revert to a previous state in the event of a server error.

## This Book's Web Site

Located at http://www.sitepoint.com/books/ajax1/, the web site supporting this book will give you access to the following facilities.

## The Code Archive

As you progress through the text, you'll note a number of references to the code archive. This is a downloadable ZIP archive that contains complete code for all the examples presented in this book. You can download the code archive from http://www.sitepoint.com/books/ajax1/code.php

## Updates and Errata

The Corrections and Typos page on the book's web site, at http://www.sitepoint.com/books/ajax1/errata.php will always have the latest information about known typographical and code errors, and necessary updates for changes to technologies.

## The SitePoint Forums

While I've made every attempt to anticipate any questions you may have, and answer them in this book, there is no way that any book could cover everything there is to know about AJAX. If you have a question about anything in this book, the best place to go for a quick answer is SitePoint's Forums[1]—SitePoint's vibrant and knowledgeable community.

## The SitePoint Newsletters

In addition to books like this one, SitePoint offers free email newsletters. The *SitePoint Tech Times* covers the latest news, product releases, trends, tips, and techniques for all technical aspects of web development. The long-running *SitePoint Tribune* is a biweekly digest of the business and moneymaking aspects of the Web. Whether you're a freelance developer looking for tips to score that dream contract, or a marketing major striving to keep abreast of changes to the major search engines, this is the newsletter for you. The *SitePoint Design View* is a monthly compilation of the best in web design. From new CSS layout methods to subtle Photoshop techniques, SitePoint's chief designer shares his years of experience in its pages. Browse the archives or sign up to any of SitePoint's free newsletters at http://www.sitepoint.com/newsletter/.

## Your Feedback

If you can't find your answer through the forums, or you wish to contact me for any other reason, the best place to write is books@sitepoint.com. SitePoint has a well-manned email support system set up to track your inquiries, and if the support staff are unable to answer your question, they send it straight to me. Suggestions for improvement as well as notices of any mistakes you may find are especially welcome.

## Acknowledgements

Any author is only as good as his editors. I'd like to extend a sincere and heartfelt thanks for the great work done by Simon Mackie, my editor, and Stuart Langridge,

---

[1] http://www.sitepoint.com/forums/

my expert reviewer. Their advice and feedback have made this book immeasurably better. Much appreciation also goes to Georgina Laidlaw, my language editor, and Craig Anderson, my tech editor, for their hard work keeping the train on the tracks.

I'd also like to express a word of thanks to a few other people who had a hand in the creation of this book either directly or indirectly: Mitch Kapor and everyone at OSAF, for being so incredibly brilliant, and giving me such a great opportunity to learn; RMS and Linus, for all the open-source goodness; all the folks in #javascript on Freenode, from the clueless to the cranky to the crazy-smart, for providing endless hours of both education and entertainment; Robbie and Will, for opportunity; Ed and Hugh, for early programming help; and Neil, Geddy, and Alex, for giving a geeky kid some inspiration back in the day, and producing some great music to write a book to.

# 1

# AJAX: the Overview

*He's escaping, idiot! Dispatch War Rocket Ajax! To bring back his body!*
—General Kala, *Flash Gordon*

So here you are, book in hand, ready to learn all about this thing called **AJAX**. But, what exactly is it? The term AJAX refers to a loose grouping of technologies that are used to create dynamic, interactive web content.

The term AJAX, originally coined by Jesse James Garrett of Adaptive Path in his essay *AJAX: A New Approach To Web Applications,*[1] is an acronym for "Asynchronous JavaScript And XML." That's a bit of a mouthful, but it's simply describing a technique that uses JavaScript to refresh a page's contents from a web server without having to reload the entire page. This is different from the traditional method of updating web pages, which requires the browser to refresh the entire page in order to display any changes to the content.

Similar techniques have been around in one form or another (often achieved with the help of some clever hacks) for quite a while. But the increasing availability of the `XMLHttpRequest` class in browsers, the coining of the catchy term AJAX, and the advent of a number of high-profile examples such as Google Maps,[2]

---

[1] http://adaptivepath.com/publications/essays/archives/000385.php
[2] http://maps.google.com/

Gmail,[3] Backpack,[4] and Flickr,[5] have allowed these kinds of highly interactive web applications to begin to gain traction in the development world.

As the term AJAX has become more widespread, its definition has expanded to refer more generally to browser-based applications that behave much more dynamically than old-school web apps. This new crop of AJAX web applications make more extensive use of interaction techniques like edit-in-place text, drag-and-drop, and CSS animations or transitions to effect changes within the user interface. This book will explain those techniques, and show you how to develop AJAX web applications of your own.

# AJAX Web Applications

AJAX can be a great solution for many web development projects—it can empower web apps to step up and take over a lot of the ground that previously was occupied almost exclusively by desktop applications.

All the same, it's important to keep in mind that AJAX is not a sort of magic fairy dust that you can sprinkle on your app to make it whizzy and cool. Like any other new development technique, AJAX isn't difficult to mis-use, and the only thing worse than a horrible, stodgy, old-school web app is a horrible, poorly executed AJAX web app.

When you apply it to the right parts of your web application, in the right ways, AJAX can enhance users' experience of your application significantly. AJAX can improve the interactivity and speed of your app, ultimately making that application easier, more fun, and more intuitive to use.

Often, AJAX applications are described as being "like a desktop application in the browser." This is a fairly accurate description—AJAX web apps are significantly more responsive than traditional, old-fashioned web applications, and they can provide levels of interactivity similar to those of desktop applications.

But an AJAX web app is still a remote application, and behaves differently from a desktop application that has access to local storage. Part of your job as an AJAX developer is to craft applications that feel responsive and easy to use despite the communication that must occur between the app and a distant server. Fortunately,

---

[3] http://mail.google.com/
[4] http://www.backpackit.com/
[5] http://flickr.com/

the AJAX toolbox gives you a number of excellent techniques to accomplish exactly that.

# The Bad Old Days

One of the first web development tasks that moved beyond serving simple, static HTML pages was the technique of building pages dynamically on the web server using data from a back-end data store.

Back in the "bad old days" of web development, the only way to create this dynamic, database-driven content was to construct the entire page on the server side, using either a CGI script (most likely written in Perl), or some server component that could interpret a scripting language (such as Microsoft's Active Server Pages). Even a single change to that page necessitated a round trip from browser to server—only then could the new content be presented to the user.

In those days, the normal model for a web application's user interface was a web form that the user would fill out and submit to the server. The server would process the submitted form, and send an entirely new page back to the browser for display as a result. So, for example, the completion of a multi-step, web-based "wizard" would require the user to submit a form—thereby prompting a round-trip between the browser and the server—for each step.

Granted, this was a huge advance on static web pages, but it was still a far cry from presenting a true "application" experience to end-users.

# Prehistoric AJAX

Early web developers immediately began to look for tricks to extend the capabilities of that simple forms-based model, as they strove to create web applications that were more responsive and interactive. These hacks, while fairly ad hoc and crude, were the first steps web developers took toward the kind of interactivity we see in today's AJAX applications. But, while these tricks and workarounds often provided serviceable, working solutions, the resulting code was not a pretty sight.

## Nesting Framesets

One way to get around the problem of having to reload the entire page in order to display even the smallest change to its content was the hideous hack of nesting framesets within other framesets, often several levels deep. This technique allowed developers to update only selected areas of the screen, and even to mimic the behavior of tab-style navigation interfaces in which users' clicking on tabs in one part of the screen changed content in another area.

This technique resulted in horrible, unmaintainable code with profusions of pages that had names like `EmployeeEditWizardMiddleLowerRight.asp`.

## The Hidden `iframe`

The addition of the `iframe` in browsers like Internet Explorer 4 made things much less painful. The ability to hide the `iframe` completely led to the development of another neat hack: developers would make HTTP requests to the server using a hidden `iframe`, then insert the content into the page using JavaScript and DHTML. This provided much of the same functionality that's available through modern AJAX, including the ability to submit data from forms without reloading the page—a feat that was achieved by having the form submit to the hidden `iframe`. The result was returned by the server to the `iframe`, where the page's JavaScript could access it.

The big drawback of this approach (beyond the fact that it was, after all, a hack) was the annoying burden of passing data back and forth between the main document and the document in the `iframe`.

## Remote Scripting

Another early AJAX-like technique, usually referred to as **remote scripting**, involved setting the `src` attribute of a `<script>` tag to load pages that contained dynamically generated JavaScript.

This had the advantage of being much cleaner than the hidden `iframe` hack, as the JavaScript generated on the server would load right into the main document. However, only simple `GET` requests were possible using this technique.

# What Makes AJAX Cool

This is why AJAX development is such an enormous leap forward for web development: instead of having to send everything to the server in a single, huge mass, then wait for the server to send back a new page for rendering, web developers can communicate with the server in smaller chunks, and selectively update specific areas of the page based on the server's responses to those requests. This is where the word **asynchronous** in the AJAX acronym originated.

It's probably easiest to understand the idea of an asynchronous system by considering its opposite—a synchronous system. In a synchronous system, everything occurs in order. If a car race was a synchronous system, it would be a very dull affair. The car that started first on the grid would be the first across the finish line, followed by the car that started second, and so on. There would be no overtaking, and if a car broke down, the traffic behind would be forced to stop and wait while the mechanics made their repairs.

Traditional web apps use a synchronous system: you must wait for the server to send you the first page of a system before you can request the second page, as shown in Figure 1.1.

## Figure 1.1. A traditional web app is a synchronous system

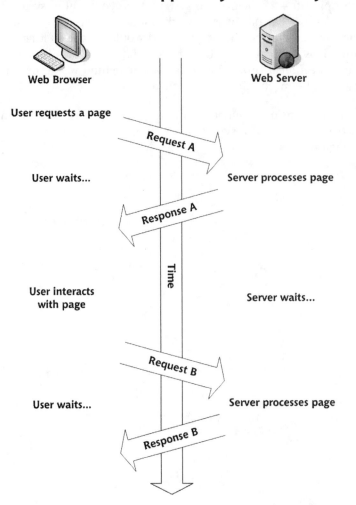

An asynchronous car race would be a lot more exciting. The car in pole position could be overtaken on the first corner, and the car that starts from the back of the grid could weave its way through the field and cross the finish line in third place. The HTTP requests from the browser in an AJAX application work in exactly this way. It's this ability to make lots of small requests to the server on a needs-basis that makes AJAX development so cool. Figure 1.2 shows an AJAX application making asynchronous requests to a web server.

## Figure 1.2. An AJAX web app is an asynchronous system

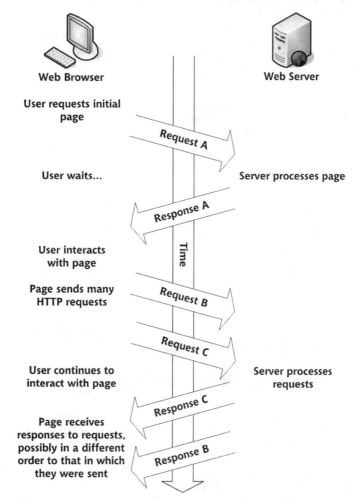

The end result is an application that feels much more responsive, as users spend significantly less time waiting for requests to process, and don't have to wait for an entire new web page to come across the wire, and be rendered by their browsers, before they can view the results.

# AJAX Technologies

The technologies that are used to build AJAX web applications encompass a number of different programming domains, so AJAX development is neither as straightforward as regular applications development, nor as easy as old-school web development.

On the other hand, the fact that AJAX development embraces so many different technologies makes it a lot more interesting and fun. Here's a brief listing of the technologies that work together to make an AJAX web application:

❑ XML

❑ the W3C DOM

❑ CSS

❑ XMLHttpRequest

❑ JavaScript

Through the rest of this chapter, we'll meet each of these technologies and discuss the roles they play in an AJAX web application.

# Data Exchange and Markup: XML

XML[6] is where AJAX gets its letter "X." This is fortunate, because tech acronyms are automatically seen as being much cooler if they contain the letter "X." (Yes, I *am* kidding!)

## Data Exchange Lingua Franca

XML often serves as the main data format used in the asynchronous HTTP requests that communicate between the browser and the server in an AJAX application. This role plays to XML's strengths as a neutral and fairly simple data exchange format, and also means that it's relatively easy to reuse or reformat content if the need arises.

---

[6]XML stands for Extensible Markup Language—not that anyone ever calls it that outside of textbooks.

There are, of course, numerous other ways to format your data for easy exchange between the browser and the server,[7] but XML is one of the most common.

# XML as Markup

The web pages in AJAX applications consist of XHTML markup, which is actually just a flavor of XML. XHTML, as the successor to HTML, is very similar to it. It's easily picked up by any developer who's familiar with old-school HTML, yet it boasts all the benefits of valid XML. There are numerous advantages to using XHTML:

❑ It offers lots of standard tools and script libraries for viewing, editing, and validating XML.

❑ It's forward-compatible with newer, XML-compatible browsers.

❑ It works with either the HTML Document Object Model (DOM) or the XML DOM.

❑ It's more easily repurposed for viewing in non-browser agents.

Some of the more pedantic folks in the development community insist that people should not yet be using XHTML. They believe very strongly that XHTML, since it is actual XML, should not be used at all unless it can be served with a proper HTTP `Content-Type` header of `application/xhtml+xml`,[8] for which, at present, there is still limited browser support. (Internet Explorer 6 and 7 do not support it at all.)

In practice, you can serve XHTML to the browser with a `Content-Type` of `text/html`, as all the mainstream browsers render correctly all XHTML documents served as `text/html`. Although browsers will treat your code as plain old HTML, other programs can still interpret it as XML, so there's no practical reason not to "future-proof" your markup by using it.

If you happen to disagree with me, you can choose instead to develop using the older HTML 4.01 standard. This is still a viable web standard, and is a perfectly legitimate choice to make in developing your web application.

---

[7] Such as CSV (comma separated values), JSON (JavaScript object notation), or simply plain text.
[8] `text/xml` and `application/xml` would also be okay, though they're less descriptive.

**XHTML and this Book**

Most of the code examples in this book will use XHTML 1.0 Strict. The `iframe` element is not available in Strict, so the few code examples we show using the `iframe` will be XHTML 1.0 Transitional.

The World Wide Web Consortium maintains an FAQ on the differences between HTML and XHTML[9].

# W3C Document Object Model

The Document Object Model (DOM) is an object-oriented representation of XML and HTML documents, and provides an API for changing the content, structure, and style of those documents.

Originally, specific browsers like Netscape Navigator and Internet Explorer provided differing, proprietary ways to manipulate HTML documents using JavaScript. The DOM arose from efforts by the World Wide Web Consortium (W3C) to provide a platform- and browser-neutral way to achieve the same tasks.

The DOM represents the structure of an XML or HTML document as an object hierarchy, which is ideal for parsing by standard XML tools.

## DOM Manipulation Methods

JavaScript provides a large API for dealing with these DOM structures, in terms of both parsing and manipulating the document. This is one of the primary ways to accomplish the smaller, piece-by-piece changes to a web page that we see in an AJAX application.[10]

## DOM Events

The other important function of the DOM is that it provides a standard means for JavaScript to attach events to elements on a web page. This makes possible much richer user interfaces, because it allows you to give users opportunities to interact with the page beyond simple links and form elements.

A great example of this is drag-and-drop functionality, which lets users drag pieces of the page around on the screen, and drop them into place to trigger specific

---

[9] http://www.w3.org/MarkUp/2004/xhtml-faq
[10]Another method is simply to change the `innerHTML` property of an element. This method is not well documented in any standard, though it's widely supported by mainstream browsers.

pieces of functionality. This kind of feature used to exist only in desktop applications, but now it works just as well in the browser, thanks to the DOM.

# Presentation: CSS

CSS (Cascading Style Sheets) provides a unified method for controlling the appearance of user interface elements in your web application. You can use CSS to change almost any aspect of the way the page looks, from font sizes, colors, and spacing, to the positioning of elements.

In an AJAX application, one very good use of CSS is to provide user-interface feedback (with CSS-driven animations and transitions), or to indicate portions of the page with which the user can interact (with changes to color or appearance triggered, for example, by mouseovers). For example, you can use CSS transitions to indicate that some part of your application is waiting for an HTTP request that's processing on the server.

CSS manipulation figures heavily in the broader definition of the term AJAX—in various visual transitions and effects, as well as in drag-and-drop and edit-in-place functionality.

# Communication: `XMLHttpRequest`

`XMLHttpRequest`, a JavaScript class with a very easy-to-use interface, sends and receives HTTP requests and responses to and from web servers. The `XMLHttpRequest` class is what makes true AJAX application development possible. The HTTP requests made with `XMLHttpRequest` work just as if the browser were making normal requests to load a page or submit a form, but without the user ever having to leave the currently loaded web page.

Microsoft first implemented `XMLHttpRequest` in Internet Explorer 5 for Windows as an ActiveX object. The Mozilla project provided a JavaScript-native version with a compatible API in the Mozilla browser, starting in version 1.0. (It's also available in Firefox, of course.) Apple has added `XMLHttpRequest` to Safari since version 1.2.

The response from the server—either an XML document or a string of text—can be passed to JavaScript to use however the developer sees fit—often to update some piece of the web application's user interface.

## Putting it All Together: JavaScript

JavaScript is the glue that holds your AJAX application together. It performs multiple roles in AJAX development:

❏ controlling HTTP requests that are made using `XMLHttpRequest`

❏ parsing the result that comes back from the server, using either DOM manipulation methods, XSLT, or custom methods, depending on the data exchange format used

❏ presenting the resulting data in the user interface, either by using DOM manipulation methods to insert content into the web page, by updating an element's `innerHTML` property, or by changing elements' CSS properties

Because of its long history of use in lightweight web programming (and at the hands of inexperienced programmers), JavaScript has not been seen by many traditional application developers as a "serious programming language," despite the fact that, in reality, it's a fully-featured, dynamic language capable of supporting object-oriented programming methodologies.

The misperception of JavaScript as a "toy language" is now changing rapidly as AJAX development techniques expand the power and functionality of browser-based applications. As a result of the advent of AJAX, JavaScript now seems to be undergoing something of a renaissance, and the explosive growth in the number of JavaScript toolkits and libraries available for AJAX development is proof of the fact.

# Summary

In this chapter, we had a quick overview of AJAX and the technologies that make it tick. We looked at some of the horrible coding contortions that developers had to endure back in the bad old days to create something resembling an interactive UI, and we saw how AJAX offers a huge improvement on those approaches. With a decent command of the building blocks of AJAX—XML, the DOM, CSS, XMLHttpRequest, and JavaScript, which ties them all together—you have everything you need to start building dynamic and accessible AJAX sites.

# Basic XMLHttpRequest

*I can't wait to share this new wonder, The people will all see its light, Let them all make their own music, The priests praise my name on this night.*
—Rush, *Discovery*

It's XMLHttpRequest that gives AJAX its true power: the ability to make asynchronous HTTP requests from the browser and pull down content in small chunks.

Web developers have been using tricks and hacks to achieve this for a long time, while suffering annoying limitations: the invisible `iframe` hack forced us to pass data back and forth between the parent document and the document in the `iframe`, and even the "remote scripting" method was limited to making `GET` requests to pages that contained JavaScript.

Modern AJAX techniques, which use `XMLHttpRequest`, provide a huge improvement over these kludgy methods, allowing your app to make both `GET` and `POST` requests without ever completely reloading the page.

In this chapter, we'll jump right in and build a simple AJAX web application—a simple site-monitoring application that pings a page on a web server to a timed schedule. But before we start making the asynchronous HTTP requests to poll the server, we'll need to simplify the use of the `XMLHttpRequest` class by taking care of all of the little browser incompatibilities, such as the different ways `XMLHttpRequest` objects are instantiated, inside a single, reusable library of code.

# A Simple AJAX Library

One approach to simplifying the use of the XMLHttpRequest class would be to use an existing library of code. Thanks to the increasing popularity of AJAX development, there are literally dozens of libraries, toolkits, and frameworks available that make XMLHttpRequest easier to use.

But, as the code for creating an instance of the XMLHttpRequest class is fairly simple, and the API for using it is easy to understand, we'll just write a very simple JavaScript library that takes care of the basic stuff we need.

Stepping through the process of creating your own library will ensure you know how the XMLHttpRequest class works, and will help you get more out of those other toolkits or libraries when you do decide to use them.

## Starting our Ajax Class

We'll start by creating a basic class, called Ajax, in which we'll wrap the functionality of the XMLHttpRequest class.

### I've Never done Object Oriented Programming in JavaScript—Help!

In this section, we'll start to create classes and objects in JavaScript. If you've never done this before, don't worry—it's quite simple as long as you know the basics of object oriented programming.

In JavaScript, we don't declare classes with complex syntax like we would in Java, C++ or one of the .NET languages; we simply write a **constructor function** to create an instance of the class. All we need to do is:

❑ provide a constructor function—the name of this function is the name of your class

❑ add properties to the object that's being constructed using the keyword this, followed by a period and the name of the property

❑ add methods to the object in the same way we'd add properties, using JavaScript's special function constructor syntax

Here's the code that creates a simple class called HelloWorld:

```
function HelloWorld() {
  this.message = 'Hello, world!';
  this.sayMessage = function() {
    window.alert(this.message);
  };
}
```

JavaScript's framework for object oriented programming is very lightweight, but functions surprisingly well once you get the hang of it. More advanced object oriented features, such as inheritance and polymorphism, aren't available in JavaScript, but these features are rarely needed on the client side in an AJAX application. The complex business logic for which these features are useful should always be on the web server, and accessed using the XMLHttpRequest class.

In this example, we create a class called HelloWorld with one property (message) and one method (sayMessage). To use this class, we simply call the constructor function, as shown below:

```
var hw = new HelloWorld();
hw.sayMessage();
hw.message = 'Goodbye';
hw.sayMessage();
```

Here, we create an instance of HelloWorld (called hw), then use this object to display two messages. The first time we call sayMessage, the default "Hello, world!" message is displayed. Then, after changing our object's message property to "Goodbye," we call sayMessage and "Goodbye" is displayed.

Don't worry if this doesn't make too much sense at the moment. As we progress through the building of our Ajax class, it will become clearer.

Here are the beginnings of our Ajax class's constructor function:

File: **ajax.js (excerpt)**

```
function Ajax() {
  this.req = null;
  this.url = null;
  this.method = 'GET';
  this.async = true;
  this.status = null;
  this.statusText = '';
  this.postData = null;
  this.readyState = null;
  this.responseText = null;
  this.responseXML = null;
```

```
    this.handleResp = null;
    this.responseFormat = 'text', // 'text', 'xml', or 'object'
    this.mimeType = null;
}
```

This code just defines the properties we'll need in our `Ajax` class in order to work with `XMLHttpRequest` objects. Now, let's add some methods to our object. We need some functions that will set up an `XMLHttpRequest` object and tell it how to make requests for us.

# Creating an `XMLHttpRequest` Object

First, we'll add an `init` method, which will create an `XMLHttpRequest` object for us. Unfortunately, `XMLHttpRequest` is implemented slightly differently in Firefox,[1] Safari, and Opera than it was in Internet Explorer's original implementation,[2] so you'll have to try instantiating the object in a number of different ways if you're not targeting a specific browser. Firefox and Safari create XMLHttpRequest objects using a class called `XMLHttpRequest`, while Internet Explorer versions 6 and earlier use a special class called `ActiveXObject` that's built into Microsoft's scripting engine. Although these classes have different constructors, they behave in the same way.

### Cross-browser Code

Fortunately, most modern browsers[3] adhere to web standards fairly well overall, so you won't have to do lots of browser-specific branching in your AJAX code.

This usually makes a browser-based AJAX application faster to develop and deploy cross-platform than a desktop application. As the power and capabilities available to AJAX applications increase, desktop applications offer fewer advantages from a user-interface perspective.

The `init` method looks like this:

File: **ajax.js** (excerpt)

```
this.init = function() {
  if (!this.req) {
```

---

[1] In this book, whenever I explain how something works in Firefox, I'm referring to all Mozilla-based browsers, including Firefox, Mozilla, Camino, and SeaMonkey.
[2] Interestingly, Internet Explorer version 7 now supports the same interface as Firefox, which promises to simplify AJAX development in the future.
[3] Internet Explorer 6, Firefox 1.0, Safari 1.2, and Opera 8, or later versions of any of these browsers.

```
  try {
    // Try to create object for Firefox, Safari, IE7, etc.
    this.req = new XMLHttpRequest();
  }
  catch (e) {
    try {
      // Try to create object for later versions of IE.
      this.req = new ActiveXObject('MSXML2.XMLHTTP');
    }
    catch (e) {
      try {
        // Try to create object for early versions of IE.
        this.req = new ActiveXObject('Microsoft.XMLHTTP');
      }
      catch (e) {
        // Could not create an XMLHttpRequest object.
        return false;
      }
    }
  }
}
  return this.req;
};
```

The init method goes through each possible way of creating an XMLHttpRequest object until it creates one successfully. This object is then returned to the calling function.

### Degrading Gracefully

Maintaining compatibility with older browsers[4] requires a lot of extra code work, so it's vital to define which browsers your application should support.

If you know your application will receive significant traffic via older browsers that don't support the XMLHtmlRequest class (e.g., Internet Explorer 4 and earlier, Netscape 4 and earlier), you will need either to leave it out completely, or write your code so that it **degrades** gracefully. That means that instead of allowing your functionality simply to disappear in less-capable browsers, you code to ensure that users of those browsers receive something that's functionally equivalent, though perhaps in a less interactive or easy-to-use format.

It's also possible that your web site will attract users who browse with JavaScript disabled. If you want to cater to these users, you should provide

---

[4]By "older" I mean anything older than the "modern browsers" I mentioned in the previous note.

an alternative, old-school interface by default, which you can then modify on-the-fly—using JavaScript—for modern browsers.

# Sending a Request

We now have a method that creates an XMLHttpRequest. So let's write a function that uses it to make a request. We start the doReq method like this:

File: ajax.js (excerpt)

```
this.doReq = function() {
  if (!this.init()) {
    alert('Could not create XMLHttpRequest object.');
    return;
  }
};
```

This first part of doReq calls init to create an instance of the XMLHttpRequest class, and displays a quick alert if it's not successful.

## Setting Up the Request

Next, our code calls the open method on this.req—our new instance of the XMLHttpRequest class—to begin setting up the HTTP request:

File: ajax.js (excerpt)

```
this.doReq = function() {
  if (!this.init()) {
    alert('Could not create XMLHttpRequest object.');
    return;
  }
  this.req.open(this.method, this.url, this.async);
};
```

The open method takes three parameters:

Method
This parameter identifies the type of HTTP request method we'll use. The most commonly used methods are GET and POST.

### Methods are Case-sensitive

According to the HTTP specification (RFC 2616), the names of these request methods are case-sensitive. And since the methods described in the spec are defined as being all uppercase, you should always make sure you type the method in all uppercase letters.

**URL**    This parameter identifies the page being requested (or posted to if the method is POST).

### Crossing Domains

Normal browser security settings will not allow you to send HTTP requests to another domain. For example, a page served from ajax.net would not be able to send a request to remotescripting.com unless the user had allowed such requests.

**Asynchronous Flag**    If this parameter is set to `true`, your JavaScript will continue to execute normally while waiting for a response to the request. As the state of the request changes, events are fired so that you can deal with the changing state of the request.

If you set the parameter to `false`, JavaScript execution will stop until the response comes back from the server. This approach has the advantage of being a little simpler than using a callback function, as you can start dealing with the response straight after you send the request in your code, but the big disadvantage is that your code pauses while the request is sent and processed on the server, and the response is received. As the ability to communicate with the server asynchronously is the whole point of an AJAX application, this should be set to `true`.

In our `Ajax` class, the `method` and `async` properties are initialized to reasonable defaults (`GET` and `true`), but you'll always have to set the target URL, of course.

## Setting Up the onreadystatechange Event Handler

As the HTTP request is processed on the server, its progress is indicated by changes to the `readyState` property. This property is an integer that represents one of the following states, listed in order from the start of the request to its finish:

**0: uninitialized**
> open has not been called yet.

**1: loading**
> send has not been called yet.

**2: loaded**
> send has been called, but the response is not yet available.

**3: interactive**
> The response is being downloaded, and the responseText property holds partial data.

**4: completed**
> The response has been loaded and the request is completed.

An XMLHttpRequest object tells you about each change in state by firing an readystatechange event. In the handler for this event, check the readyState of the request, and when the request completes (i.e., when the readyState changes to 4), you can handle the server's response.

A basic outline for our Ajax code would look like this:

File: **ajax.js (excerpt)**
```
this.doReq = function() {
  if (!this.init()) {
    alert('Could not create XMLHttpRequest object.');
    return;
  }
  this.req.open(this.method, this.url, this.async);
  var self = this; // Fix loss-of-scope in inner function
  this.req.onreadystatechange = function() {
    if (self.req.readyState == 4) {
      // Do stuff to handle response
    }
  };
};
```

We'll discuss how to "do stuff to handle response" in just a bit. For now, just keep in mind that you need to set up this event handler before the request is sent.

# Sending the Request

Use the `send` method of the `XMLHttpRequest` class to start the HTTP request, like so:

File: **ajax.js (excerpt)**

```
this.doReq = function() {
  if (!this.init()) {
    alert('Could not create XMLHttpRequest object.');
    return;
  }
  this.req.open(this.method, this.url, this.async);
  var self = this; // Fix loss-of-scope in inner function
  this.req.onreadystatechange = function() {
    if (self.req.readyState == 4) {
      // Do stuff to handle response
    }
  };
  this.req.send(this.postData);
};
```

The `send` method takes one parameter, which is used for `POST` data. When the request is a simple `GET` that doesn't pass any data to the server, like our current request, we set this parameter to `null`.

## Loss of Scope and `this`

You may have noticed that `onreadystatechange` includes a weird-looking variable assignment:

File: **ajax.js (excerpt)**

```
var self = this; // Fix loss-of-scope in inner function
```

This new variable, `self`, is the solution to a problem called "loss of scope" that's often experienced by JavaScript developers using asynchronous event handlers. Asynchronous event handlers are commonly used in conjunction with `XMLHttpRequest`, and with functions like `setTimeout` or `setInterval`.

The `this` keyword is used as shorthand in object-oriented JavaScript code to refer to "the current object." Here's a quick example—a class called `ScopeTest`:

```
function ScopeTest() {
  this.message = 'Greetings from ScopeTest!';
```

```
  this.doTest = function() {
    alert(this.message);
  };
}
var test = new ScopeTest();
test.doTest();
```

This code will create an instance of the ScopeTest class, then call that object's doTest method, which will display the message "Greetings from ScopeTest!" Simple, right?

Now, let's add some simple XMLHttpRequest code to our ScopeTest class. We'll send a simple GET request for your web server's home page, and, when a response is received, we'll display the content of both this.message and self.message.

```
function ScopeTest() {
  this.message = 'Greetings from ScopeTest!';
  this.doTest = function() {
    // This will only work in Firefox, Opera and Safari.
    this.req = new XMLHttpRequest();
    this.req.open('GET', '/index.html', true);
    var self = this;
    this.req.onreadystatechange = function() {
      if (self.req.readyState == 4) {
        var result = 'self.message is ' + self.message;
        result += '\n';
        result += 'this.message is ' + this.message;
        alert(result);
      }
    }
    this.req.send(null);
  };
}
var test = new ScopeTest();
test.doTest();
```

So, what message is displayed? The answer is revealed in Figure 2.1.

We can see that self.message is the greeting message that we're expecting, but what's happened to this.message?

Using the keyword this is a convenient way to refer to "the object that's executing this code." But this has one small problem—its meaning changes when it's called from outside the object. This is the result of something called **execution context**. All of the code inside the object runs in the same execution context, but code that's run from other objects—such as event handlers—runs in the calling object's execution context. What this means is that, when you're writing object-oriented JavaScript, you won't be able to use the `this` keyword to refer to the object in code for event handlers (like `onreadystatechange` above). This problem is called **loss of scope**.

If this concept isn't 100% clear to you yet, don't worry too much about it. We'll see an actual demonstration of this problem in the next chapter. In the meantime, just kind of keep in mind that if you see the variable `self` in code examples, it's been included to deal with a loss-of-scope problem.

## Figure 2.1. Message displayed by `ScopeTest` class

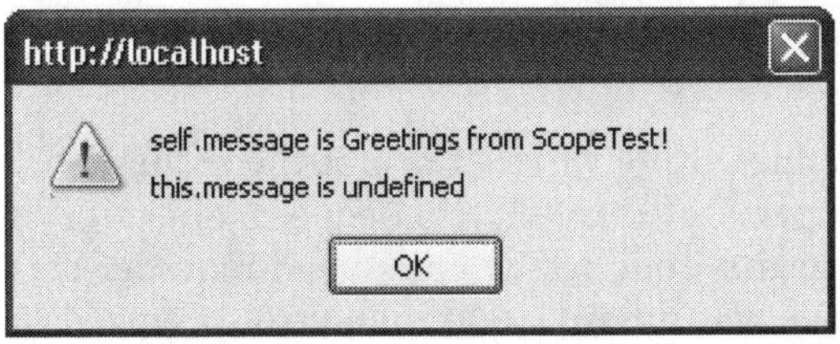

```
http://localhost                               ⊠

     ⚠   self.message is Greetings from ScopeTest!
          this.message is undefined

                    ┌──────────────┐
                    │      OK      │
                    └──────────────┘
```

# Processing the Response

Now we're ready to write some code to handle the server's response to our HTTP request. Remember the "do stuff to handle response" comment that we left in the `onreadystatechange` event handler? We'll, it's time we wrote some code to do that stuff! The function needs to do three things:

1.  Figure out if the response is an error or not.

2.  Prepare the response in the desired format.

3.  Pass the response to the desired handler function.

Include the code below in the inner function of our `Ajax` class:

File: **ajax.js (excerpt)**

```javascript
this.req.onreadystatechange = function() {
  var resp = null;
  if (self.req.readyState == 4) {
    switch (self.responseFormat) {
      case 'text':
        resp = self.req.responseText;
        break;
      case 'xml':
```

```
      resp = self.req.responseXML;
      break;
  case 'object':
    resp = req;
    break;
}
if (self.req.status >= 200 && self.req.status <= 299) {
  self.handleResp(resp);
}
else {
  self.handleErr(resp);
}
  }
};
```

When the response completes, a code indicating whether or not the request succeeded is returned in the `status` property of our `XMLHttpRequest` object. The `status` property contains the HTTP status code of the completed request. This could be code 404 if the requested page was missing, 500 if an error occurred in the server-side script, 200 if the request was successful, and so on. A full list of these codes is provided in the HTTP Specification (RFC 2616).[5]

### No Good with Numbers?

*Tip*

If you have trouble remembering the codes, don't worry: you can use the `statusText` property, which contains a short message that tells you a bit more detail about the error (e.g., "Not Found," "Internal Server Error," "OK").

Our `Ajax` class will be able to provide the response from the server in three different formats: as a normal JavaScript string, as an XML document object accessible via the W3C XML DOM, and as the actual `XMLHttpRequest` object that was used to make the request. These are controlled by the `Ajax` class's `responseFormat` property, which can be set to `text`, `xml` or `object`.

The content of the response can be accessed via two properties of our `XMLHttpRequest` object:

**responseText**    This property contains the response from the server as a normal string. In the case of an error, it will contain the web server's error page HTML. As long as a response is returned (that is,

---

[5] http://www.w3.org/Protocols/rfc2616/rfc2616-sec10.html#sec10

readyState becomes 4), this property will contain data, though it may not be what you expect.

responseXML    This property contains an XML document object. If the response is not XML, this property will be empty.

Our Ajax class initializes its responseFormat property to text, so by default, your response handler will be passed the content from the server as a JavaScript string. If you're working with XML content, you can change the responseFormat property to xml, which will pull out the XML document object instead.

There's one more option you can use if you want to get really fancy: you can return the actual XMLHttpRequest object itself to your handler function. This gives you direct access to things like the status and statusText properties, and might be useful in cases in which you want to treat particular classes of errors differently—for example, completing extra logging in the case of 404 errors.

## Setting the Correct Content-Type

Implementations of XMLHttpRequest in all major browsers require the HTTP response's Content-Type to be set properly in order for the response to be handled as XML. Well-formed XML, returned with a content type of text/xml (or application/xml, or even application/xhtml+xml), will properly populate the responseXML property of an XMLHttpRequest object; non-XML content types will result in values of null or undefined for that property.

However, Firefox, Safari, and Internet Explorer 7 provide a way around XMLHttpRequest's pickiness over XML documents: the overrideMimeType method of the XMLHttpRequest class. Our simple Ajax class hooks into this with the setMimeType method:

File: **ajax.js (excerpt)**

```
this.setMimeType = function(mimeType) {
  this.mimeType = mimeType;
};
```

This method sets the mimeType property.

Then, in our doReq method, we simply call overrideMimeType inside a try ... catch block, like so:

File: **ajax.js (excerpt)**

```
req.open(this.method, this.url, this.async);
if (this.mimeType) {
  try {
    req.overrideMimeType(this.mimeType);
  }
  catch (e) {
    // couldn't override MIME type -- IE6 or Opera?
  }
}
var self = this; // Fix loss-of-scope in inner function
```

Being able to override `Content-Type` headers from uncooperative servers can be very important in environments in which you don't have control over both the front and back ends of your web application. This is especially true since many of today's apps access services and content from a lot of disparate domains or sources. However, as this technique won't work in Internet Explorer 6 or Opera 8, you may not find it suitable for use in your applications today.

# Response Handler

According to the HTTP 1.1 specification, any response that has a code between 200 and 299 inclusive is a successful response.

The `onreadystatechange` event handler we've defined looks at the `status` property to get the status of the response. If the code is within the correct range for a successful response, the `onreadystatechange` event handler passes the response to the response handler method (which is set by the `handleResp` property).

The response handler will need to know what the response was, of course, so we'll pass it the response as a parameter. We'll see this process in action later, when we talk about the `doGet` method.

Since the handler method is user-defined, the code also does a cursory check to make sure the method has been set properly before it tries to execute the method.

# Error Handler

If the `status` property indicates that there's an error with the request (i.e., it's outside the 200 to 299 code range), the server's response is passed to the error handler in the `handleErr` property. Our `Ajax` class already defines a reasonable default for the error handler, so we don't have to make sure it's defined before we call it.

The `handleErr` property points to a function that looks like this:

File: **ajax.js** (excerpt)

```
this.handleErr = function() {
  var errorWin;
  try {
    errorWin = window.open('', 'errorWin');
    errorWin.document.body.innerHTML = this.responseText;
  }
  catch (e) {
    alert('An error occurred, but the error message cannot be '
      + 'displayed. This is probably because of your browser\'s '
      + 'pop-up blocker.\n'
      + 'Please allow pop-ups from this web site if you want to '
      + 'see the full error messages.\n'
      + '\n'
      + 'Status Code: ' + this.req.status + '\n'
      + 'Status Description: ' + this.req.statusText);
  }
};
```

This method checks to make sure that pop-ups are not blocked, then tries to display the full text of the server's error page content in a new browser window. This code uses a `try … catch` block, so if users have blocked pop-ups, we can show them a cut-down version of the error message and tell them how to access a more detailed error message.

This is a decent default for starters, although you may want to show less information to the end-user—it all depends on your level of paranoia. If you want to use your own custom error handler, you can use `setHandlerErr` like so:

File: **ajax.js** (excerpt)

```
this.setHandlerErr = function(funcRef) {
  this.handleErr = funcRef;
}
```

## Or, the One True Handler

It's possible that you might want to use a single function to handle both successful responses and errors. `setHandlerBoth`, a convenience method in our `Ajax` class, sets this up easily for us:

File: **ajax.js (excerpt)**

```
this.setHandlerBoth = function(funcRef) {
  this.handleResp = funcRef;
  this.handleErr = funcRef;
};
```

Any function that's passed as a parameter to `setHandlerBoth` will handle both successful responses and errors.

This setup might be useful to a user who sets your class's `responseFormat` property to `object`, which would cause the `XMLHttpRequest` object that's used to make the request—rather than just the value of the `responseText` or `responseXML` properties—to be passed to the response handler.

# Aborting the Request

Sometimes, as you'll know from your own experience, a web page will take a very long time to load. Your web browser has a Stop button, but what about your `Ajax` class? This is where the `abort` method comes into play:

File: **ajax.js (excerpt)**

```
this.abort = function() {
  if (this.req) {
    this.req.onreadystatechange = function() { };
    this.req.abort();
    this.req = null;
  }
};
```

This method changes the `onreadystate` event handler to an empty function, calls the `abort` method on your instance of the `XMLHttpRequest` class, then destroys the instance you've created. That way, any properties that have been set exclusively for the request that's being aborted are reset. Next time a request is made, the `init` method will be called and those properties will be reinitialized.

So, why do we need to change the `onreadystate` event handler? Many implementations of `XMLHttpRequest` will fire the `onreadystate` event once `abort` is called, to indicate that the request's state has been changed. What's worse is that those events come complete with a `readyState` of `4`, which indicates that everything completed as expected (which is partly true, if you think about it: as soon as we call `abort`, everything should come to a stop and our instance of `XMLHttpRequest` should be ready to send another request, should we so desire).

Obviously, we don't want our response handler to be invoked when we abort a request, so we remove the existing handler just before we call `abort`.

# Wrapping it Up

Given the code we have so far, the `Ajax` class needs just two things in order to make a request:

❏ a target URL

❏ a handler function for the response

Let's provide a method called `doGet` to set both of these properties, and kick off the request:

File: **ajax.js (excerpt)**

```
this.doGet = function(url, hand, format) {
  this.url = url;
  this.handleResp = hand;
  this.responseFormat = format || 'text';
  this.doReq();
};
```

You'll notice that, along with the two expected parameters, *url* and *hand*, the function has a third parameter: *format*. This is an optional parameter that allows us to change the format of the server response that's passed to the handler function.

If we don't pass in a value for *format*, the `responseFormat` property of the `Ajax` class will default to a value of `text`, which means your handler will be passed the value of the `responseText` property. You could, instead, pass `xml` or `object` as the *format*, which would change the parameter that's being passed to the response handler to an XML DOM or `XMLHttpRequest` object.

# Example: a Simple Test Page

It's finally time to put everything we've learned together! Let's create an instance of this `Ajax` class, and use it to send a request and handle a response.

Now that our class's code is in a file called `ajax.js`, any web pages in which we want to use our `Ajax` class will need to include the `Ajax` code with a `<script`

`type="text/javascript" src="ajax.js">` tag. Once our page has access to the Ajax code, we can create an Ajax object.

File: **ajaxtest.html (excerpt)**

```
<!DOCTYPE html PUBLIC "-//W3C//DTD XHTML 1.0 Strict//EN"
    "http://www.w3.org/TR/xhtml1/DTD/xhtml1-strict.dtd">
<html xmlns="http://www.w3.org/1999/xhtml">
  <head>
    <meta http-equiv="Content-Type"
        content="text/html; charset=iso-8859-1" />
    <title>A Simple AJAX Test</title>
    <script type="text/javascript" src="ajax.js"></script>
    <script type="text/javascript">
      var ajax = new Ajax();
    </script>
  </head>
  <body>
  </body>
</html>
```

This script gives us a shiny, new instance of the Ajax class. Now, let's make it do something useful.

To make the most basic request with our Ajax class, we could do something like this:

File: **ajaxtest.html (excerpt)**

```
<script type="text/javascript">
  var hand = function(str) {
    alert(str);
  }
  var ajax = new Ajax();
  ajax.doGet('/fakeserver.php', hand);
</script>
```

This creates an instance of our Ajax class that will make a simple GET request to a page called fakeserver.php, and pass the result back as text to the hand function. If fakeserver.php returned an XML document that you wanted to use, you could do so like this:

File: **ajaxtest.html (excerpt)**

```
<script type="text/javascript">
  var hand = function(str) {
    // Do XML stuff here
  }
```

```
  var ajax = new Ajax();
  ajax.doGet('/fakeserver.php', hand);
</script>
```

You would want to make *absolutely sure* in this case that `somepage.php` was really serving valid XML and that its `Content-Type` HTTP response header was set to `text/xml` (or something else that was appropriate).

## Creating the Page

Now that we have created the `Ajax` object, and set up a simple handler function for the request, it's time to put our code into action.

## The Fake Server Page

In the code above, you can see that the target URL for the request is set to a page called `fakeserver.php`. To use this demonstration code, you'll need to serve both `ajaxtest.html` and `fakeserver.php` from the same PHP-enabled web server. You can do this from an IIS web server with some simple ASP, too. The fake server page is a super-simple page that simulates the varying response time of a web server using the PHP code below:

File: **fakeserver.php**

```
<?php
header('Content-Type: text/plain');
sleep(rand(3, 12));
print 'ok';
?>
```

That's all this little scrap of code does: it waits somewhere between three and 12 seconds, then prints `ok`.

The `fakeserver.php` code sets the `Content-Type` header of the response to `text/plain`. Depending on the content of the page you pass back, you might choose another `Content-Type` for your response. For example, if you're passing an XML document back to the caller, you would naturally want to use `text/xml`.

This works just as well in ASP, although some features (such as `sleep`) are not as easily available, as the code below illustrates:

File: **fakeserver.asp**

```
<%
Response.ContentType = "text/plain"
```

```
' There is no equivalent to sleep in ASP.
Response.Write "ok"
%>
```

Throughout this book, all of our server-side examples will be written in PHP, although they could just as easily be written in ASP, ASP.NET, Java, Perl, or just about any language that can serve content through a web server.

 *Tip*

### Use the `setMimeType` Method

Imagine that you have a response that you know contains a valid XML document that you want to parse as XML, but the server insists on serving it to you as `text/plain`. You can force that response to be parsed as XML in Firefox and Safari by adding an extra call to `setMimeType`, like so:

```
var ajax = new Ajax();
ajax.setMimeType('text/xml');
ajax.doGet('/fakeserver.php', hand, 'xml');
```

Naturally, you should use this approach only when you're certain that the response from the server will be valid XML, and you can be sure that the browser is Firefox or Safari.

# Hitting the Page

Now comes the moment of truth! Hit your local web server, load up `ajaxtest.html`, and see what you get. If everything is working properly, there will be a few moments' delay, and then you'll see a standard JavaScript `alert` like the one in Figure 2.2 that says simply `ok`.

## Figure 2.2. Confirmation that your `Ajax` class is working as expected

```
┌─────────────────────────────────────┐
│ http://localhost              [X]    │
├─────────────────────────────────────┤
│  ⚠  ok                               │
│                                       │
│         ┌──────────┐                 │
│         │    OK    │                 │
│         └──────────┘                 │
└─────────────────────────────────────┘
```

Now that all is well and our `Ajax` class is functioning properly, it's time to move to the next step.

# Example: a Simple AJAX App

Okay, so using the awesome power of AJAX to spawn a tiny little JavaScript `alert` box that reads "ok" is probably not exactly what you had in mind when you bought this book. Let's implement some changes to our example code that will make this `XMLHttpRequest` stuff a little more useful. At the same time, we'll create that simple monitoring application I mentioned at the start of this chapter. The app will ping a web site and report the time it takes to get a response back.

## Laying the Foundations

We'll start off with a simple HTML document that links to two JavaScript files: `ajax.js`, which contains our library, and `appmonitor1.js`, which will contain the code for our application.

File: **appmonitor1.html**

```
<!DOCTYPE html PUBLIC "-//W3C//DTD XHTML 1.0 Strict//EN"
    "http://www.w3.org/TR/xhtml1/DTD/xhtml1-strict.dtd">
<html xmlns="http://www.w3.org/1999/xhtml">
  <head>
    <meta http-equiv="Content-Type"
        content="text/html; charset=iso-8859-1" />
    <title>App Monitor</title>
    <script type="text/javascript" src="ajax.js"></script>
    <script type="text/javascript" src="appmonitor1.js"></script>
  </head>
  <body>
    <div id="pollDiv"></div>
  </body>
</html>
```

You'll notice that there's virtually no content in the `body` of the page—there's just a single `div` element. This is fairly typical of web apps that rely on AJAX functions. Often, much of the content of AJAX apps is created by JavaScript dynamically, so we usually see a lot less markup in the body of the page source than we would in a non-AJAX web application for which all the content was generated by the server. However, where AJAX is not an absolutely essential part of the application, a plain HTML version of the application should be provided.

We'll begin our `appmonitor1.js` file with some simple content that makes use of our `Ajax` class:

File: **appmonitor1.js (excerpt)**

```
var start = 0;
var ajax = new Ajax();

var doPoll = function() {
  start = new Date();
  start = start.getTime();
  ajax.doGet('/fakeserver.php?start=' + start, showPoll);
}

window.onload = doPoll;
```

We'll use the start variable to record the time at which each request starts—this figure will be used to calculate how long each request takes. We make start a global variable so that we don't have to gum up the works of our Ajax class with extra code for timing requests—we can set the value of start immediately before and after our calls to the Ajax object.

The ajax variable simply holds an instance of our Ajax class.

The doPoll function actually makes the HTTP requests using the Ajax class. You should recognize the call to the doGet method from our original test page.

Notice that we've added to the target URL a query string that has the start value as a parameter. We're not actually going to use this value on the server; we're just using it as a random value to deal with Internet Explorer's overzealous caching. IE caches all GET requests made with XMLHttpRequest, and one way of disabling that "feature" is to append a random value into a query string. The milliseconds value in start can double as that random value. An alternative to this approach is to use the setRequestHeader method of the XMLHttpRequest class to set the If-Modified-Since header on the request.

Finally, we kick everything off by attaching doPoll to the window.onload event.

# Handling the Result with showPoll

The second parameter we pass to doGet tells the Ajax class to pass responses to the function showPoll. Here's the code for that function:

File: **appmonitor1.js (excerpt)**

```
var showPoll = function(str) {
  var pollResult = '';
  var diff = 0;
```

```
    var end = new Date();
    if (str == 'ok') {
      end = end.getTime();
      diff = (end - start) / 1000;
      pollResult = 'Server response time: ' + diff + ' seconds';
    }
    else {
      pollResult = 'Request failed.';
    }
    printResult(pollResult);
    var pollHand = setTimeout(doPoll, 15000);
}
```

This is all pretty simple: the function expects a single parameter, which should be the string ok returned from fakeserver.php if everything goes as expected. If the response is correct, the code does the quick calculations needed to figure out how long the response took, and creates a message that contains the result. It passes that message to pollResult for display.

In this very simple implementation, anything other than the expected response results in a fairly terse and unhelpful message: Request failed. We'll make our handling of error conditions more robust when we upgrade this app in the next chapter.

Once pollResult is set, it's passed to the printResult function:

File: **appmonitor1.js (excerpt)**

```
function printResult(str) {
  var pollDiv = document.getElementById('pollDiv');
  if (pollDiv.firstChild) {
    pollDiv.removeChild(pollDiv.firstChild);
  }
  pollDiv.appendChild(document.createTextNode(str));
}
```

The printResult function displays the message that was sent from showPoll inside the lone div in the page.

Note the test in the code above, which is used to see whether our div has any child nodes. This checks for the existence of any text nodes, which could include text that we added to this div in previous iterations, or the text that was contained inside the div in the page markup, and then removes them. If you don't remove existing text nodes, the code will simply append the new result to the page as a new text node: you'll display a long string of text to which more text is continually being appended.

> **Why Not Use `innerHTML`?**
>
> *note*
>
> You could simply update the `innerHTML` property of the `div`, like so:
>
> ```
> document.getElementById('pollDiv').innerHTML = str;
> ```
>
> The `innerHTML` property is not a web standard, but all the major browsers support it. And, as you can see from the fact that it's a single line of code (as compared with the four lines needed for DOM methods), sometimes it's just easier to use than the DOM methods. Neither way of displaying content on your page is inherently better.
>
> In some cases, you may end up choosing a method based on the differences in rendering speeds of these two approaches (`innerHTML` can be faster than DOM methods). In other cases, you may base your decision on the clarity of the code, or even on personal taste.

# Starting the Process Over Again

Finally, `showPoll` starts the entire process over by scheduling a call to the original `doPoll` function in 15 seconds time using `setTimeout`, as shown below:

File: **appmonitor1.js (excerpt)**
```
var pollHand = setTimeout(doPoll, 15000);
```

The fact that the code continuously invokes the `doPoll` function means that once the page loads, the HTTP requests polling the `fakeserver.php` page will continue to do so until that page is closed. The `pollHand` variable is the interval ID that allows you to keep track of the pending operation, and cancel it using `clearTimeout`.

The first parameter of the `setTimeout` call, `doPoll`, is a pointer to the main function of the application; the second represents the length of time, in seconds, that must elapse between requests.

# Full Example Code

Here's all the code from our first trial run with this simple monitoring application.

File: **appmonitor1.js**

```
var start = 0;
var ajax = new Ajax();

var doPoll = function() {
  start = new Date();
  start = start.getTime();
  ajax.doGet('/fakeserver.php?start=' + start, showPoll);
}

window.onload = doPoll;

var showPoll = function(str) {
  var pollResult = '';
  var diff = 0;
  var end = new Date();
  if (str == 'ok') {
    end = end.getTime();
    diff = (end - start)/1000;
    pollResult = 'Server response time: ' + diff + ' seconds';
  }
  else {
    pollResult = 'Request failed.';
  }
  printResult(pollResult);
  var pollHand = setTimeout(doPoll, 15000);
}

function printResult(str) {
  var pollDiv = document.getElementById('pollDiv');
  if (pollDiv.firstChild) {
    pollDiv.removeChild(pollDiv.firstChild);
  }
  pollDiv.appendChild(document.createTextNode(str));
}
```

In a bid to follow good software engineering principles, I've separated the JavaScript code from the markup, and put them in two different files.

I'll be following a similar approach with all the example code for this book, separating each example's markup, JavaScript code, and CSS into separate files. This little monitoring app is so basic that it has no CSS file. We'll be adding a few styles to make it look nicer in the next chapter.

# Running the App

Try loading the page in your browser. Drop it into your web server's root directory, and open the page in your browser.

If the `fakeserver.php` page is responding properly, you'll see something like the display shown in Figure 2.3.

## Figure 2.3. Running the simple monitoring application

# Further Reading

Here are some online resources that will help you learn more about the techniques and concepts in this chapter.

## JavaScript's Object Model

http://docs.sun.com/source/816-6409-10/obj.htm
http://docs.sun.com/source/816-6409-10/obj2.htm

> Check out these two chapters on objects from the *Client-Side JavaScript Guide* for version 1.3 of JavaScript, hosted by Sun Microsystems. The first chapter explains all the basic concepts you need to understand how to work with objects in JavaScript. The second goes into more depth about JavaScript's prototype-based inheritance model, allowing you to leverage more of the power of object-oriented coding with JavaScript.

http://www.crockford.com/javascript/private.html
> This is a brief introduction to creating private instance variables with JavaScript objects. It will help you get a deeper understanding of JavaScript's prototype-based inheritance scheme.

## XMLHttpRequest

http://developer.apple.com/internet/webcontent/xmlhttpreq.html
> Here's a good reference page from the Apple Developer Connection. It gives a nice overview of the `XMLHttpRequest` class, and a reference table of its methods and properties.

http://jibbering.com/2002/4/httprequest.html
> This article, originally posted in 2002, continues to be updated with new information. It includes information on making `HEAD` requests (instead of just `GET` or `POST`), as well as JavaScript Object Notation (JSON), and SOAP.

http://www.xulplanet.com/references/objref/XMLHttpRequest.html
> This is XULPlanet's exhaustive reference on the `XMLHttpRequest` implementation in Firefox.

http://kb.mozillazine.org/XMLHttpRequest
> Here's another nice overview, which also shows some of the lesser-used methods of the `XMLHttpRequest` object, such as `overrideMimeType`, `setRequestHeader`, and `getResponseHeader`. Again, this reference is focused on implementation in Firefox.

http://msdn.microsoft.com/library/en-us/xmlsdk/html/xmobjxmlhttprequest.asp
> This is Microsoft's documentation on MSDN of its implementation of `XMLHttpRequest`.

## Summary

`XMLHttpRequest` is at the heart of AJAX. It gives scripts within the browser the ability to make their own requests and get content from the server. The simple AJAX library we built in this chapter provided a solid understanding of how `XMLHttpRequest` works, and that understanding will help you when things go wrong with your AJAX code (whether you're using a library you've built yourself, or one of the many pre-built toolkits and libraries listed in Appendix A). The sample app we built in this chapter gave us a chance to dip our toes into the AJAX pool—now it's time to dive in and learn to swim.

# The "A" in AJAX

*It's flying over our heads in a million pieces.*
—Willy Wonka, *Willy Wonka & the Chocolate Factory*

The "A" in AJAX stands for "asynchronous," and while it's not nearly as cool as the letter "X," that "A" is what makes AJAX development so powerful. As we discussed in Chapter 1, AJAX's ability to update sections of an interface asynchronously has given developers a much greater level of control over the interactivity of the apps we build, and a degree of power that's driving web apps into what was previously the domain of desktop applications alone.

Back in the early days of web applications, users interacted with data by filling out forms and submitting them. Then they'd wait a bit, watching their browser's "page loading" animation until a whole new page came back from the server. Each data transaction between the browser and server was large and obvious, which made it easy for users to figure out what was going on, and what state their data was in.

As AJAX-style development becomes more popular, users can expect more interactive, "snappy" user interfaces. This is a good thing for users, but presents new challenges for the developers working to deliver this increased functionality. In an AJAX application, users alter data in an ad hoc fashion, so it's easy for both the user and the application to become confused about the state of that data.

The solution to both these issues is to display the application's status, which keeps users informed about what the application is doing. This makes the application seem very responsive, and gives users important guidance about what's happening to their data. This critical part of AJAX web application development is what separates the good AJAX apps from the bad.

# Planned Application Enhancements

To create a snappy user interface that keeps users well-informed of the application's status, we'll take the monitoring script we developed in the previous chapter, and add some important functionality to it. Here's what we're going to add:

❏ a way for the system administrator to configure the interval between polls and the timeout threshold

❏ an easy way to start and stop the monitoring process

❏ a bar graph of response times for previous requests; the number of entries in the history list will be user-configurable

❏ user notification when the application is in the process of making a request

❏ graceful handling of request timeouts

Figure 3.1 shows what the running application will look like once we're done with all the enhancements.

The code for this application is broken up into three files: the markup in appmonitor2.html, the JavaScript code in appmonitor2.js, and the styles in appmonitor2.css. To start with, we'll link all the required files in to appmonitor2.html:

File: **appmonitor2.html (excerpt)**

```
<!DOCTYPE html PUBLIC "-//W3C//DTD XHTML 1.0 Strict//EN"
    "http://www.w3.org/TR/xhtml1/DTD/xhtml1-strict.dtd">
<html xmlns="http://www.w3.org/1999/xhtml">
  <head>
    <meta http-equiv="Content-Type"
        content="text/html; charset=iso-8859-1" />
    <title>App Monitor</title>
    <script type="text/javascript" src="ajax.js"></script>
    <script type="text/javascript" src="appmonitor2.js"></script>
    <link rel="stylesheet" href="appmonitor2.css"
```

```
        type="text/css" />
  </head>
  <body>
  </body>
</html>
```

## Figure 3.1. The running application

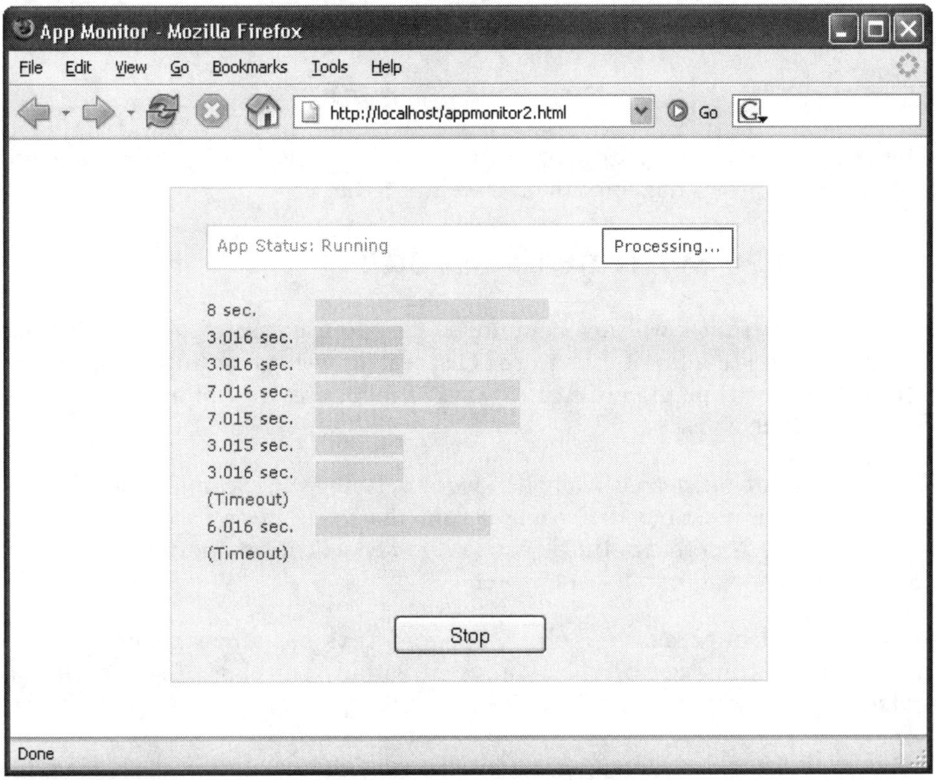

# Organizing the Code

All this new functionality will add a lot more complexity to our app, so this is a good time to establish some kind of organization within our code (a much better option than leaving everything in the global scope). After all, we're building a fully functional AJAX application, so we'll want to have it organized properly.

We'll use object-oriented design principles to organize our app. And we'll start, of course, with the creation of a base class for our application—the `Monitor` class.

Typically, we'd create a class in JavaScript like this:

```
function Monitor() {
  this.firstProperty = 'foo';
  this.secondProperty = true;
  this.firstMethod = function() {
    // Do some stuff here
  };
}
```

This is a nice, normal constructor function, and we could easily use it to create a `Monitor` class (or a bunch of them if we wanted to).

# Loss of Scope with `setTimeout`

Unfortunately, things will not be quite so easy in the case of our application. We're going to use a lot of calls to `setTimeout` (as well as `setInterval`) in our app, so the normal method of creating JavaScript classes may prove troublesome for our `Monitor` class.

The `setTimeout` function is really handy for delaying the execution of a piece of code, but it has a serious drawback: it runs that code in an execution context that's different from that of the object. (We talked a little bit about this problem, called **loss of scope**, in the last chapter.)

This is a problem because the object keyword `this` has a new meaning in the new execution context. So, when you use it within your class, it suffers from a sudden bout of amnesia—it has no idea what it is!

This may be a bit difficult to understand; let's walk through a quick demonstration so you can actually see this annoyance in action. You might remember the `ScopeTest` class we looked at in the last chapter. To start with, it was a simple class with one property and one method:

```
function ScopeTest() {
  this.message = "Greetings from ScopeTest!";
  this.doTest = function() {
    alert(this.message);
  };
}
```

```
var test = new ScopeTest();
test.doTest();
```

The result of this code is the predictable JavaScript alert box with the text "Greetings from ScopeTest!"

Let's change the doTest method so that it uses setTimeout to display the message in one second's time.

```
function ScopeTest() {
  this.message = "Greetings from ScopeTest!";
  this.doTest = function() {
    var onTimeout = function() {
      alert(this.message);
    };
    setTimeout(onTimeout, 1000);
  };
}
var test = new ScopeTest();
test.doTest();
```

Instead of our greeting message, the alert box that results from this version of the code will read "undefined." Because we called onTimeout with setTimeout, onTimeout is run within a new execution context. In that execution context, this no longer refers to an instance of ScopeTest, so this.message has no meaning.

The simplest way to deal with this problem of loss of scope is by making the Monitor class a special kind of class, called a **singleton**.

## Singletons with JavaScript

A "singleton" is called that because only a "single" instance of that class exists at any time. Making a class into a singleton is surprisingly easy:

```
var ScopeTest = new function() {
  this.message = "Greetings from ScopeTest!";
  this.doTest = function() {
    var onTimeout = function() {
      alert(this.message);
    };
    setTimeout(onTimeout, 1000);
  };
}
```

Using the keyword new before `function` creates a "one-shot" constructor. It creates a single instance of `ScopeTest`, and it's done: you can't use it to create any more `ScopeTest` objects.

To call the `doTest` method of this singleton object, you must use the actual name of the class (since there's only the one instance of it):

```
ScopeTest.doTest();
```

That's all well and good, but we haven't solved our loss of scope problem. If you were to try the code now, you'd get the same "undefined" message you saw before, because `this` doesn't refer to an instance of `ScopeTest`. However, using a singleton gives us an easy way to fix the problem. All we have to do is use the actual name of the object—instead of the keyword `this`—inside onTimeout, instead of the keyword `this`:

```
var ScopeTest = new function() {
  this.message = "Greetings from ScopeTest!";
  this.doTest = function() {
    var onTimeout = function() {
      alert(ScopeTest.message);
    };
    setTimeout(onTimeout, 1000);
  };
}
```

There's only one instance of `ScopeTest`, and we're using its actual name instead of `this`, so there's no confusion about which instance of `ScopeTest` is being referred to here.

When you execute *this* code, you'll see the expected value of "Greetings from ScopeTest!" in the JavaScript alert box.

Now, I get tired of using the actual object name throughout my object code, and I like to use a shortcut keyword like `this` wherever I possibly can. So, usually I create a variable `self` that I can use in place of `this`, and point it to the object name at the top of each method, like so:

```
var onTimeout = function() {
  var self = ScopeTest();
  alert(self.message);
};
```

This looks a bit silly in a method that's as short as that, but in longer chunks of code it's nice to have a shorthand solution similar to `this` that you can use to refer to your object. I use `self`, but you could use `me`, or `heyYou`, or `darthVader` if you wanted to.

# Creating the Monitor Object

Now that we have a plan for code organization that will fix the loss-of-scope problem from `setTimeout`, it's time to create our base `Monitor` class:

File: appmonitor2.js (excerpt)

```
var Monitor = new function(){
  this.targetURL = null;
  this.pollInterval = null;
  this.maxPollEntries = null;
  this.timeoutThreshold = null;
  this.ajax = new Ajax();
  this.start = 0;
  this.pollArray = [];
  this.pollHand = null;
  this.timeoutHand = null;
  this.reqStatus = Status;
}
```

The first four properties, `targetURL`, `pollInterval`, `maxPollEntries`, and `timeoutThreshold`, will be initialized as part of the class's initialization. They will take on the values defined in the application's configuration, which we'll look at in the next section.

Here's a brief rundown on the other properties:

**ajax**  The instance of our `Ajax` class that makes the HTTP requests to the server we're monitoring.

**start**  Used to record the time at which the last request was sent.

**pollArray**  An array that holds the server response times; the constant `MAX_POLL_ENTRIES` determines the number of items held in this array.

**pollHand**
**timeoutHand**  Interval IDs returned by the `setTimeout` calls for two different processes—the main polling process, and the timeout watcher, which controls a user-defined timeout period for each request.

**reqStatus**  Used for the status animation that notifies the user when a request is in progress. The code that achieved this is fairly complicated, so we'll be writing another singleton class to take care of it. The `reqStatus` property points to the single instance of that class.

# Configuring and Initializing our Application

A webmaster looking at this application may think that it was quite cool, but one of the first things he or she would want is an easy way to configure the app's **polling interval**, or the time that elapses between requests the app makes to the site it's monitoring. It's easy to configure the polling interval using a global constant.

To make it very simple for any user of this script to set the polling interval, we'll put this section of the code in a `script` element within the `head` of `appmonitor2.html`:

File: **appmonitor2.html** (excerpt)

```
<script type="text/javascript">
  // URL to monitor
  var TARGET_URL = '/fakeserver.php';
  // Seconds between requests
  var POLL_INTERVAL = 5;
  // How many entries bars to show in the bar graph
  var MAX_POLL_ENTRIES = 10;
  // Seconds to wait for server response
  var TIMEOUT_THRESHOLD = 10;
</script>
```

You'll notice that these variable names are written in all-caps. This is an indication that they should act like **constants**—values that are set early in the code, and do not change as the code executes. Constants are a feature of many programming languages but, unfortunately, JavaScript is not one of them.[1] Note that these constants relate directly to the first four properties of our class: `targetURL`, `pollInterval`, `maxPollEntries`, and `timeoutThreshold`. These properties will be initialized in our class's `init` method:

---

[1]Newer versions of JavaScript allow you to set real constants with the `const` keyword, but this facility isn't widely supported (even by many modern browsers).

File: **appmonitor2.js** (excerpt)

```
this.init = function() {
  var self = Monitor;
  self.targetURL = TARGET_URL;
  self.pollInterval = POLL_INTERVAL;
  self.maxPollEntries = MAX_POLL_ENTRIES;
  self.timeoutThreshold = TIMEOUT_THRESHOLD;
  self.toggleAppStatus(true);
  self.reqStatus.init();
};
```

As well as initializing some of the properties of our class, the `init` method also calls two methods: `toggleAppStatus`, which is responsible for starting and stopping the polling, and the `init` method of the `reqStatus` object. `reqStatus` is the instance of the `Status` singleton class that we discussed a moment ago.

This `init` method is tied to the `window.onload` event for the page, like so:

File: **appmonitor2.js** (excerpt)

```
window.onload = Monitor.init;
```

# Setting Up the UI

The first version of this application started when the page loaded, and ran until the browser window was closed. In this version, we want to give users a button that they can use to toggle the polling process on or off. The `toggleAppStatus` method handles this for us:

File: **appmonitor2.js** (excerpt)

```
this.toggleAppStatus = function(stopped) {
  var self = Monitor;
  self.toggleButton(stopped);
  self.toggleStatusMessage(stopped);
};
```

Okay, so `toggleAppStatus` doesn't *really* do the work, but it calls the methods that do: `toggleButton`, which changes Start buttons into Stop buttons and vice versa, and `toggleStatusMessage`, which updates the application's status message. Let's take a closer look at each of these methods.

# The `toggleButton` Method

This method toggles the main application between its "Stop" and "Start" states. It uses DOM-manipulation methods to create the appropriate button dynamically, assigning it the correct text and an `onclick` event handler:

File: **appmonitor2.js (excerpt)**

```
this.toggleButton = function(stopped) {
  var self = Monitor;
  var buttonDiv = document.getElementById('buttonArea');
  var but = document.createElement('input');
  but.type = 'button';
  but.className = 'inputButton';
  if (stopped) {
    but.value = 'Start';
    but.onclick = self.pollServerStart;
  }
  else {
    but.value = 'Stop';
    but.onclick = self.pollServerStop;
  }
  if (buttonDiv.firstChild) {
    buttonDiv.removeChild(buttonDiv.firstChild);
  }
  buttonDiv.appendChild(but);
  buttonDiv = null;
};
```

The only parameter to this method, *stopped*, can either be `true`, indicating that the polling has been stopped; or `false`, indicating that polling has started.

As you can see in the code for this method, the button is created, and is set to display Start if the application is stopped, or Stop if the application is currently polling the server. It also assigns either `pollServerStart` or `pollServerStop` as the button's `onclick` event handler. These event handlers will start or stop the polling process respectively.

When this method is called from `init` (via `toggleAppStatus`), *stopped* is set to `true` so the button will display Start when the application is started.

As this code calls for a `div` with the ID `buttonArea`, let's add that to our markup now:

File: **appmonitor2.html** (excerpt)

```
<body>
  <div id="buttonArea"></div>
</body>
```

# The `toggleStatusMessage` Method

Showing a button with the word "Start" or "Stop" on it might be all that programmers or engineers need to figure out the application's status, but most normal people need a message that's a little clearer and more obvious in order to work out what's going on with an application.

This upgraded version of the application will display a status message at the top of the page to tell the user about the overall state of the application (stopped or running), and the status of the polling process. To display the application status, we'll place a nice, clear message in the application's status bar that states App Status: Stopped or App Status: Running.

In our markup, let's insert the status message above where the button appears. We'll include only the "App Status" part of the message in our markup. The rest of the message will be inserted into a span with the ID currentAppState:

File: **appmonitor2.html** (excerpt)

```
<body>
  <div id="statusMessage">App Status:
     <span id="currentAppState"></span>
  </div>
  <div id="buttonArea"></div>
</body>
```

The `toggleStatusMessage` method toggles between the words that can display inside the `currentAppState` span:

File: **appmonitor2.js** (excerpt)

```
this.toggleStatusMessage = function(stopped) {
  var statSpan = document.getElementById('currentAppState');
  var msg;
  if (stopped) {
    msg = 'Stopped';
  }
  else {
    msg = 'Running';
  }
```

```
  if (statSpan.firstChild) {
    statSpan.removeChild(statSpan.firstChild);
  }
  statSpan.appendChild(document.createTextNode(msg));
};
```

Once the UI is set up, the application is primed and ready to start polling and recording response times.

# Checking your Work In Progress

Now that you've come this far, it would be nice to be able to see your work in action, right? Well, unfortunately, we've still got a lot of loose ends in our application—we've briefly mentioned a singleton class called `Status` but we haven't created it yet, and we still have event handlers left to write. But never fear! We can quickly get the application up and running with a few class and function stubs.

We'll start by creating that `Status` singleton class with one empty method.

File: **appmonitor2.js (excerpt)**

```
var Status = new function() {
  this.init = function() {
    // don't mind me, I'm just a stub ...
  };
}
```

Since the `Status` class is used by the `Monitor` class, we must declare `Status` before `Monitor`.

Then, we'll add our button's `onclick` event handlers to the `Monitor` class. We'll have them display alert dialogs so that we know what would be going on if there was anything happening behind the scenes.

File: **appmonitor2.js (excerpt)**

```
this.pollServerStart = function() {
  alert('This will start the application polling the server.');
};
this.pollServerStop = function() {
  alert('This will stop the application polling the server.');
};
```

With these two simple stubs in place, your application should now be ready for a test-drive.

## Figure 3.2. Humble beginnings

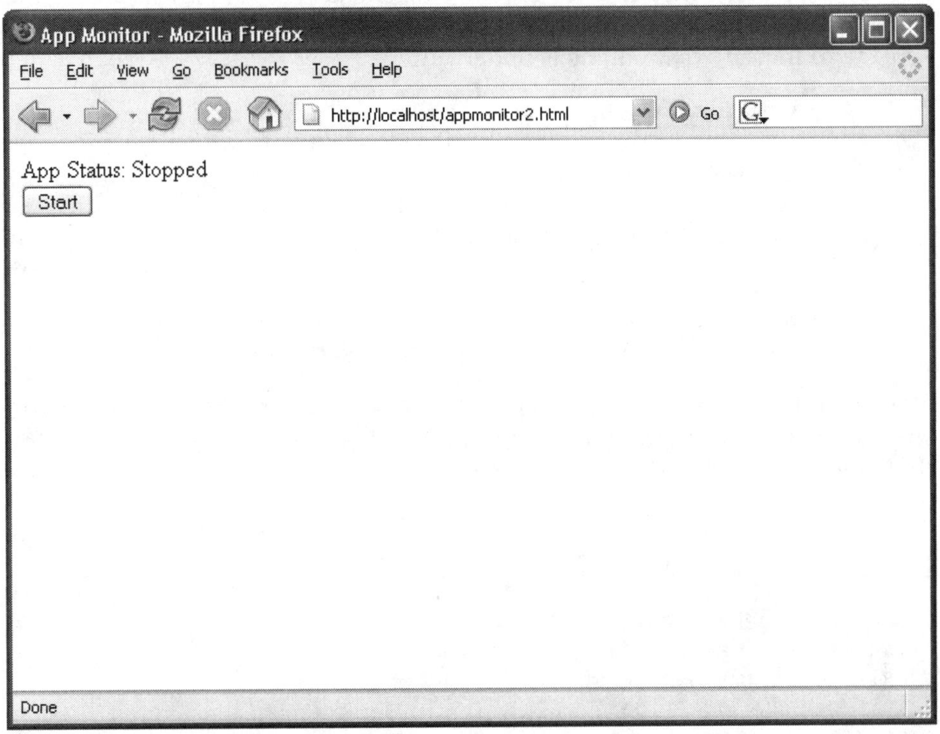

When you click the Start button in the display shown in Figure 3.2, you're presented with an alert box that promises greater things to come. Let's get started making good on those promises.

# Polling the Server

The first step is to flesh out the Start button's onclick event handler, pollServer-Start:

File: **appmonitor2.js (excerpt)**

```
this.pollServerStart = function() {
  var self = Monitor;
  self.doPoll();
  self.toggleAppStatus(false);
};
```

This code immediately calls the `doPoll` method, which, like the app monitor we built in Chapter 2, will be responsible for making an HTTP request to poll the server. Once the request has been sent, the code calls `toggleAppStatus`, passing it `false` to indicate that polling is underway.

### Where's the Poll Interval?

You might wonder why, after all this talk about setting a poll interval, our code jumps right in with a request to the server; where's the time delay? The answer is that we don't want a time delay on the very first request. If users click the button and there's a ten-second delay before anything happens, they'll think the app is broken. We want delays between all the subsequent requests that occur once the application is running, but when the user first clicks that button, we want the polling to start right away.

The only difference between `doPoll` in this version of our app monitor and the one we saw in the last chapter is the use of `self` to prefix the properties of the class, and the call to `setTimeout`. Take a look:

File: **appmonitor2.js (excerpt)**

```
this.doPoll = function() {
  var self = Monitor;
  var url = self.targetURL;
  var start = new Date();
  self.reqStatus.startProc();
  self.start = start.getTime();
  self.ajax.doGet(self.targetURL + '?start=' + self.start,
      self.showPoll);
  self.timeoutHand = setTimeout(self.handleTimeout,
      self.timeoutThreshold * 1000);
};
```

Our call to `setTimeout` instructs the browser to call `handleTimeout` once the timeout threshold has passed. We're also keeping track of the interval ID that's returned, so we can cancel our call to `handleTimeout` when the response is received by `showPoll`.

Here's the code for the `showPoll` method, which handles the response from the server:

File: **appmonitor2.js (excerpt)**

```
this.showPoll = function(str) {
  var self = Monitor;
  var diff = 0;
  var end = new Date();
```

```
  clearTimeout(self.timeoutHand);
  self.reqStatus.stopProc(true);
  if (str == 'ok') {
    end = end.getTime();
    diff = (end - self.start) / 1000;
  }
  if (self.updatePollArray(diff)) {
    self.printResult();
  }
  self.doPollDelay();
};
```

The first thing this method does is cancel the delayed call to handleTimeout that was made at the end of doPoll. After this, we tell our instance of the Status class to stop its animation (we'll be looking at the details of this a little later).

After these calls, showPoll checks to make sure that the response is ok, then calculates how long that response took to come back from the server. The error handling capabilities of the Ajax class should handle errors from the server, so our script shouldn't return anything other than ok … though it never hurts to make sure!

Once it has calculated the response time, showPoll records that response time with updatePollArray, then displays the result with printResult. We'll look at both of these methods in the next section.

Finally, we schedule another poll in doPollDelay—a very simple method that schedules another call to doPoll once the poll interval has passed:

File: **appmonitor2.js (excerpt)**

```
this.doPollDelay = function() {
  var self = Monitor;
  self.pollHand = setTimeout(self.doPoll,
      self.pollInterval * 1000);
};
```

To check our progress up to this point, we'll need to add a few more stub methods. First, let's add startProc and stopProc to the Status class:

File: **appmonitor2.js (excerpt)**

```
var Status = new function() {
  this.init = function() {
    // don't mind me, I'm just a stub ...
  };
  this.startProc = function() {
```

```
    // another stub function
  };
  this.stopProc = function() {
    // another stub function
  };
}
```

Let's also add a few stub methods to our `Monitor` class:

File: **appmonitor2.js (excerpt)**

```
this.handleTimeout = function() {
  alert("Timeout!");
};
this.updatePollArray = function(responseTime) {
  alert("Recording response time: " + responseTime);
};
this.printResult = function() {
  // empty stub function
};
```

Now we're ready to test our progress. Open `appmonitor2.html` in your web browser, click Start, and wait for `fakeserver.php` to wake from its sleep and send `ok` back to your page.

You can expect one of two outcomes: either a response is received by your page, and you see a dialog similar to the one shown in Figure 3.3, or you see the timeout message shown in Figure 3.4.

## Figure 3.3. A response received by your AJAX application

Don't worry if you receive the timeout message shown in Figure 3.4. Keep in mind that in our AJAX application, our timeout threshold is currently set to ten seconds, and that `fakeserver.php` is currently sleeping for a randomly selected number of seconds between three and 12. If the random number is ten or greater, the AJAX application will report a timeout.

## Figure 3.4. Your AJAX application giving up hope

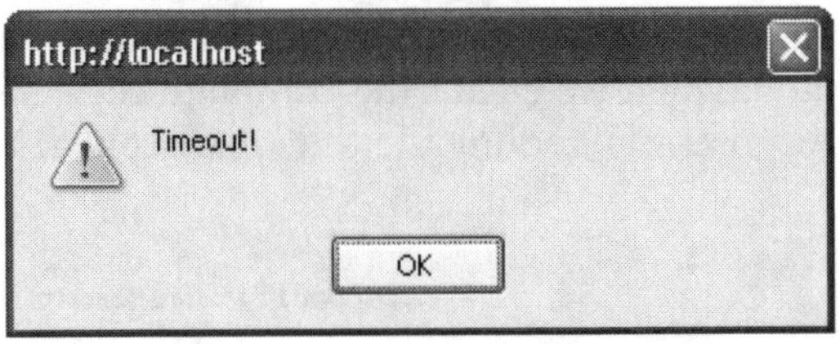

At the moment, we haven't implemented a way to stop the polling, so you'll need to stop it either by reloading the page or closing your browser window.

# Handling Timeouts

If you've run the code we've written so far, you've probably noticed that even when a timeout is reported, you see a message reporting the request's response time soon afterward. This occurs because handleTimeout is nothing but a simple stub at the moment. Let's look at building on that stub so we don't get this side-effect.

handleTimeout is basically a simplified version of showPoll: both methods are triggered by an asynchronous event (a call to setTimeout and an HTTP response received by an XMLHttpRequest object respectively), both methods need to record the response time (in a timeout's case, this will be 0), both methods need to update the user interface, and both methods need to trigger the next call to doPoll. Here's the code for handleTimeout:

File: **appmonitor2.js (excerpt)**

```
this.handleTimeout = function() {
  var self = Monitor;
  if (self.stopPoll()) {
    self.reqStatus.stopProc(true);
    if (self.updatePollArray(0)) {
      self.printResult();
    }
    self.doPollDelay();
  }
};
```

Here, handleTimeout calls stopPoll to stop our application polling the server. It records that a timeout occurred, updates the user interface, and finally sets up another call to doPoll via doPollDelay. We moved the code that stops the polling into a separate function because we'll need to revisit it later and beef it up. At present, the `stopPoll` method merely aborts the HTTP request via the `Ajax` class's `abort` method; however, there are a few scenarios that this function doesn't handle. We'll address these later, when we create the complete code to stop the polling process, but for the purposes of handling the timeout, `stopPoll` is fine.

File: **appmonitor2.js (excerpt)**

```
this.stopPoll = function() {
  var self = Monitor;
  if (self.ajax) {
    self.ajax.abort();
  }
  return true;
};
```

Now, when we reload our application, the timeouts perform exactly as we expect them to.

# The Response Times Bar Graph

Now, to the meat of the new version of our monitoring app! We want the application to show a list of past response times, not just a single entry of the most recent one, and we want to show that list in a way that's quickly and easily readable. A running bar graph display is the perfect tool for the job.

## The Running List in `pollArray`

All the response times will go into an array that's stored in the `pollArray` property of the `Monitor` class. We keep this array updated with the intuitively named `updatePollArray` method. It's a very simple method that looks like this:

File: **appmonitor2.js (excerpt)**

```
this.updatePollArray = function(pollResult) {
  var self = Monitor;
  self.pollArray.unshift(pollResult);
  if (self.pollArray.length > self.maxPollEntries) {
    self.pollArray.pop();
  }
  return true;
};
```

The code is very straightforward, although some of the functions we've used in it have slightly confusing names.

The unshift method of an Array object puts a new item in the very first element of the array, and shifts the rest of the array's contents over by one position, as shown in Figure 3.5.

## Figure 3.5. Inserting fruit using unshift

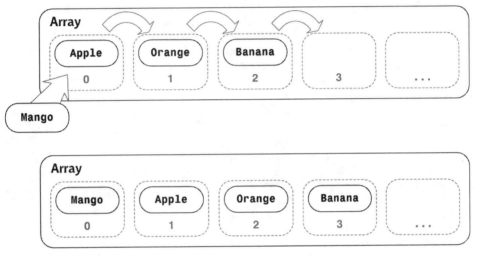

When the array exceeds the user-defined maximum length, updatePollArray truncates it by "popping" an item off the end. This is achieved by the pop method, which simply deletes the last item of an array.[2] The reason why we append items to the top and remove items from the bottom of the array is that, in our display, we want the most recent entries to appear at the top, and older entries to gradually move down to the bottom.

# Displaying the Results

Once we've updated the results in pollArray, we can display them using the printResult method. This is actually the cool part: the user will experience first-

---

[2] The method name pop may seem quite odd, but it makes more sense once you understand a data structure called a **stack**, which stores a number of items that can be accessed only in the reverse of the order in which they were added to the stack. We "push" an item onto a stack to add it, and "pop" an item from a stack to retrieve it. The pop method was originally designed for developers who were using arrays as stacks, but here we've repurposed it simply to delete the last item in an array.

hand the difference between our AJAX application and an older-style app that requires an entire page refresh to update content.

### Rendering Page Partials

In AJAX jargon, the chunk of the page that holds the list of response times is called a **page partial**. This refers to an area of a web page that's updated separately from the rest of the page.

Updating a chunk of a web page in response to an asynchronous request to the server is called "rendering a page partial."

The `printResult` method iterates through `pollArray`, and uses DOM methods to draw the list of poll results inside a `div` with the ID `pollResults`. We'll start by adding that `div` to our markup:

File: **appmonitor2.html** (excerpt)

```
<body>
  <div id="statusMessage">App Status:
    <span id="currentAppState"></span>
  </div>
  <div id="pollResults"></div>
  <div id="buttonArea"></div>
</body>
```

Now we're ready for the `printResult` method:

File: **appmonitor2.js** (excerpt)

```
this.printResult = function() {
  var self = Monitor;
  var polls = self.pollArray;
  var pollDiv = document.getElementById('pollResults');
  var entryDiv = null;
  var messageDiv = null;
  var barDiv = null;
  var clearAll = null;
  var msgStr = '';
  var txtNode = null;
  while (pollDiv.firstChild) {
    pollDiv.removeChild(pollDiv.firstChild);
  }
  for (var i = 0; i < polls.length; i++) {
    if (polls[i] == 0) {
      msgStr = '(Timeout)';
    }
```

```
    else {
      msgStr = polls[i] + ' sec.';
    }
    entryDiv = document.createElement('div');
    messageDiv = document.createElement('div');
    barDiv = document.createElement('div');
    clearAll = document.createElement('br');
    entryDiv.className = 'pollResult';
    messageDiv.className = 'time';
    barDiv.className = 'bar';
    clearAll.className = 'clearAll';
    if (polls[i] == 0) {
      messageDiv.style.color = '#933';
    }
    else {
      messageDiv.style.color = '#339';
    }
    barDiv.style.width = (parseInt(polls[i] * 20)) + 'px';
    messageDiv.appendChild(document.createTextNode(msgStr));
    barDiv.appendChild(document.createTextNode('\u00A0'));
    entryDiv.appendChild(messageDiv);
    entryDiv.appendChild(barDiv);
    entryDiv.appendChild(clearAll);
    pollDiv.appendChild(entryDiv);
  }
};
```

There's quite a bit here, so let's look at this method step by step.

File: **appmonitor2.js** (excerpt)

```
while (pollDiv.firstChild) {
  pollDiv.removeChild(pollDiv.firstChild);
}
```

After initializing some variables, this method removes everything from pollDiv: the while loop uses removeChild repeatedly to delete all the child nodes from pollDiv.

Next comes a simple for loop that jumps through the updated array of results and displays them.

We generate a message for the result of each item in this array. As you can see below, timeouts (which are recorded as a 0) generate a message of (Timeout).

File: **appmonitor2.js** (excerpt)

```
if (polls[i] == 0) {
  msgStr = '(Timeout)';
}
else {
  msgStr = polls[i] + ' sec.';
}
```

Next, we use DOM methods to add the markup for each entry in the list dynamically. In effect, we construct the following HTML in JavaScript for each entry in the list:

```
<div class="pollResult">
    <div class="time" style="color: #339;">8.031 sec.</div>
    <div class="bar" style="width: 160px;"> </div>
    <br class="clearAll"/>
</div>
```

The width of the `bar` `div` changes to reflect the actual response time, and timeouts are shown in red, but otherwise all entries in this list are identical. Note that you have to put something in the `div` to cause its background color to display. Even if you give the `div` a fixed width, the background color will not show if the `div` is empty. This is annoying, but it's easy to fix: we can fill in the `div` with a non-breaking space character.

Let's take a look at the code we'll use to insert this markup:

File: **appmonitor2.js** (excerpt)

```
entryDiv = document.createElement('div');
messageDiv = document.createElement('div');
barDiv = document.createElement('div');
clearAll = document.createElement('br');
entryDiv.className = 'pollResult';
messageDiv.className = 'time';
barDiv.className = 'bar';
clearAll.className = 'clearAll';
if (polls[i] == 0) {
  messageDiv.style.color = '#933';
}
else {
  messageDiv.style.color = '#339';
}
barDiv.style.width = (parseInt(polls[i] * 20).) + 'px';
messageDiv.appendChild(document.createTextNode(msgStr));
barDiv.appendChild(document.createTextNode('\u00A0'));
```

```
entryDiv.appendChild(messageDiv);
entryDiv.appendChild(barDiv);
entryDiv.appendChild(clearAll);
pollDiv.appendChild(entryDiv);
```

This code may seem complicated if you've never used DOM manipulation functions, but it's really quite simple. We use the well-named `createElement` method to create elements; then we assign values to the properties of each of those element objects.

Just after the `if` statement, we can see the code that sets the pixel width of the bar `div` according to the number of seconds taken to generate each response. We multiply that time figure by 20 to get a reasonable width, but you may want to use a higher or lower number depending on how much horizontal space is available on the page.

To add text to elements, we use `createTextNode` in conjunction with `appendChild`, which is also used to place elements inside other elements.

 *Tip*

### createTextNode and Non-breaking Spaces

In the code above, we create a non-breaking space using \u00A0. If we try to use the normal   entity here, `createTextNode` will attempt to be "helpful" by converting the ampersand to &amp;; the result of this is that   is displayed on your page. The workaround is to use the escaped unicode non-breaking space: \u00A0.

### Figure 3.6. The application starting to take shape

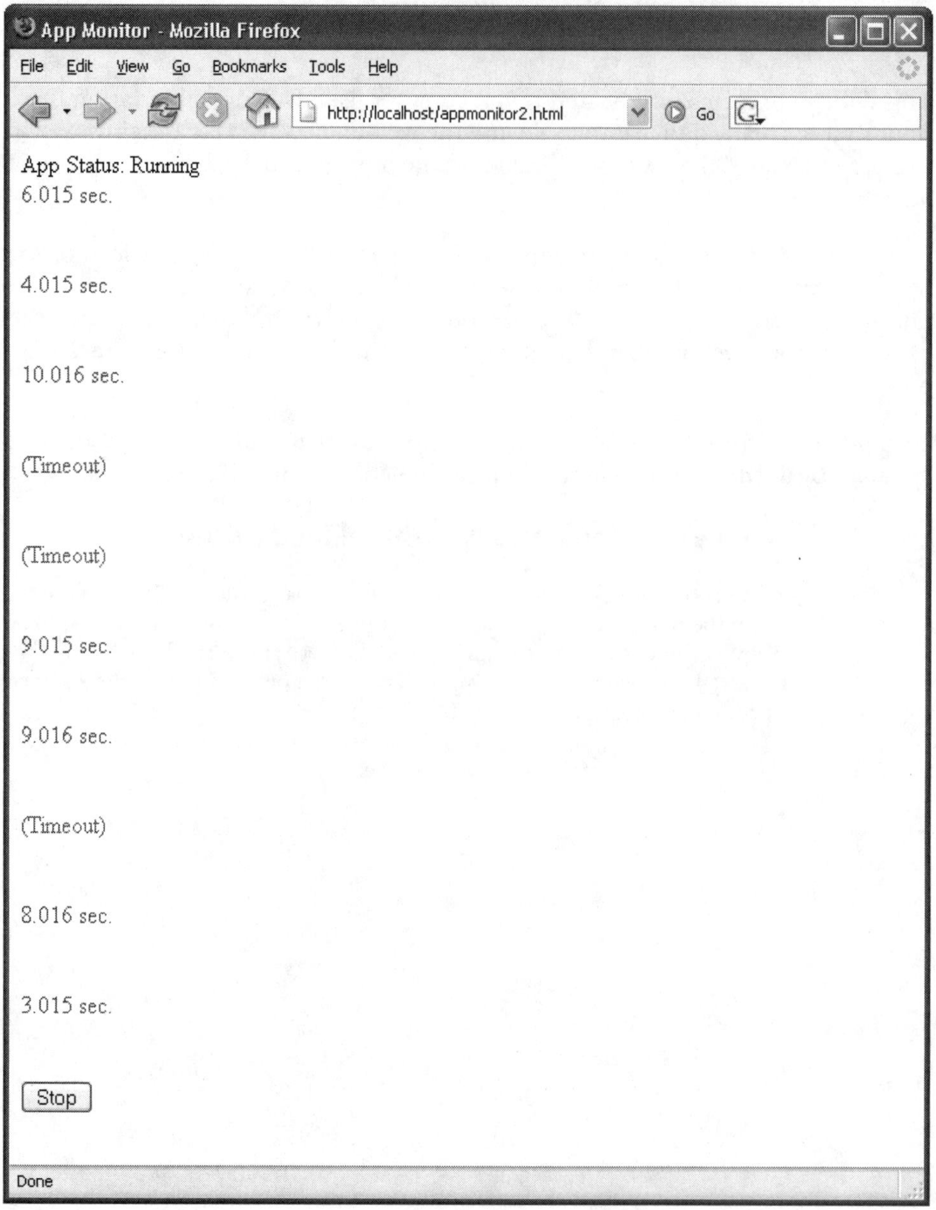

The last piece of the code puts all the `div` elements together, then places the `pollResult div` inside the `pollResults div`. Figure 3.6 shows the running application.

"Hold on a second," you may well be thinking. "Where's the bar graph we're supposed to be seeing?"

The first bar is there, but it's displayed in white on white, which is pretty useless. Let's make it visible through our application's CSS:

File: **appmonitor2.css** (excerpt)

```
.time {
  width: 6em;
  float: left;
}
.bar {
  background: #ddf;
  float: left;
}
.clearBoth {
  clear: both;
}
```

The main point of interest in the CSS is the `float: left` declarations for the `time` and `bar div` elements, which make up the time listing and the colored bar in the bar graph. Floating them to the left is what makes them appear side by side. However, for this positioning technique to work, an element with the `clearBoth` class must appear immediately after these two `divs`.

This is where you can see AJAX in action. It uses bits and pieces of all these different technologies—`XMLHttpRequest`, the W3C DOM, and CSS—wired together and controlled with JavaScript. Programmers often experience the biggest problems with CSS and with the practicalities of building interface elements in their code.

As an AJAX programmer, you can either try to depend on a library to take care of the CSS for you, or you can learn enough to get the job done. It's handy to know someone smart who's happy to answer lots of questions on the topic, or to have a good book on CSS (for example, SitePoint's *The CSS Anthology: 101 Essential Tips, Tricks & Hacks*[3]).

---

[3] http://www.sitepoint.com/books/cssant1/

**Figure 3.7. The beginnings of our bar graph**

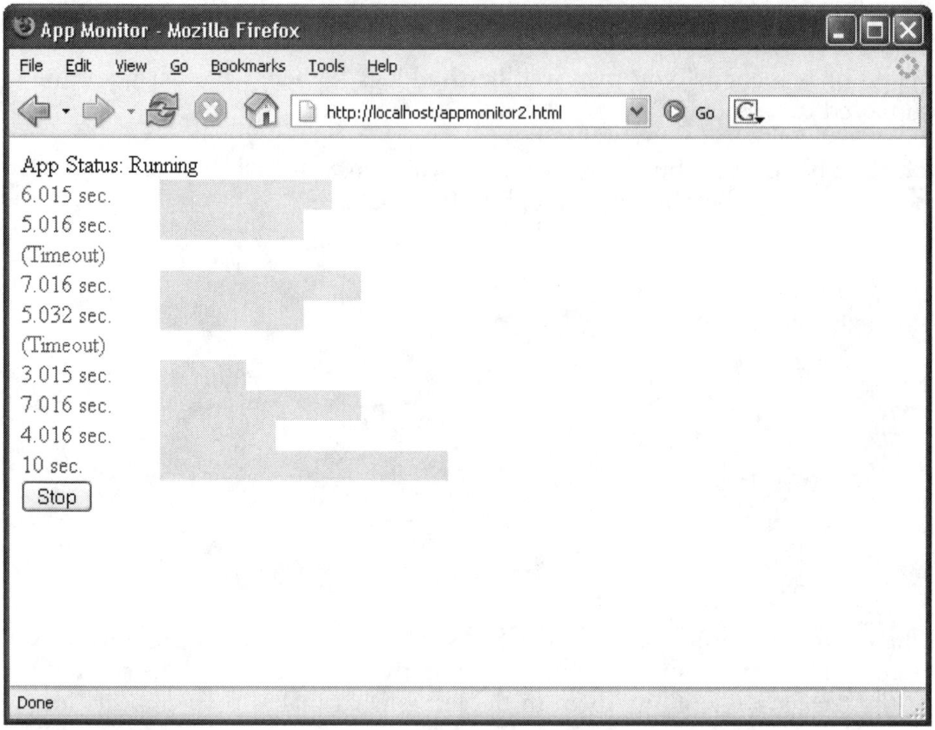

Now that our CSS is in place, we can see the bar graph in our application display, as Figure 3.7 illustrates.

# Stopping the Application

The final action of the `pollServerStart` method, after getting the app running, is to call `toggleAppStatus` to toggle the appearance of the application. `toggleAppStatus` changes the status display to App Status: Running, switches the Start button to a Stop button, and attaches the `pollServerStop` method to the button's `onclick` event.

The `pollServerStop` method stops the ongoing polling process, then toggles the application back so that it looks like it's properly stopped:

File: **appmonitor2.js** (excerpt)

```
this.pollServerStop = function() {
  var self = Monitor;
  if (self.stopPoll()) {
    self.toggleAppStatus(true);
  }
  self.reqStatus.stopProc(false);
};
```

This code reuses the `stopPoll` method we added earlier in the chapter. At the moment, all that method does is abort the current HTTP request, which is fine while we're handling a timeout. However, this method needs to handle two other scenarios as well.

The first of these scenarios occurs when the method is called during the poll interval (that is, after we receive a response to an HTTP request, but before the next request is sent). In this scenario, we need to cancel the delayed call to `doPoll`.

The second scenario that this method must be able to handle arises when `stopPoll` is called after it has sent a request, but before it receives the response. In this scenario, the timeout handler needs to be canceled.

As we keep track of the interval IDs of both calls, we can modify `stopPoll` to handle these scenarios with two calls to `clearTimeout`:

File: **appmonitor2.js** (excerpt)

```
this.stopPoll = function() {
  var self = Monitor;
  clearTimeout(self.pollHand);
  if (self.ajax) {
    self.ajax.abort();
  }
  clearTimeout(self.timeoutHand);
  return true;
};
```

Now, you should be able to stop and start the polling process just by clicking the Start/Stop button beneath the bar graph.

# Status Notifications

The ability of AJAX to update content asynchronously, and the fact that updates may affect only small areas of the page, make the display of status notifications a critical part of an AJAX app's design and development. After all, your app's users need to know what the app is doing.

Back in the old days of web development, when an entire page had to reload in order to reflect any changes to its content, it was perfectly clear to end users when the application was communicating with the server. But our AJAX web apps can talk to the server in the background, which means that users don't see the complete page reload that would otherwise indicate that something was happening.

So, how will users of your AJAX app know that the page is communicating with the server? Well, instead of the old spinning globe or waving flag animations that display in the browser chrome, AJAX applications typically notify users that processing is under way with the aid of small animations or visual **transitions**. Usually achieved with CSS, these transitions catch users' eyes—without being distracting!—and provide hints about what the application is doing. An important aspect of the good AJAX app design is the development of these kinds of notifications.

# The Status Animation

Since we already have at the top of our application a small bar that tells the user if the app is running or stopped, this is a fairly logical place to display a little more status information.

Animations like twirling balls or running dogs are a nice way to indicate that an application is busy—generally, you'll want to display an image that uses movement to indicate activity. However, we don't want to use a cue that's going to draw users' attention away from the list, or drive people to distraction as they're trying to read the results, so we'll just go with the slow, pulsing animation shown in Figure 3.8.

This animation has the added advantages of being lightweight and easy to implement in CSS—no Flash player is required, and there's no bulky GIF image to download frame by tedious frame.

The far right-hand side of the white bar is unused space, which makes it an ideal place for this kind of notification: it's at the top of the user interface, so it's easy to see, but it's off to the right, so it's out of the way of people who are trying to read the list of results.

## Figure 3.8. Our pulsing status animation

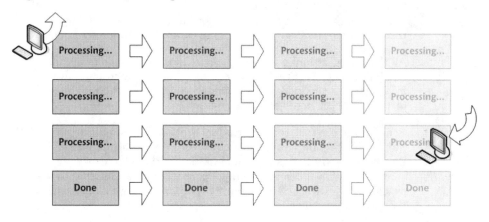

To host this animation, we'll add a div with the ID pollingMessage just below the status message div in our document:

File: **appmonitor2.html** (excerpt)

```
<body>
  <div id="statusMessage">App Status:
    <span id="currentAppState"></span>
  </div>
  <div id="pollingMessage"></div>
  <div id="pollResults"></div>
  <div id="buttonArea"></div>
</body>
```

Add a CSS rule to your style sheet to position this div:

File: **appmonitor2.css** (excerpt)

```
#pollingMessage {
  float: right;
  width: 80px;
  padding: 0.2em;
  text-align: center;
}
```

This animation is now positioned to the right of the page.

When you open the page in your browser, you won't be able to see the animation—it's nothing but a white box on a white background at the moment. If you'd like to, add some content to pollingMessage to see where it's positioned.

### setInterval and Loss of Scope

The JavaScript `setInterval` is an obvious and easy way to handle a task that occurs repeatedly—for instance, to control a pulsing animation.

All the CSS gyrations with `setInterval` result in some fairly interesting and bulky code. So, as I mentioned before, it makes sense to put the code for the status animation into its own class—`Status`—that we can reference and use from the `Monitor` class.

Some of the clever developers reading this may already have guessed that `setInterval` suffers from the same loss-of-scope problems as `setTimeout`: the object keyword `this` becomes lost. Since we have to deal with only one status animation in our monitoring application, it makes sense to take the expedient approach, and make our `Status` class a singleton class, just as we did for the `Monitor` class.

# Setting Up Status

Let's start by adding some properties to the `Status` stub we've already written, in order to get the previous code working:

File: **appmonitor2.js (excerpt)**

```
var Status = new function() {
  this.currOpacity = 100;
  this.proc = 'done'; // 'proc', 'done' or 'abort'
  this.procInterval = null;
  this.div = null;
  this.init = function() {
    // don't mind me, I'm just a stub ...
  };
  this.startProc = function() {
    // another stub function
  };
  this.stopProc = function() {
    // another stub function
  };
}
```

The `Status` object has four properties:

❑ The `currOpacity` property tracks the opacity of the `pollingMessage` div. We use `setInterval` to change the opacity of this `div` rapidly, which produces the pulsing and fading effect.

❏ The `proc` property is a three-state switch that indicates whether an HTTP request is currently in progress, has been completed successfully, or was aborted before completion.

❏ The `procInterval` property is for storing the interval ID for the `setInterval` process that controls the animation. We'll use it to stop the running animation.

❏ The `div` property is a reference to the `pollingMessage` div. The `Status` class manipulates the `pollingMessage` div's CSS properties to create the animation.

## Initialization

An `init` method is needed to bind the `div` property to `pollingMessage`:

File: **appmonitor2.js (excerpt)**

```
this.init = function() {
  var self = Status;
  self.div = document.getElementById('pollingMessage');
  self.setAlpha();
};
```

The `init` method also contains a call to a method named `setAlpha`, which is required for an IE workaround that we'll be looking at a bit later.

# Internet Explorer Memory Leaks

DOM element references (variables that point to `div`, `td`, or `span` elements and the like) that are used as class properties are a notorious cause of memory leaks in Internet Explorer. If you destroy an instance of a class without clearing such properties (by setting them to `null`), memory will not be reclaimed.

Let's add to our `Monitor` class a cleanup method that handles the `window.onunload` event, like so:

File: **appmonitor2.js (excerpt)**

```
window.onunload = Monitor.cleanup;
```

This method cleans up the `Status` class by calling that class's `cleanup` method and setting the `reqStatus` property to `null`:

File: **appmonitor2.js (excerpt)**

```
this.cleanup = function() {
  var self = Monitor;
```

```
  self.reqStatus.cleanup();
  self.reqStatus = null;
};
```

The `cleanup` method in the `Status` class does the IE housekeeping:

*File: **appmonitor2.js** (excerpt)*

```
this.cleanup = function() {
  Status.div = null;
};
```

If we don't set that `div` reference to `null`, Internet Explorer will keep the memory it allocated to that variable in a death grip, and you'll see memory use balloon each time you reload the page.

In reality, this wouldn't be much of a problem for our tiny application, but it can become a serious issue in large web apps that have a lot of DHTML. It's good to get into the habit of cleaning up DOM references in your code so that this doesn't become an issue for you.

# The `displayOpacity` Method

The central piece of code in the `Status` class lives in the `displayOpacity` method. This contains the browser-specific code that's necessary to change the appropriate CSS properties of the `pollingMessage` div. Here's the code:

*File: **appmonitor2.js** (excerpt)*

```
this.displayOpacity = function() {
  var self = Status;
  var decOpac = self.currOpacity / 100;
  if (document.all && typeof window.opera == 'undefined') {
    self.div.filters.alpha.opacity = self.currOpacity;
  }
  else {
    self.div.style.MozOpacity = decOpac;
  }
  self.div.style.opacity = decOpac;
};
```

The `currOpacity` property of the object represents the opacity to which the `pollingMessage` div should be set. Our implementation uses an integer scale ranging from 0 to 100, which is employed by Internet Explorer, rather than the fractional scale from zero to one that's expected by Mozilla and Safari. This choice is just a personal preference; if you prefer to use fractional values, by all means do.

In the method, you'll see a test for `document.all`—a property that's supported only by IE and Opera—and a test for `window.opera`, which, unsurprisingly, is supported only by Opera. As such, only IE should execute the `if` clause of this `if` statement. Inside this IE branch of the `if` statement, the proprietary `alpha.opacity` property is used to set opacity, while in the `else` clause, we use the older `MozOpacity` property, which is supported by older Mozilla-based browsers.

Finally, this method sets the opacity in the standards-compliant way: using the `opacity` property, which should ultimately be supported in all standards-compliant browsers.

## IE Gotchas

Internet Explorer version 6, being an older browser, suffers a couple of issues when trying to render opacity-based CSS changes.

Fortunately, the first of these is easily solved by an addition to our `pollingMessage` CSS rule:

File: **appmonitor2.css** (excerpt)

```
#pollingMessage {
  float: right;
  width: 80px;
  padding: 0.2em;
  text-align: center;
  background: #fff;
}
```

The addition of the `background` property fixes the first specific problem with Internet Explorer. We must set the background color of an element if we want to change its opacity in IE, or the text will display with jagged edges. Note that setting `background` to `transparent` will not work: it must be set to a specific color.

The second problem is a little trickier if you want your CSS files to be valid. IE won't let you change the `style.alpha.opacity` unless it's declared in the style sheet first. Now, if you don't mind preventing your style sheets from being passed by the W3C validator, it's easy to fix this problem by adding another declaration:

File: **appmonitor2.css** (excerpt)

```css
#pollingMessage {
  float: right;
  width: 80px;
  padding: 0.2em;
  text-align: center;
  background: #fff;
  filter: alpha(opacity = 100);
}
```

Unfortunately, this approach generates CSS warnings in browsers that don't support that proprietary property, such as Firefox 1.5, which displays CSS warnings in the JavaScript console by default. A solution that's better than inserting IE-specific style information into your global style sheet is to use JavaScript to add that declaration to the pollingMessage div's style attribute in IE only. That's what the setAlpha method that's called in init achieves. Here's the code for that method:

File: **appmonitor2.js** (excerpt)

```javascript
this.setAlpha = function() {
  var self = Status;
  if (document.all && typeof window.opera ==
      'undefined') {
    var styleSheets = document.styleSheets;
    for (var i = 0; i < styleSheets.length; i++) {
      var rules = styleSheets[i].rules;
      for (var j = 0; j < rules.length; j++) {
        if (rules[j].selectorText ==
            '#pollingMessage') {
          rules[j].style.filter =
              'alpha(opacity = 100)';
          return true;
        }
      }
    }
  }
  return false;
};
```

This code, which executes only in Internet Explorer, uses the document.styleSheets array to iterate through each style sheet that's linked to the current page. It accesses the rules in each of those style sheets using the rules property, and finds the style we want by looking at the selectorText property. Once it has the right style in the rules array, it gives the filter property the value it needs to change the opacity.

**Opacity in Opera?**

Unfortunately, at the time of writing, even the latest version of Opera (version 8.5) doesn't support CSS opacity, so such an animation does not work in that browser. However, this feature is planned for Opera version 9.

# Running the Animation

The code for the processing animation consists of five methods: the first three control the "Processing …" animation, while the remaining two control the "Done" animation. The three methods that control the "Processing …" animation are:

❑ startProc, which sets up the "Processing …" animation and schedules repeated calls to doProc with setInterval

❑ doProc, which monitors the properties of this class and sets the current frame of the "Processing …" animation appropriately

❑ stopProc, which signals that the "Processing …" animation should cease

The two that control the "Done" animation are:

❑ startDone sets up the "Done" animation and schedules repeated calls to doDone with setInterval

❑ doDone sets the current frame of the "Done" animation and terminates the animation once it's completed

## Starting it Up

Setting the animation up and starting it are jobs for the startProc method:

File: **appmonitor2.js (excerpt)**

```
this.startProc = function() {
  var self = Status;
  self.proc = 'proc';
  if (self.setDisplay(false)) {
    self.currOpacity = 100;
    self.displayOpacity();
    self.procInterval = setInterval(self.doProc, 90);
  }
};
```

After setting the `proc` property to `proc` (processing), this code calls the `setDisplay` method, which sets the color and content of the `pollingMessage` div. We'll take a closer look at `setDisplay` next.

Once the code sets the color and content of the `pollingMessage` div, it initializes the div's opacity to 100 (completely opaque) and calls `displayOpacity` to make this setting take effect.

Finally, this method calls `setInterval` to schedule the next step of the animation process. Note that, as with `setTimeout`, the `setInterval` call returns an interval ID. We store this in the `procInterval` property so we can stop the process later.

Both the "Processing ..." and "Done" animations share the `setDisplay` method:

File: **appmonitor2.js (excerpt)**

```
this.setDisplay = function(done) {
  var self = Status;
  var msg = '';
  if (done) {
    msg = 'Done';
    self.div.className = 'done';
  }
  else {
    msg = 'Processing...';
    self.div.className = 'processing';
  }
  if (self.div.firstChild) {
    self.div.removeChild(self.div.firstChild);
  }
  self.div.appendChild(document.createTextNode(msg));
  return true;
};
```

Since the only differences between the "Processing ..." and "Done" states of the `pollingMessage` div are its color and text, it makes sense to use this common function to toggle between the two states of the `pollingMessage` div. The colors are controlled by assigning classes to the `pollingMessage` div, so we'll need to add CSS class rules for the `done` and `processing` classes to our style sheet:

File: **appmonitor2.css (excerpt)**

```
.processing {
  color: #339;
  border: 1px solid #339;
}
```

```
.done {
  color:#393;
  border:1px solid #393;
}
```

# Making it Stop

Stopping the animation smoothly requires some specific timing. We don't want the animation to stop abruptly right in the middle of a pulse. We want to stop it in the natural break, when the "Processing …" image's opacity is down to zero.

So the stopProc method for stopping the animation doesn't actually stop it per se—it just sets a flag to tell the animation process that it's time to stop when it reaches a convenient point. This is a lot like the phone calls received by many programmers at the end of the day from wives and husbands reminding them to come home when they get to a logical stopping point in their code.

Since very little action occurs here, the method is pretty short:

File: **appmonitor2.js** (excerpt)

```
this.stopProc = function(done) {
  var self = Status;
  if (done) {
    self.proc = 'done';
  }
  else {
    self.proc = 'abort';
  }
};
```

This method does have to distinguish between two types of stopping: a successfully completed request (done) and a request from the user to stop the application (abort).

The doProc method uses this flag to figure out whether to display the "Done" message, or just to stop.

# Running the Animation with doProc

The doProc method, which is invoked at 90 millisecond intervals, changes the opacity of the pollingMessage div to produce the pulsing effect of the processing animation. Here's the code:

File: **appmonitor2.js** (excerpt)

```
this.doProc = function() {
  var self = Status;
  if (self.currOpacity == 0) {
    if (self.proc == 'proc') {
      self.currOpacity = 100;
    }
    else {
      clearInterval(self.procInterval);
      if (self.proc == 'done') {
        self.startDone();
      }
      return false;
    }
  }
  self.currOpacity = self.currOpacity - 10;
  self.displayOpacity();
};
```

This method is dead simple—its main purpose is simply to reduce the opacity of the pollingMessage div by 10% every time it's called.

The first if statement looks to see if the div has completely faded out. If it has, and the animation is still supposed to be running, it resets the opacity to 100 (fully opaque). Executing this code every 90 milliseconds produces a smooth effect in which the pollingMessage div fades out, reappears, and fades out again—the familiar pulsing effect that shows that the application is busy doing something.

If the animation is not supposed to continue running, we stop the animation by calling clearInterval, then, if the proc property is done, we trigger the "Done" animation with a call to startDone.

## Starting the "Done" Animation with startDone

The startDone method serves the same purpose for the "Done" animation that the startProc method serves for the "Processing …" animation. It looks remarkably similar to startProc, too:

File: **appmonitor2.js** (excerpt)

```
this.startDone = function() {
  var self = Status;
  if (self.setDisplay(true)) {
    self.currOpacity = 100;
    self.displayOpacity();
```

```
    self.procInterval = setInterval(self.doDone, 90);
  }
};
```

This time, we pass true to setDisplay, which will change the text to "Done" and the color to green.

We then set up calls to doDone with setInterval, which actually performs the fadeout.

## The Final Fade

The code for doDone is significantly simpler than the code for doProc. It doesn't have to process continuously until told to stop, like doProc does. It just keeps on reducing the opacity of the pollingMessage div by 10% until it reaches zero, then stops itself. Pretty simple stuff:

File: **appmonitor2.js** (excerpt)

```
this.doDone = function() {
  var self = Status;
  if (self.currOpacity == 0) {
    clearInterval(self.procInterval);
  }
  self.currOpacity = self.currOpacity - 10;
  self.displayOpacity();
};
```

## Figure 3.9. The application with a pulsing status indicator

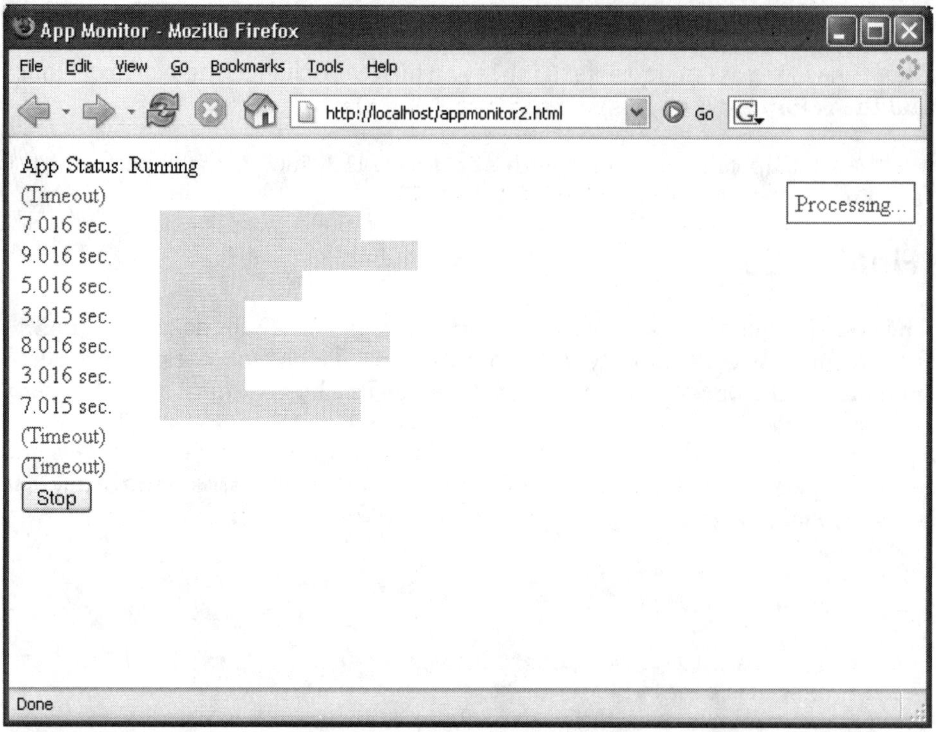

Finally, we're ready to test this code in our browser. Open `appmonitor2.html` in your browser, click the Start button, and you should see a pulsing Processing … message near the top right-hand corner of the browser's viewport, like the one shown in Figure 3.9.

**Tip**

### Be Careful with that Poll Interval!

Now that we have an animation running in the page, we need to be careful that we don't start the animation again before the previous one stops. For this reason, it's highly recommended that you don't set `POLL_INTERVAL` to anything less than two seconds.

# Styling the Monitor

Now that we've got our application up and running, let's use CSS to make it look good. We'll need to add the following markup to achieve our desired layout:

File: **appmonitor2.html (excerpt)**

```
<body>
  <div id="wrapper">
    <div id="main">
      <div id="status">
        <div id="statusMessage">App Status:
          <span id="currentAppState"></span>
        </div>
        <div id="pollingMessage"></div>
        <br class="clearBoth" />
      </div>
      <div id="pollResults"></div>
      <div id="buttonArea"></div>
    </div>
  </div>
</body>
```

As you can see, we've added three divs from which we can hang our styles, and a line break to clear the floated application status message and animation. The completed CSS for this page is as follows; the styled interface is shown in Figure 3.10:

File: **appmonitor2.css**

```
body, p, div, td, ul {
  font-family: verdana, arial, helvetica, sans-serif;
  font-size:12px;
}
#wrapper {
  padding-top: 24px;
}
#main {
  width: 360px;
  height: 280px;
  padding: 24px;
  text-align: left;
  background: #eee;
  border: 1px solid #ddd;
  margin:auto;
}
#status {
  width: 358px;
  height: 24px;
  padding: 2px;
  background: #fff;
  margin-bottom: 20px;
```

```css
  border: 1px solid #ddd;
}
#statusMessage {
  font-size: 11px;
  float: left;
  height: 16px;
  padding: 4px;
  text-align: left;
  color: #999;
}
#pollingMessage {
  font-size: 11px;
  float: right;
  width: 80px;
  height: 14px;
  padding: 4px;
  text-align: center;
  background: #fff;
}
#pollResults {
  width: 360px;
  height: 210px;
}
#buttonArea {
  text-align: center;
}
.pollResult {
  padding-bottom: 4px;
}
.time {
  font-size: 11px;
  width: 74px;
  float: left;
}
.processing {
  color: #339;
  border: 1px solid #333399;
}
.done {
  color: #393;
  border: 1px solid #393;
}
.bar {
  background: #ddf;
  float: left;
}
```

```
.inputButton {
  width: 8em;
  height: 2em;
}
.clearBoth {
  clear: both;
}
```

**Figure 3.10. The completed App Monitor**

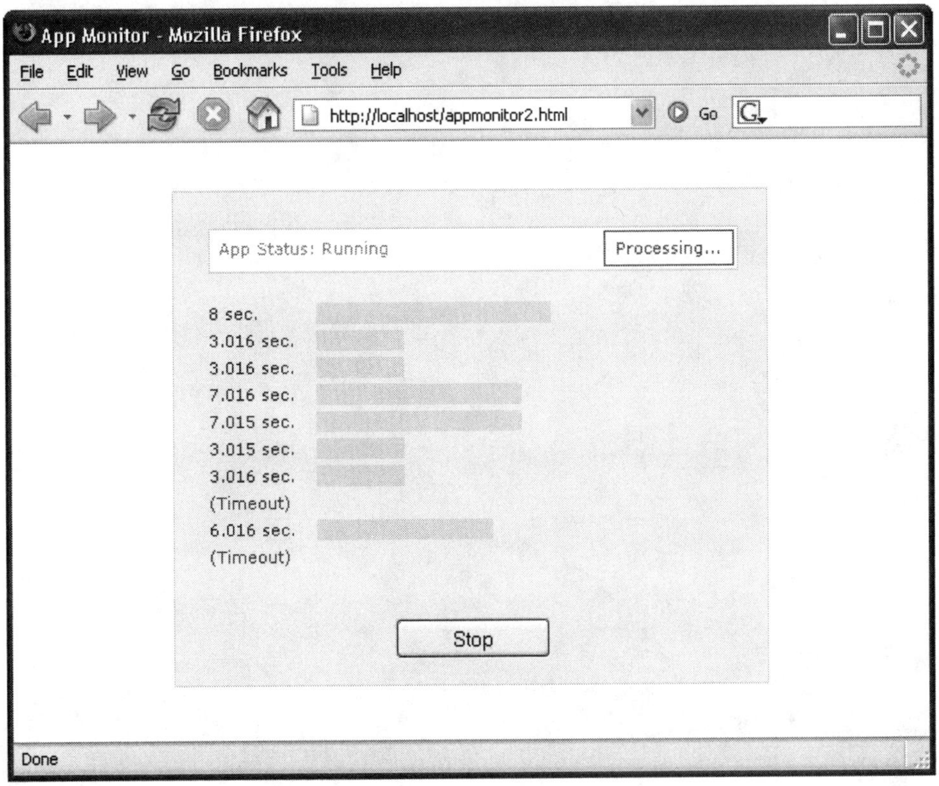

# Summary

Our first working application showed how AJAX can be used to make multiple requests to a server without the user ever leaving the currently loaded page. It also gave a fairly realistic picture of the kind of complexity we have to deal with when performing multiple tasks asynchronously. A good example of this complexity was our use of `setTimeout` to time the `XMLHttpRequest` requests. This example provided a good opportunity to explore some of the common problems you'll encounter as you develop AJAX apps, such as loss of scope and connection timeouts, and provided practical solutions to help you deal with them.

# 4

# AJAX and POST Requests

*I do not sit at the kiddie table. Now you either give me the big toys or you send me home.*
—John Crichton, *Farscape*

We spent the last two chapters working with AJAX and basic HTTP GET requests. We built a very simple monitoring application that pings a web site and reports the server's response time. In this chapter, we'll move up to the next level as we begin to work with POST requests. Here, we'll build a web application login screen that uses AJAX to send users' login information back to the server in a POST request.

Generally, a login page for a web application involves only two form fields, so it's legitimate to ask if there's any real advantage in using AJAX techniques to build such a form. Why wouldn't we just keep things basic and use a normal form? Actually, this is a very important question. AJAX development is fairly new, and right now the biggest problem with it seems to be that people immediately begin to ask *how* to achieve a task using AJAX when they should first ask *if* they should achieve that task using AJAX.

You should only pull AJAX out of your web development toolbox if it's going to provide tangible value for the end user. In the case of a web application login system, AJAX can deliver some real benefits in terms of efficiency and ease of use. With the login form we'll be building in this chapter, incomplete form submissions are near-impossible, and incorrect logins can be reported in as little time as it takes to send and receive a few hundred bytes of data. This is a big improvement on the tens of thousands of bytes that would need to be sent and received in an non-AJAX web application.

But, before we dive into the process of POSTing data, let's review how we work with query strings, and how we send data back to the server with the request.

# Review: Sending Data with GET

An easy way to send a little data back to the server involves sending a simple GET request with a query string tacked onto the end of the target URL. Doing so using our Ajax library is easy:

```
var ajax = new Ajax();
var handlerFunc = function(str) {
  // Do something with the response
}
ajax.doGet('/some_url.php?bass=Geddy&guitar=Alex&drums=Neil',
    handlerFunc);
```

Using GET makes it very easy to send a little extra information to the web server.

# Sending Data with POST

Let's have a look at how our Ajax class sends POST requests, then apply that to our web application login.

The POST method sends the extra data in a package that's separate from the page location, so it's not as easy to use as GET. However, it's the preferred option in the following types of situations:

❑ You need to send a large amount of data back to the server.

❑ The data needs to be formatted in a very specific way (e.g., XML-RPC).

❑ You're sending sensitive data such as passwords.

We need to take the following, additional steps in order to use our Ajax class to send POST requests:

❑ Set the request method for our instance of XMLHttpRequest to POST (of course).

❏ Pass the POST data to the send method of the XMLHttpRequest object.

❏ Set the Content-Type header for the request to application/x-www-form-urlencoded.

To perform these actions, we'll add to the Ajax class a method called doPost, which will be very similar to doGet:

File: **ajax.js (excerpt)**

```
this.doPost = function(url, postData, hand, format) {
  this.url = url;
  this.handleResp = hand;
  this.responseFormat = format || 'text';
  this.method = 'POST';
  this.postData = postData;
  this.doReq();
};
```

The first three lines of this method are the same as those in the doGet method, and should be familiar to you by now. The fourth line sets the value of the method property, which is used in the call to the XMLHttpRequest class's open method in doReq:

File: **ajax.js (excerpt)**

```
this.req.open(this.method, this.url, this.async);
```

In order to set the POST data for this request, we simply set the postData property. This data should consist of a string that's formatted in variable-value pairs and is URL-encoded—just like a normal query string.

Finally, we need to set the ContentType of the request to application/x-www-form-urlencoded. We'll add this to the doReq method using the setRequestMethod method:

File: **ajax.js (excerpt)**

```
this.doReq = function() {
  if (!this.init()) {
    alert('Could not create XMLHttpRequest object.');
    return;
  }
  this.req.open(this.method, this.url, this.async);
  if (this.method == "POST") {
    this.req.setRequestHeader('Content-Type',
        'application/x-www-form-urlencoded');
```

```
    }
    var self = this; // Fix loss-of-scope in inner function
    this.req.onreadystatechange = function() {
      if (self.req.readyState == 4) {
        ⋮
      }
    };
    this.req.send(this.postData);
};
```

Now, let's look at a quick example that pulls data from an actual form.

# A Quick Form POST

Imagine that you have a web page that displays the following form, which contains information about 80s-era progressive rock bands:

```
<form id="band" action="/handle_input.php">
  <input type="text" name="bass" id="bass" value="Geddy"/>
  <input type="text" name="guitar" id="guitar" value="Alex"/>
  <input type="text" name="drums" id="drums" value="Neil"/>
</form>
```

You could pull out the form data and POST it with our Ajax object, like this:

```
var bandForm = document.getElementById('band');
var ajax = new Ajax();
var handlerFunc = function(str) {
  // Do something with the response
}
var formData = '';
formData += 'bass=' + escape(bandForm.bass.value);
formData += '&guitar=' + escape(bandForm.guitar.value);
formData += '&drums=' + escape(bandForm.drums.value);
ajax.doPost('/handle_input.php', formData, handlerFunc);
```

This seems fairly easy. The only difference between this and the doGet method is the extra parameter, which passes the query string-formatted data for POSTing.

# Using formData2QueryString

When you're working with more complicated forms, you're not very likely to want to craft query strings laboriously, pulling in the data from form elements.

This is where `formData2QueryString`[1] comes in handy. `formData2QueryString`, an external library, contains a handy function that scrapes a web form of all its data and creates a string of name-value pairs; we can use `formData2QueryString` for our `POST`.

Using `formData2QueryString` is easy: just pass it a reference to the `form` from which you want to pull data, and it returns a properly formatted string that contains the values of all the elements in the form.

Using `formData2QueryString`, we could modify the previous example to look like this:

```
var bandForm = document.getElementById('band');
var ajax = new Ajax();
var handlerFunc = function(str) {
  // Do something with the input
}
var formData = '';
formData = formData2QueryString(bandForm);
ajax.doPost('/handle_input.php', formData, handlerFunc);
```

By simplifying the process of packaging data for `POST` requests, `formData2QueryString` allows you to continue to use web forms as you always have, while taking advantage of the power of AJAX.

---

[1] `formData2QueryString` is available under the Apache License, Version 2.0, at http://www.fleegix.org/downloads/formdata2querystring.js.

# An Application Login

## Figure 4.1. The web application login

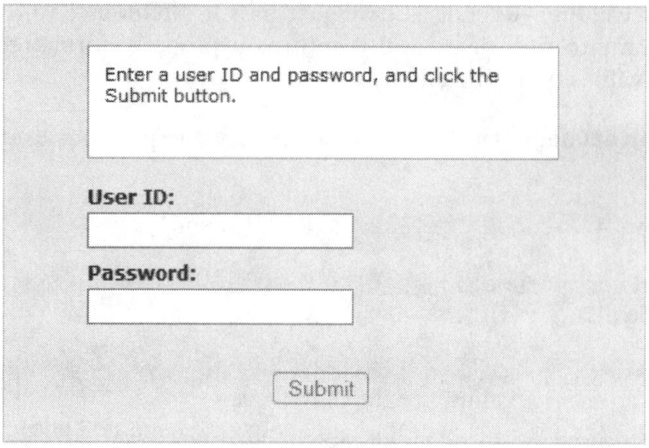

By AJAX-ifying a web application's login form you can provide your users an experience that's much closer to that of a traditional desktop application than a typical web application. AJAX improves the developer's ability to insert notifications—such as processing animations or error messages—inline into the page, which quickly and conveniently lets users know what's happening with the login process. Figure 4.1 shows what the login page will look like.

# Accessibility and Backward Compatibility

In some cases, AJAX web application code is so complicated that it makes sense to maintain two separate versions—a "hi-fi" version that contains all the AJAX bells and whistles for modern browsers, and a low-fi version, made up of text-only web pages generated on the server side, for users of older browsers, text browsers, and low-end mobile devices. This all-or-nothing approach is less than optimal, because it requires us to relegate all users who don't have the ideal browser configuration to the text-only "ghetto," even though many of their systems may support a lot of the app's functionality.

That's why the principle of **progressive enhancement** (which, in the web application context, is also known as "unobtrusive DHTML") should underpin the design of our code. This principle proposes that we should build our app's more advanced features on top of a foundation that will support less-capable clients, enabling the same code to function in the widest possible range of client apps. Actually, this approach can save you work—if you adopt it, you'll avoid needing to maintain two separate versions of your application.

We'll apply the principle of progressive enhancement to the AJAX code in this login form, as we work to ensure that it degrades gracefully in less-capable clients.

## Screen Readers

There's a common misconception that screen readers can't use JavaScript or read dynamic content. Actually, most screen readers work along similar lines to a normal web browser, so despite some special limitations, they are capable of reading DHTML content.

You'll see a few brief mentions of accessibility and screen readers throughout the example code that follows, but we'll save most of that discussion for the section at the end of the chapter that's devoted specifically to creating AJAX that works with screen readers.

# Markup and CSS

Let's take a quick look at the markup and CSS with which we'll start. Note that, in this code, we've included the `formData2QueryString` library with another `script` element:

File: **applogin.html**

```
<!DOCTYPE html PUBLIC "-//W3C//DTD XHTML 1.0 Strict//EN"
    "http://www.w3.org/TR/xhtml1/DTD/xhtml1-strict.dtd">
<html xmlns="http://www.w3.org/1999/xhtml">
  <head>
    <meta http-equiv="Content-Type"
        content="text/html; charset=iso-8859-1" />
    <title>Application Login</title>
    <script type="text/javascript" src="ajax.js"></script>
    <script type="text/javascript"
        src="formdata2querystring.js"></script>
    <script type="text/javascript" src="applogin.js"></script>
    <link rel="stylesheet" href="applogin.css" type="text/css"/>
  </head>
  <body>
    <div id="uiDiv">
      <form id="loginForm" method="POST" action="applogin.html">
```

```
            <div id="promptDiv" class="basePrompt">
              <span id="msgSpan"></span>
              <span id="dotSpan"></span>
            </div> <!-- promptDiv -->
            <div id="fieldDiv">
              <div class="fieldTitle">Login ID:</div>
              <div class="fieldEntry">
                <input type="text" name="LoginId" id="LoginId"
                    size="24" maxlength="100" value=""/>
              </div>
              <div class="fieldTitle">Password:</div>
              <div class="fieldEntry">
                <input type="password" name="Pass" id="Pass"
                    size="24" maxlength="100" value=""/>
              </div>
            </div> <!-- fieldDiv -->
            <div id="buttonDiv">
              <input type="submit" id="submitButton"
                  name="submitButton" value="Submit"/>
            </div>
          </form>
        </div>
      </body>
    </html>
```

File: **applogin.css (excerpt)**

```
body, p, div, td, ul {
  font-family: verdana, arial, helvetica, sans-serif;
  font-size: 12px;
}
form {
  display: inline;
}
#mainDiv {
  padding-top: 24px;
}
#uiDiv {
  width: 360px;
  height: 220px;
  padding: 24px;
  background: #eeeeee;
  border: 1px solid #dddddd;
  margin: auto;
}
#formDiv {
  width: 300px;
```

```
    height: 200px;
    margin: auto;
}
#promptDiv {
    width: 278px;
    height: 48px;
    padding: 10px;
    margin-bottom: 16px;
    background: #ffffff;
    text-align: left;
    font-size: 11px;
}
#fieldDiv {
    width: 300px;
    text-align: left;
}
#buttonDiv {
    text-align: center;
}
#hintDiv {
    width: 380px;
    padding: 14px;
    border: 1px solid #dddddd;
    color: #666666;
    margin: auto;
    margin-top: 36px;
}
.fieldTitle {
    margin-bottom: 3px;
    font-weight: bold;
    color: #666666;
}
.fieldEntry {
    margin-bottom: 8px;
}
.basePrompt {
    color: #666666;
    border: 1px solid #cccccc;
}
.procPrompt {
    color: #333399;
    border: 1px solid #ccccee;
}
.errPrompt {
    color: #993333;
    border: 1px solid #eecccc;
```

```
}
.inputButtonActive {
  cursor: pointer;
}
.inputButtonDisabled {
  cursor: default;
}
.readerText {
  position: absolute;
  top: -1000px;
  left: -1000px;
  width: 1px;
  height: 1px;
  overflow: hidden;
  z-index: -1000;
}
.clearBoth {
  clear: both;
}
```

# Creating the Login Class

Let's start off by creating a Login class to organize the code.

We'll include in our app the code for a processing animation that makes use of setInterval, so we're likely to experience those loss-of-scope problems we discussed in the previous chapter. And, since we're going to display only one login form on-screen at any time, it makes sense to make our Login class a singleton class—a type of class that can only have one instance:

File: **applogin.js (excerpt)**

```
var Login = new function() {
  this.ajax = null;
  this.form = null;
  this.promptDiv = null;
  this.dotSpan = null;
  this.button = null;
  this.enabled = true;
  this.dots = '';
  this.promptInterval = null;
};
```

Remember that, by defining a class with the new keyword, you make that class a singleton.

## DOM-element References

Note that `promptDiv`, `dotSpan`, and `button` are DOM-element references, and remember that when our login page unloads, we need to be sure to clean up these references to avoid the IE memory leak situation we discussed in Chapter 3. As with the monitoring application we created in the last chapter, we'll clean up our DOM-element references using a `cleanup` method that's attached to the `window.onunload` event handler:

File: **applogin.js** (excerpt)

```
window.onunload = Login.cleanup;
```

Here's the `cleanup` method code:

File: **applogin.js** (excerpt)

```
this.cleanup = function() {
  var self = Login;
  self.form = null;
  self.promptDiv = null;
  self.dotSpan = null;
  self.button = null;
};
```

It's good to get into the habit of keeping track of your DOM-element references, and disposing of them when you're done with them. This may seem like a huge hassle, but you don't want to find out halfway through a huge project that your app leaks like a sieve in IE. There are no good tools for tracking memory leak issues like these, so being proactive as you go can save you serious headaches later on.

# Setting it Up with `init`

Now that we have our basic properties in place, let's set up the object with an `init` method, which will be pegged to the `window.onload` event:

File: **applogin.js** (excerpt)

```
this.init = function() {
  var self = Login;
  self.ajax = new Ajax();
  self.form = document.getElementById('loginForm');
  self.promptDiv = document.getElementById('promptDiv');
  self.dotSpan = document.getElementById('dotSpan');
  self.button = document.getElementById('submitButton');
```

```
  self.setPrompt('base', 'Enter a login ID and password, and ' +
    'click the Submit button.');
  self.form.LoginId.focus();
  self.toggleEnabled(false);
  self.form.onsubmit = function() { return false; }
  self.clearCookie('userId');
};
```

File: **applogin.js (excerpt)**

```
window.onload = Login.init;
```

After setting some references to DOM elements that will be used in the interface, this code sets up the user interface.

First, it calls the `setPrompt` method to display the initial login prompt. This text instructs users to enter their login information and click the Submit button. Next, the code gives focus to the first field on the form—the Login ID field. This may seem like a small or unnecessary detail, but it's the kind of detail that's important in using AJAX to develop a truly usable application interface.

## Get Focused!

When the page loads in an ideal world, the user should not be forced to click in the first field to begin typing. Sure, setting the focus to the first form field will only save the user a tiny amount of time, effort, and inconvenience, but it will save every user that inconvenience every single time they log in. For an app that's to be used by many, many people, over and over again, that time (and frustration!) can add up.

You can set the focus to a field simply by calling that field's `focus` method from the `window.onload` event handler. In a lightweight page, this will prepare the form for user input in the blink of an eye—your users *will* be grateful.

However, actions associated with `window.onload` can sometimes take a while to trigger, as the event will not fire until all of the HTML, CSS, JavaScript, and images associated with a page have loaded. On a page with a number of images, quite some time can pass before the event is fired. And in the case of a login form, it's quite possible that users have seen the login form, entered their usernames, and are halfway through entering their passwords by the time your pretty background graphics have loaded. If we shift the focus to the username field while the user is interacting with the form, the user is going to be annoyed.

As our login form is very lightweight, we'll set the focus to the username field without concerning ourselves with the users' own focus—they're not likely to have begun to type by the time we set focus. However, this is an issue that you'll need to consider as you develop your own AJAX applications.

Next, `init` calls `toggleEnabled` to disable the Submit button—we'll take a look at that method shortly—and sets a dummy `onsubmit` event handler for the form. This event handler does nothing but return `false`, which disables form submission. This allows our form to do double-duty for people who come to this page without JavaScript support. For such users, the page will behave like a normal, old-school web form. For users with JavaScript, this scrap of code preempts that normal submission process and, instead, allows us to send the data using AJAX.

Finally, `init` calls a method called `clearCookie` to wipe the `userId` cookie, which we'll use to keep track of an authenticated user. `clearCookie` uses `document.cookie` to set the cookie's expiration date to January 1, 1970, which causes the browser to remove it as an expired cookie. Here's the code:

File: **applogin.js** (excerpt)

```
this.clearCookie = function(name) {
  var expireDate = new Date(0);
  document.cookie = name + '=; expires=' +
      expireDate.toGMTString() + '; path=/';
};
```

### January 1, 1970

JavaScript `Date` objects can be initialized with a single millisecond value, instead of separate values for the year, month, and so on. Initializing an instance of the `Date` class to zero milliseconds sets the date to January 1, 1970. This convention started in the Unix world and is common to a number of programming languages and operating systems, including JavaScript and Mac OS X. A date that's measured in milliseconds like this is often referred to as a "Unix timestamp."

# Setting the Login Prompt

As we saw above, the `init` method calls the `setPrompt` method to set a message at the top of the login form. This prompt is an example of a page partial that our `Login` class can render separately from the rest of the page, making it an easy and convenient way to keep the user informed of what the application is doing. Here's the code for `setPrompt`:

File: **applogin.js (excerpt)**

```
this.setPrompt = function(stat, msg) {
  var self = Login;
  var promptDiv = self.promptDiv;
  var msgSpan = document.getElementById('msgSpan');
  var statusClass = '';
  promptDiv.className = stat + 'Prompt'; // base, proc or err
  if (msgSpan.firstChild) {
    msgSpan.removeChild(msgSpan.firstChild);
  }
  msgSpan.appendChild(document.createTextNode(msg));
};
```

The setPrompt method can display three different kinds of color-coded prompts to emphasize the status of the login process. Each prompt type is tied to a CSS class in applogin.css:

❑ The basePrompt class is gray, and indicates the default status of the login page. This is the color of the initial prompt that the user sees when the page first loads.

❑ The procPrompt class is blue. It indicates that the login has submitted the user's authentication information to the server, and is waiting for a response. We can add an animation effect to a div to which this class is applied, to emphasize the fact that the application is "busy." Instead of the pulsing CSS opacity effects we used in our monitoring application, we'll create this animation using an all-text effect: an animated line of dots that looks a bit like a string of Christmas lights.

❑ The errPrompt class is red, and indicates an error of some kind.

The classes are made up of simple CSS declarations:

File: **applogin.css (excerpt)**

```
.basePrompt {
  color: #666;
  border: 1px solid #ccc;
}
.procPrompt {
  color: #339;
  border: 1px solid #cce;
}
.errPrompt {
  color: #933;
```

```
    border: 1px solid #ecc;
}
```

The setPrompt method accepts two parameters. The first is *stat*, which specifies the state of the message as base, proc, or err. The other parameter is *msg*—the message to be displayed.

Having set the style of the message, the code uses DOM-manipulation methods to delete the current contents of the message box and display the message inside the span with the ID msgSpan.

# Ensuring Valid Input

In old-fashioned web applications, the server was the only place we could reliably validate user input. The user had to submit the form, wait for it to be processed on the server, then wait to see whether the submission was a success, or had included some bad data such as a missed field or incorrectly formatted number.

While the server remains the only reliable place to validate user input, we can greatly reduce the likelihood of a user submitting invalid data with some clever use of AJAX techniques. With modern browsers and solid JavaScript support, it's much easier to make an initial pass at input validation right there on the client, to save the user from waiting. However, this approach still puts users in a potentially irritating position: they have to click the Submit button to find out that the input they entered was wrong in some way.

In our login form, we'll disable the Submit button by default, and enable it when the user types something into both of the form fields. This is a different—and much more user-friendly—way to ensure proper input than the more common method of validating inputs after the user submits the form. Ours is a more active approach to providing feedback to users—they can't even click the Submit button until they've entered data into both form fields.

### *Always* Validate Input on the Server Side

Never assume that client-side validation will make data input from the client safe. You should think of client-side validation purely as a convenience for end-users—something to reduce the likelihood of errors as they enter form data. Always validate data inputs on the server side to make sure that the data you're processing is safe. Make sure you don't end up being the victim of an attack!

# Capturing and Using Keyboard Input

In order to capture changes to the text in each field, we'll add a method called keyup to handle the document.onkeyup event.

File: **appmonitor.js** (excerpt)

```
document.onkeyup = Login.keyup;
```

keyup will watch the user's typing and activate the Submit button when the user has entered data into both fields. Here's the code:

File: **appmonitor.js** (excerpt)

```
this.keyup = function(e) {
  var self = Login;
  if (!e) {
    e = window.event;
  }
  if (e.keyCode != 13) {
    self.evalFormFieldState();
  }
  else {
    if (self.enabled) {
      self.submitData();
    }
  }
};
```

Notice that this method takes one parameter called **e**. In Firefox, Safari, and Opera, this parameter contains information about the source of the event, such as the key that was pressed to trigger it. In Internet Explorer, the same information can be accessed via window.event.

To check which key was pressed to trigger this event, we check **e**'s keyCode property, which contains the key's unicode value. In keyup, we check to see if the **Enter** key (which has a unicode value of 13) was pressed. If it was, we send the data off to the server (more on this later). Otherwise, keyup calls evalFormFieldState to check the state of the form fields and set the Submit button to its appropriate state.

File: **appmonitor.js** (excerpt)

```
this.evalFormFieldState = function() {
  var self = Login;
  if (self.form.LoginId.value.length > 0 &&
      self.form.Pass.value.length > 0) {
```

```
    self.toggleEnabled(true);
  }
  else {
    self.toggleEnabled(false);
  }
};
```

If the code determines that the user has properly entered some data into both fields, it calls the `toggleEnabled` method we originally used in `init`, and passes it a value of `true` to enable the Submit button. Similarly, on every keystroke, if the code sees that either form field is empty, it deactivates the Submit button by calling `toggleEnabled` with a value of `false`.

Incidentally, if we wanted to, we could create conditions about the kinds of data we wanted users to enter into the field, and perform much more complicated validation (for example, using regular expressions) for things like telephone numbers or email addresses.

### Screen Readers and onkeyup

Screen readers may interfere with the functioning of the `onkeyup` event when users of these devices enter data into form fields, so you shouldn't depend on code triggered by `onkeyup` alone to determine whether to enable or disable important elements of the UI. Later in the chapter, we'll attach the `evalFormFieldState` method directly to the `onchange` event for the password form field, to make sure that the button is properly turned on for people using screen readers.

Here's the `toggleEnabled` method:

File: **appmonitor.js (excerpt)**

```
this.toggleEnabled = function(able) {
  var self = Login;
  if (able) {
    self.button.onclick = self.submitData;
    self.button.disabled = false;
    self.button.className = 'inputButtonActive';
    self.enabled = true;
  }
  else {
    self.button.onclick = null;
    self.button.disabled = true;
    self.button.className = 'inputButtonDisabled';
    self.enabled = false;
```

```
    }
};
```

Passing this method a value of `true` enables the Submit button: it assigns an `on-click` event handler, sets the button's `disabled` property to `false` and its `class` property to `inputButtonActive`, and, finally, sets the `Login` class's `enabled` property to `true`.

If `toggleEnable` is passed a value of `false`, the reverse of all this will occur. So, if the user fills out the form—enabling the button—but then deletes one of the form field entries, the Submit button will revert to its original state.

At this point, we should be able to check our progress simply by adding the empty stub for `submitData` shown below, then loading the page in a web browser.

File: **applogin.js (excerpt)**

```
this.submitData = function() { };
```

## Figure 4.2. The login user interface

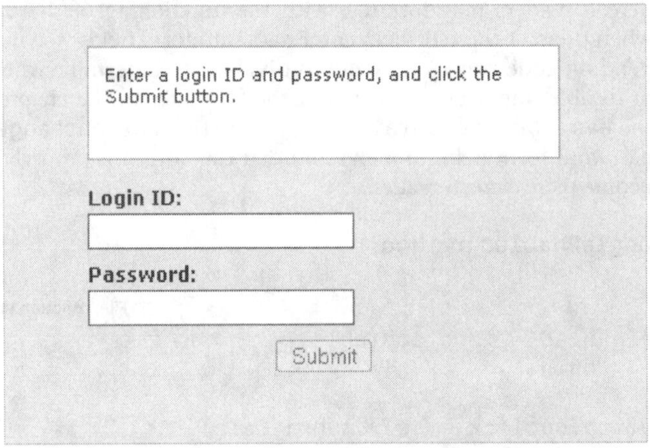

Once the page has loaded, and you've entered something in the Login ID and Password fields, the Submit button should be enabled, signifying that you've entered all the details that the application needs, and we're ready to check the login ID and password against our list of users on the server.

# Submitting the Form Data

Now that the Submit button is active, it's time for the user to take a shot at logging in to our web app. We'll use our Ajax class to send the user's login information to the server via an HTTP POST request. Here's the code:

File: **applogin.js** (excerpt)

```
this.submitData = function() {
  var self = Login;
  var postData = '';
  postData = formData2QueryString(self.form);
  self.ajax.doPost('/applogin.php', postData,
      self.handleLoginResp);
  self.showStatusPrompt();
  self.toggleEnabled(false);
};
```

This method uses formData2QueryString to pull the values out of the form and put them into a string, which we then pass to the Ajax class for POSTing. Next, the code sends the POST request that contains the data string using the Ajax class's doPost method. This method takes three parameters:

❏ the target URL

❏ the data string

❏ the function that you want to handle the response

After the POST request has gone off to the server, the code switches on the processing animation in the prompt box, and deactivates the Submit button to prevent multiple submissions.

**IMPORTANT**

### Securing your Login Details

As we're not submitting real login details to a real web application, we're not too concerned about securing users' data at this point. However, with a real-world login, it's vital to make sure that malicious snoopers can't peek at your users' personal data, including their login IDs and passwords. In fact, many users won't use applications that don't encrypt personal or sensitive data with SSL.

Submitting your data using **SSL** (secure sockets layer), an industry-standard encryption technology, is the most common way to lock down your users' precious personal information. Pages that are served over an SSL connection have URLs that begin with `https:` instead of `http:`.

A wealth of information that explains how to set up your web server to use SSL is available online. Free implementations of SSL, such as OpenSSL,[2] also mean that you can set up a web server with industrial-strength encryption—the same encryption that the big boys use—with no cost other than the price of a digital certificate.

## Submitting Data without Touching the Mouse

Obviously, clicking the Submit button is a good bet for kicking off the submit process, and for those who prefer to use the mouse, clicking that little button is no big deal. But let's pause for a moment to take some pity on the poor keyboard junkies who also want to log in to our fake application. We've got some extra mojo up our sleeves that we can apply to make things even easier for those guys and girls. Remember: users like it when we make things easier for them. And if your users are happy, you're happy.

Remember when we wrote the `keyup` method? You'll recall that we treated the **Enter** key as a special case. When the **Enter** key is pressed and the Submit button is enabled, the `submitData` method is called.

This is a nicety akin to the results of our work with the `init` method, which gave focus to the login ID field on initial page load. These may seem like quite small things, but for people who use the keyboard a lot, some extra effort on your part can save your users significant time and effort in the long run. Indeed, it's this kind of attention to usability detail that separates the good AJAX applications from the mediocre and even bad ones. Take the time to get these details right!

# Processing the Submission

Normally, a web application login form submits the login ID and password to the web server, which checks the data against a list of login IDs and encrypted passwords. To fake this process with our processing page, `applogin.php`, we'll simply hard-code some values against which the login ID and password can be checked. To make it seem like the server is having to think about this validation a little, we'll also add a call to `sleep` for three seconds.

---

[2] http://www.openssl.org

Here's how our fake back-end code looks in PHP. Again, remember that this code could be written in any server-side language; we've chosen to use PHP here only because it's freely available for most popular web servers.

File: **applogin.php (excerpt)**

```php
<?php
$loginId = $_POST['LoginId'];
$password = $_POST['Pass'];
$respType = '';
$respMsg = '';
$separator = ',';
sleep(3);
if ($loginId == 'user' && $password == 'password') {
  setcookie('userId', 12345);
  $respType = 'success';
  $respMsg = '/appmainpage.php';
}
else {
  $respType = 'error';
  $respMsg = 'Could not verify your login information.';
}
header('Content-Type: text/plain');
print $respType;
print $separator;
print $respMsg;
?>
```

The first two variables hold the inputs from our login screen, which were extracted from the POST request. When XMLHttpRequest submits POST data with its request, the data behaves exactly like any data that might be submitted through a normal web form, even though it's originally packed to look like a query string.

IMPORTANT

### Validate your Data!

In this login demonstration, we're not doing anything to validate the data that's coming from the client. If this were the login to a production application, you would, of course, run any input from the browser through some sort of validation process to ensure that it was safe, and was the type of data you were expecting. Unvalidated data could give malicious hackers a way to attack your application, and incorrect data types or formats could do serious damage to your app. Always validate data from the client.

# CSV Data Format

The last three variables—`$respType`, `$respMsg`, and `$separator`—come into play when we print out the response for the client.

The response can be pretty brief: all the client needs from this page is a notice of success or failure, and a short message. And, since `XMLHttpRequest` can work happily with a range of data formats other than XML (despite its name), we'll use something a lot more lightweight: **CSV** (comma separated values).

CSV is a good choice for small or simple sets of data. It provides a nice, easy way to break information into multiple fields when you don't really need the extra complexity that XML provides, and comes with an added bonus in that it works well with popular spreadsheet and database programs.

In this case, we have only two data fields. The `$respType` variable tells us whether the login process worked or not, and `$respMsg` contains either the error message that we'll display to the user, or the redirect path for a successful login. The `$separator` variable contains the character we'll use as the delimiter to separate the two fields (in this case, a comma).

## Setting the Values

Once the variables are declared, and the program insists on resting for a few seconds, the user's login ID and password are checked against a hard-coded pair of values. Then, `$respType` and `$respMsg` are set. If the values match, `$respType` is set to `success` and `$respMsg` is set to the address of the page to which the login form will redirect; if the values do not match, `$respType` is set to `error` and `$respMsg` is set to a message that explains the error.

Upon successful login, the code also sets a cookie called `userId` that indicates that the user is actually logged into the app. In our page, the code sets the cookie to a fictitious number, but a real application would set it to something useful—such as a user identifier.

## Printing the Response

Lastly, our fake back-end code prints out the response, which goes back to the client. This page is very simple, and there are only two possible outputs:

- ❑ `success,/appmainpage.php`

❏ `error,Could not verify your login information.`

Our client-side code parses this result and either redirects to the main application page, or displays the error message for the user.

Also note that we set `Content-Type` to `text/plain`, so `XMLHttpRequest` won't expect the response to contain valid XML.

Of course, this is a really basic example. You could certainly expand it to return different error messages or codes, or to direct different classes of users to different parts of the application (for example, logging administrative users into an admin console). You could also choose a different separator character. Sometimes, your data will contain commas, so using a comma as a separator may not be a good idea. The pipe character ( | ) is another popular choice.

The CSV format is simple, yet flexible enough to deal with a wide range of uses—any case in which you have a limited number of data fields and you control the code on both the back end and the front. XML is better suited to more complicated types of data, and situations in which your application has to communicate with other applications.

# Showing Processing Status

While our fake processing page is pretending to authenticate the submitted data, users will be staring at the login screen, wondering what the heck is going on. This is where status notification again comes to the fore. It's vital to let users know what's going on with an application, but it's particularly important in the case of an AJAX app, as users have to sit and wait for processes on the server to finish. If the application is busy performing some task, it should *look* busy to the user.

On this login page, we'll use an animation effect to indicate that the application is processing the user's request, but we'll take a slightly different approach to the one we used last time. Rather than creating a sense of movement by changing the animation's opacity, we'll use a line of dots similar to an ellipsis (…), animating them a bit like a line of Christmas lights, as shown in Figure 4.3. This is a pretty common look for a processing animation, and it has the advantage of being very lightweight, since it's all text.

## Figure 4.3. Creating animation by appending a string of dots

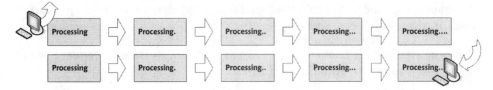

The `showStatusPrompt` method starts off the status animation. This code sets the prompt message to "Processing," then starts up the `setInterval` process that animates the dots.

Here's the code:

File: **applogin.js** (excerpt)

```
this.showStatusPrompt = function() {
  var self = Login;
  self.dots = '';
  self.setPrompt('proc', 'Processing');
  self.promptInterval = setInterval(self.showStatusDots, 200);
};
```

Again, the return value of the `setInterval` call is the interval ID we'll need to turn off the animation, so we save it for future use in the `promptInterval` property. The `setInterval` process is set to call `showStatusDots` every 200 milliseconds.

Here's the `showStatusDots` code:

File: **applogin.js** (excerpt)

```
this.showStatusDots = function() {
  var self = Login;
  var dotSpan = self.dotSpan;
  self.dots += '.';
  if (self.dots.length > 4) {
    self.dots = '';
  }
  if (dotSpan.firstChild) {
    dotSpan.removeChild(dotSpan.firstChild);
  }
  dotSpan.appendChild(document.createTextNode(' ' + self.dots));
};
```

The action in this code occurs in two parts. The first part sets up the dot string for display; the second part displays the string after the word "Processing" in the prompt box.

The process of animating the dots starts with an empty string; a dot is appended to this string over and over, so that the line of dots grows. When the number of dots exceeds four, the code resets the string to be empty, and starts the process over. These dots appear in a span element that appears immediately to the right of the word "Processing" in the prompt, so it looks like the entire string of text is animated. The movement of the dots draws the user's eye to the word "Processing," which makes it more likely that the user will read and understand the prompt. The constantly changing row of dots provides another hint to the user that the application is busy doing something.

# Handling the Server Response

When the response arrives back from the server, the result is passed to the handleLoginResp method as a string. This method parses the CSV-formatted result string by splitting it at the comma and restoring the respType and respMsg values we had on the server side in applogin.php:

File: **applogin.js (excerpt)**

```
this.handleLoginResp = function(str) {
  var self = Login;
  var respArr = str.split(',');
  var respType = respArr[0].toLowerCase();
  var respMsg = respArr[1];
  if (respType == 'success') {
    location = respMsg;
  }
  else {
    self.showErrorPrompt(respMsg);
  }
};
```

This provides the status of the response in respType, and the meat of the response—either an error message or redirect path—in respMsg.

Once we know whether this response indicates success or an error, we know what to do with the response content in respMsg.

If the login was successful, the code will redirect the browser to whatever path the server returned in respMsg. If the response indicates an error, respMsg will instead contain an error message, and `handleLoginResp` will hand it off to the `showErrorPrompt` method for display.

### Taking Care of Case-sensitivity

With a string variable like `respType` that contains some sort of named status (e.g., `success` or `error`), it's usually a good idea to get into the habit of converting the string to upper- or lowercase before checking the value. This takes care of any case-sensitivity issues that might occur if either you, or someone you work with, use the wrong case or mixed case somewhere else in the code.

# Dealing with Login Failures

The `showErrorPrompt` method displays an error to users when their logins fail, and resets the login interface to make it easy for them to try logging in again:

File: applogin.js (excerpt)

```
this.showErrorPrompt = function(str) {
  var self = Login;
  var dotSpan = self.dotSpan;
  clearInterval(self.promptInterval);
  if (dotSpan.firstChild) {
    dotSpan.removeChild(dotSpan.firstChild);
  }
  self.setPrompt('err', str);
  self.form.Pass.value = '';
};
```

After declaring and initializing a couple of variables, `showErrorPrompt` stops the moving dots animation by calling `clearInterval` with the animation process's interval ID. Then, as the animation may have been stopped while displaying dots, `showErrorPrompt` uses `removeChild` to clear any dots that may be left in the animation's `span`.

The next thing we need to do is to set the prompt to the error text that's come back from the server, and to set the prompt type to `err` so it will display in the proper style. We achieve this with a call to `setPrompt`.

Last of all, the code resets the user interface by clearing out the Password field so that users can quickly and easily re-enter their passwords and attempt another login. This is another addition that's important to the usability of the app, as it saves your users time and irritation. Most often, login errors (for valid users) arise from the mistyping of passwords, so when a login attempt fails, the code empties the text in the password field, to save the user from having to delete it manually.

Now that we've sent the request, set up an animation to indicate that the server is busy, and handled both successful and unsuccessful login attempts, our basic login application is ready to go! Open `applogin.html` in your web browser and try to log in with bogus details. You should see the animated dots, followed by the "Could not verify your login information" message shown in Figure 4.4.

## Figure 4.4. A failed login attempt

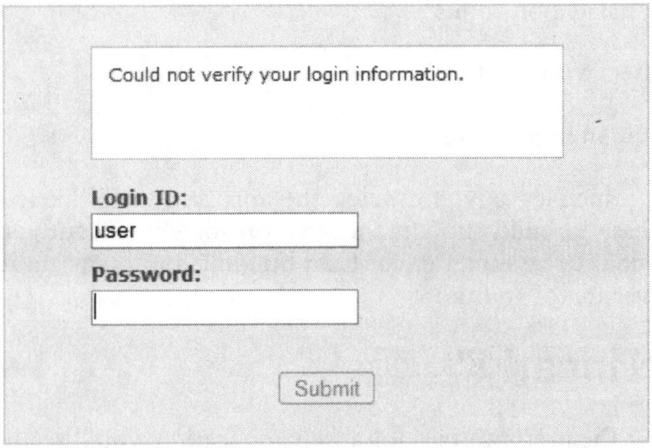

If you log in using the login ID **user** and the password **password**, you'll be redirected away from `applogin.html` to a page named `appmainpage.php`—the main page of your application.

Great! You now have a fully functional application login form. There's no chance that users can submit details without filling in both the Login ID and Password fields, and the app keeps users informed about what's going on behind the scenes. It also works in modern versions of Internet Explorer, Firefox, Safari, and Opera. In fact, the only browsers on which it doesn't work are screen readers used by the vision-impaired. However, contrary to popular belief, there's no reason why our AJAX can't work in those browsers, too.

# AJAX and Screen Readers

Making the login page accessible to screen readers requires a little more work than did the relatively simple task of dealing with non-JavaScript browsers, but it won't be much of a chore if you keep some basic principles in mind as you design your code. Here's a quick list; we'll discuss each point in detail in a moment:

❏  Think "linearly."

❏  Use "skip navigation" links.

❏  Provide users with notification about dynamic content.

❏  Test the app in multiple readers.

Follow these principles as you develop the app, and you'll likely find that it's surprisingly easy to build support for screen readers into your code. In fact, it has the potential to be much easier than building and maintaining a separate, "accessible" version of your app.

# Thinking "Linearly"

As you look at the user interface for a web application, you'll see buttons, links, and form elements placed all over your browser window. However, view the page's source and you'll see a very different picture—line after line of markup that reads from top to bottom. That's exactly how a screen reader views your page: in a **linear** fashion, from top to bottom, left to right.

In designing a web app interface, and creating page elements (especially tables and web forms), for screen reader access, you must think about how your markup will appear when read from top to bottom. Here's a quick example.

## Example: a Two-column Web Form

Imagine that you want to create a web form that allows users to provide their names and address information. To save vertical space on the page, you want to display the inputs in two columns. If you were of the old school of table-based web design, an obvious way to do that would be to use a big table with columns for the form field labels and text inputs, like so:

```
<table>
  <tr>
    <th colspan="2">Name Info</th>
    <th colspan="2">Address Info</th>
  </tr>
  <tr>
    <td>First Name:</td>
    <td><input type="text" id="First" name="First" value=""/></td>
    <td>Address:</td>
    <td><input type="text" id="Addr" name="Addr" value=""/></td>
  </tr>
  <tr>
    <td>Last Name:</td>
    <td><input type="text" id="Last" name="Last" value=""/></td>
    <td>City:</td>
    <td><input type="text" id="City" name="City" value=""/></td>
  </tr>
</table>
```

I'm sure you already know where I'm going with this: the form will look fine in the browser, as shown in Figure 4.5, but a screen reader will read the markup from top to bottom, so the fields will be out of order: First Name, Address, Last Name, City.

## Figure 4.5. Form with a table-based layout

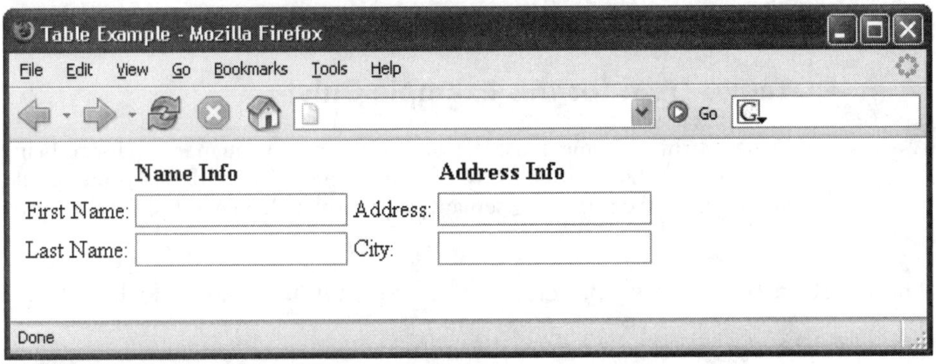

Instead, you could use two tables and a little CSS "float" magic; you'd see exactly the same visual result, but the markup would be better suited to linearization. Here's the markup:

```
<div id="formDiv">
  <table class="floatTable">
```

```
    <tr>
      <th colspan="2">Name Info</th>
    </tr>
    <tr>
      <td>First Name:</td>
      <td><input type="text" id="First" name="First" value=""/>
          </td>
    </tr>
    <tr>
      <td>Last Name:</td>
      <td><input type="text" id="Last" name="Last" value=""/></td>
    </tr>
  </table>
  <table class="floatTable">
    <tr>
      <th colspan="2">Address Info</th>
    </tr>
    <tr>
      <td>Address:</td>
      <td><input type="text" id="Addr" name="Addr" value=""/></td>
    </tr>
    <tr>
      <td>City:</td>
      <td><input type="text" id="City" name="City" value=""/></td>
    </tr>
  </table>
  <div class="clearBoth"></div>
</div>
```

*note*

## Tables Used for this Example Only!

Don't try this at home, kids! We don't recommend you mark up forms using tables unless those forms really are made up of tabular data. Forms should always be marked up using semantically correct elements, then styled using CSS.

The `floatTable` CSS class that creates the two-column layout looks like this:

```
.floatTable {
  width: 230px;
  float: left;
}
```

The end result, shown in Figure 4.6, is a form that looks identical to the one built using a single large table.

This is just a single example, but the same top-to-bottom, left-to-right principle of linearization applies to the layout of any elements on the screen. Fortunately, CSS gives you plenty of freedom to place on-screen elements wherever you want them to appear, so if you give your layout a little thought early in the process, you can create web application interfaces whose elements are logically grouped top-to-bottom in the markup, but still display in intuitive locations on the screen.

We'll be talking later about testing your code in screen readers, but of course the best way to get a visceral feel for the linear way in which a screen reader reads your site or app is to try using these tools for yourself. You'll be surprised (and possibly appalled) at the difference between these and visually-based browsers.

# Skip Navigation Links

What usually appears at the very top or far-left of the vast majority of web pages? That's right: navigation links. Now, knowing what you know about the top-to-bottom way a screen reader digests markup, imagine what it must be like for users of screen readers who, every time they move to a new page, have to sit through a list of every navigation link on the web site before they can get to the actual content of the page.

That's the kind of annoyance that vision-impaired people using screen readers have to endure when sites don't implement **"skip navigation" links**. These are internal page links that allow the screen reader to jump over the annoying, repetitive navigation and get to the content the users are really looking for.

Providing this kind of internal navigation to allow screen reader users to skip around on the page makes the browsing experience much easier and more enjoyable for these users. And your application of these links needn't be confined to skipping over page navigation. Many screen readers start off by giving the user a brief "scan" of the page, and although some readers wrap back to the top from the bottom of the page, not all do, so it can be a big help to provide an easy way for users to jump back to the top of the page.

## Hiding Screen Reader Content

At this point, you might be curious about the idea of sprinkling internal navigation links all over your page, and wondering what's that's going to do to your nice, clean design. Well, fear not! CSS can help you out here, as well. All you have to do is define a class that's for use by screen readers only, and use CSS to make it invisible to everyone else.

## Figure 4.6. A two-column form built with a table or CSS

| Table Example - Mozilla Firefox |
|---|
| File    Edit    View    Go    Bookmarks    Tools    Help |

| Name Info | | Address Info | |
|---|---|---|---|
| First Name: | | Address: | |
| Last Name: | | City: | |

Done

The web app login code we've been working with in this chapter uses the following style for its screen reader-only class:

File: **applogin.css (excerpt)**

```
.screenReader {
  position: absolute;
  top: -1000px;
  left: -1000px;
  width: 1px;
  height: 1px;
  overflow: hidden;
  z-index: -1000;
}
```

Applying this class to a `div` or any other block-level element effectively makes it invisible, though it's still readable by screen readers. This is what we use to set up the internal page navigation anchors that will allow readers to jump from the bottom of the page to the top.

### Avoid Using `display: none`

Don't set the CSS `display` property to `none` for your screen reader class. Many screen readers will ignore elements with a `display` of `none`, which is correct behavior, as this property indicates that the element is not to be "shown."

Here's the markup we use as the target link at the top of the login screen:

File: **applogin.html** (excerpt)

```
<body>
  <div class="readerText">
    <a id="pageTop" name="pageTop">Page top</a>
  </div>
  <div id="uiDiv">
```

It doesn't show up on-screen, but screen readers see this perfectly, and report it as an internal page link. And at the very bottom of the page, we add this:

File: **applogin.html** (excerpt)

```
  </div>
  <div class="readerText">
    <a href="#pageTop">Back to form top</a>
    End of page
  </div>
</body>
```

When a screen reader reads this markup, users knows that they're at the end of the page, and that there's an easy way to jump to the top.

# Notification for Dynamic Content

A lot of discussion about screen readers assumes that they can't handle JavaScript or content that's created dynamically on the client-side. In reality, screen readers work in conjunction with a regular browser like Internet Explorer, so they're dependent on the browser for their JavaScript support.

The problem screen readers have is not with dynamic content itself. The problem is that with AJAX-style updates to the page, such as those that occur when our app login page displays an error message that's returned from the server, the screen reader has no way to know that the content has changed, or where on the page the changes have occurred.

## Giving an alert

A good solution to this problem is to provide some kind of notification for screen reader users when content on the page changes. Screen readers will read `alert` dialog boxes, so a good technique is to give screen reader users the option to receive an `alert` when you perform a partial page refresh with AJAX.

A neat way to give users this option is to add to your form a checkbox that's visible only to screen readers, and turns these alerts on and off. This gives users the ability to choose for themselves whether or not they want to be alerted when page content changes.

Here are a couple of points that you should keep in mind when you implement this type of solution:

❑ This is probably not an ideal solution for an app in which content is constantly changing (e.g., a stock ticker application)—you don't want to bombard users with `alert` after `alert`.

❑ Consider what information should appear in the `alert` dialog. In the case of our simple login form, the only content change is a short error message, so you can put that right there in the `alert`. If the changed content included a long list of search results, you'd just want to tell the user that the search had completed, and direct them to the area on the page where they can find the results (we'll see an example of this in Chapter 7).

Without JavaScript, this login form acts like a plain, old-school web form. This means that we only need to add the notification of dynamic content changes for people who use their screen readers in conjunction with JavaScript-enabled browsers. We achieve this using JavaScript as the application loads. You'll see how this works in just a moment, when we step through the screen reader-specific code.

# Testing in Multiple Readers

The single most important thing you can do to make your code work in screen readers is, of course, to sit down and use your app with screen readers. Here's a brief list of some commercial screen reader applications you might try:

**Home Page Reader from IBM**[3]

This application is a specialized screen reader that's used in place of a web browser. The current version requires Internet Explorer 6 be installed.

**JAWS from Freedom Scientific**[4]

The most popular screen reader software worldwide, JAWS works with a variety of programs including web browsers.

---

[3] http://www.ibm.com/
[4] http://www.freedomscientific.com/

**Window-Eyes from GW Micro**[5]

Another general screen reader program, Windows-Eyes works with a variety of programs including web browsers.

**Hal from Dolphin Computer Access**[6]

Hal is another general screen reader program that works with a variety of programs including web browsers.

Some screen readers offer trial versions that you can use, so you can take them for a spin and see how well your application works—or doesn't—with them. These trial versions are time-limited (i.e., they'll run for about half an hour before they shut down), so they're not really suitable for serious testing, but the trial versions are more than sufficient for getting a feel for the ways these tools work, and learning how to create accessible user interfaces for your AJAX applications.

Just as you wouldn't develop your site in Firefox and deploy it without testing it in your other supported browsers (especially if IE was one of those browsers), you can't test your app successfully in one screen reader and expect it to work flawlessly in all the others.

---

[5] http://www.gwmicro.com/
[6] http://www.dolphincomputeraccess.com/

## Figure 4.7. Testing the app login in IBM Home Page Reader

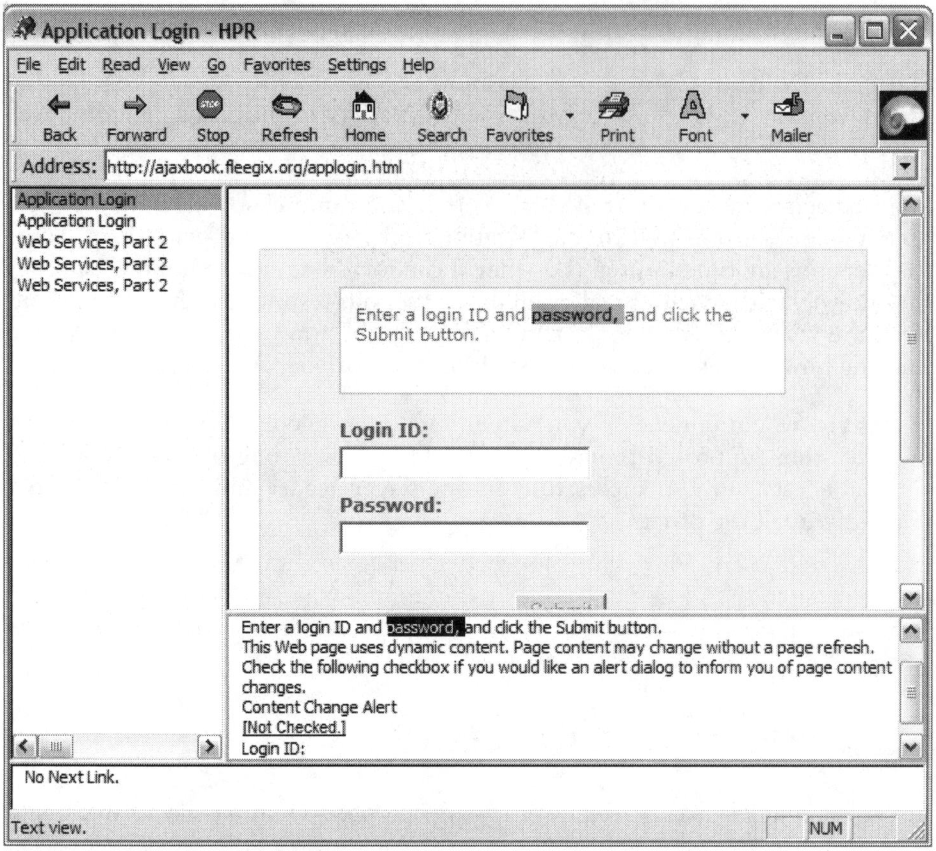

In that respect, supporting a specific screen reader is very much like supporting a new browser. They have differences and individual quirks. For example, IBM's Home Page Reader uses IE as its browsing engine, but runs like a separate program. Figure 4.7 shows a screen capture of the app login system we developed in this chapter as accessed through IBM Home Page Reader. The JAWS screen reader, on the other hand, opens in a small window and runs in the background, reading the text for the active application. Figure 4.8 shows the JAWS application window.

## Figure 4.8. The JAWS application window

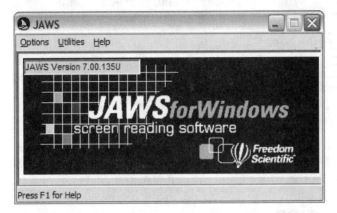

I would strongly encourage you to sit down and try this: fire up a screen reader program, pull up your web application, and literally turn off your monitor while you use it.

Spend some time fighting with some inaccessible user interfaces in a few screen reader programs, and you'll get a very different perspective on the situation; in fact, that visceral understanding of what it's like may boost your motivation to build better accessibility into your AJAX web app.

# The Screen Reader Code

Let's take a quick look at the code that allows our web app login to work with screen reader programs. Note that these extra features are unnecessary for users who have no JavaScript support, or have JavaScript turned off, since the markup for the web form itself is made up of a set of simple, reader-friendly `div` elements.

The full AJAX version of the display needs these extra features to work with screen readers, though, so we'll add them into the mix by calling the `enableScreenReaderFeatures` method in the `init` code at application startup:

File: **applogin.js** (excerpt)

```
this.init = function() {
  var self = Login;
  self.ajax = new Ajax();
  self.form = document.getElementById('loginForm');
  self.promptDiv = document.getElementById('promptDiv');
  self.dotSpan = document.getElementById('dotSpan');
```

```
   self.button = document.getElementById('submitButton');
   self.setPrompt('base', 'Enter a login ID and password, and ' +
      'click the Submit button.');
   self.form.LoginId.focus();
   self.toggleEnabled(false);
   self.form.onsubmit = function() { return false; }
   self.clearCookie('userId');
   self.enableScreenReaderFeatures();
};
```

This method sets up all the reader-specific functionality for the login code, including the notifications for active content. Note that we're putting all the screen reader-specific interface elements into the markup with the `readerText` CSS class, so they don't appear in the UI for users without screen readers.

# Setting Up Notification

Before we start to notify users with screen readers about partial page refreshes, they need to know that the page uses dynamic content. Then, they can decide for themselves whether or not they want to receive alerts when the page content changes. Let's add a warning about the dynamic content, alongside the checkbox that allows them to choose whether or not to receive an `alert` for AJAX-style updates of the page. The markup for this warning and checkbox is as follows:

```
<div class="readerText">
  This web page uses dynamic content. Page content may change
  without a page refresh. Check the following checkbox if you
  would like an alert dialog to inform you of page content
  changes.
</div>
<div class="readerText">
  <label>
    Content Change Alert
    <input type="checkbox" name="ChangeAlert" id="ChangeAlert"
        value="true" title="Content Change Alert"/>
  </label>
</div>
```

We won't be adding this code to the actual markup of the page; instead, we'll inject it into the page using DOM methods inside the `enableScreenReaderFeatures` method. Here's the code:

File: **applogin.js** (excerpt)

```
this.enableScreenReaderFeatures = function() {
  var self = Login;
  var fieldDiv = document.getElementById('fieldDiv');
  var msgDiv = null;
  var checkboxDiv = null;
  var label = null;
  var checkbox = null;
  var msg = 'This web page uses dynamic content. Page content' +
      ' may change without a page refresh. Check the following' +
      ' checkbox if you would like an alert dialog to inform' +
      ' you of page content changes.';
  msgDiv = document.createElement('div');
  msgDiv.className = 'readerText';
  msgDiv.appendChild(document.createTextNode(msg));
  self.form.insertBefore(msgDiv, fieldDiv);
  checkboxDiv = document.createElement('div');
  checkboxDiv.className = 'readerText';
  label = document.createElement('label');
  label.appendChild(document.createTextNode('Content Change ' +
      'Alert'));
  checkbox = document.createElement('input');
  checkbox.type = 'checkbox';
  checkbox.id = 'ChangeAlert';
  checkbox.name = 'ChangeAlert';
  checkbox.value = 'true';
  checkbox.title = 'Content Change Alert';
  label.appendChild(checkbox);
  checkboxDiv.appendChild(label);
  self.form.insertBefore(checkboxDiv, fieldDiv);
};
```

DOM methods can get a little verbose and hard to follow, so I usually do an initial pass of the markup I want, then translate it into the appropriate DOM method code, which is what I've done here.

Again, since all of these elements are wrapped in div elements that have the readerText class, they will be "visible" only to users with screen readers.

# Showing Notifications

This application displays only one notification: the error that tells users that their login information couldn't be verified. If the change to the page content was more substantial, we'd likely just tell users about the change, and tell them where to find it (e.g., "in the main content area," "below the search form," or whatever). But, since this is a nice, short little message, we'll go ahead and display it right there in the `alert` dialog, to save users the trouble of surfing around the page in an effort to find the message. Figure 4.9 shows this error message popped up in Home Page Reader.

## Figure 4.9. Changed content alert in IBM Home Page Reader

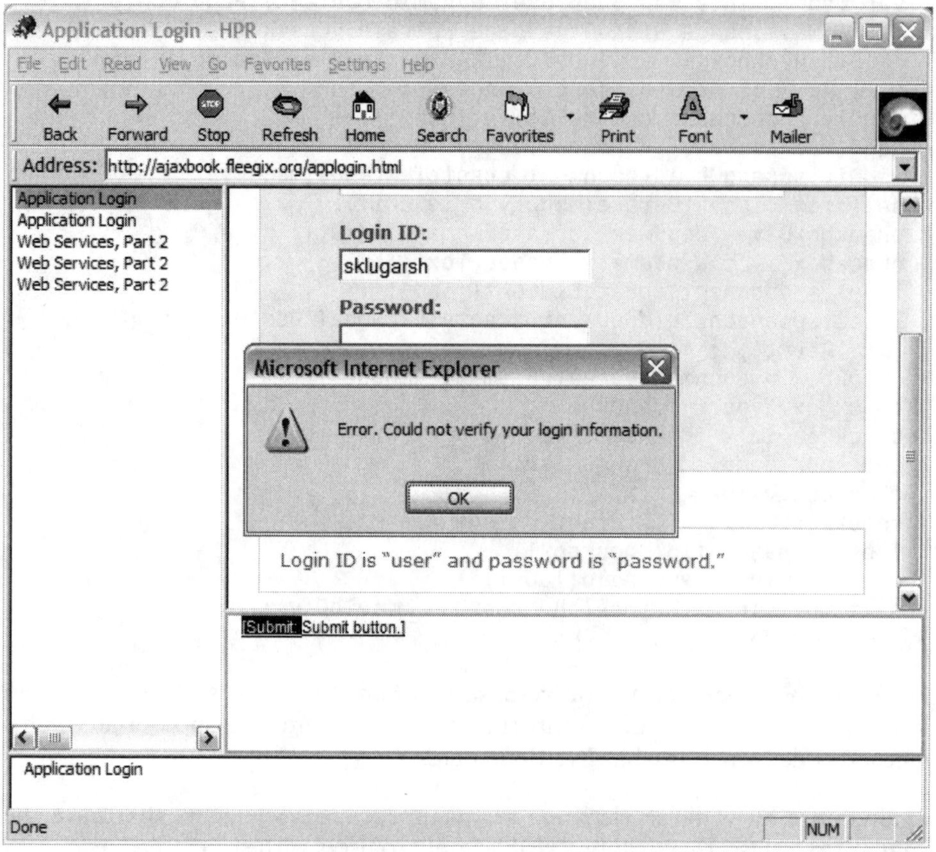

To get this effect, we add the following lines to the `showErrorPrompt` method:

File: **applogin.js (excerpt)**

```
this.showErrorPrompt = function(str) {
  var self = Login;
  var dotSpan = self.dotSpan;
  clearInterval(self.promptInterval);
```

```
    if (dotSpan.firstChild) {
      dotSpan.removeChild(dotSpan.firstChild);
    }
    self.setPrompt('err', str);
    self.form.Pass.value = '';
    if (self.form.ChangeAlert.checked) {
      alert('Error. ' + str);
    }
};
```

This code checks to see whether or not the user has checked the `ChangeAlert` checkbox—an interface element that only screen reader users will know exists—and dumps the error text into a standard JavaScript `alert` box.

The same message is written into the main prompt `div`, and if the screen reader re-reads the page from the top, it will pick up the changed content. But with the `alert` dialog box, a user with a screen reader can enjoy the same instant feedback received by users of visually-based browsers. When the `alert` pops up, the screen reader will read the contents of the dialog box. Then, the user can dismiss the box and try entering login information again.

# Enabling the Submit Button

Having set up the warning and checkbox to provide notifications about AJAX-style partial page updates, we still have a couple more things to do in `enableScreenReaderFeatures` to make the app screen reader-ready.

Earlier, I showed how you can set an event listener to watch users' keyboard inputs and call `evalFormFieldState` to activate the Submit button when values have been entered into both the Login ID and Password fields. Unfortunately, screen readers can interfere with the `onkeyup` event when the user enters text in form fields, so we can't count on that event to trigger checks on the form fields' contents. Figure 4.10 shows Home Page Reader in Text Entry mode. Note that it opens a completely new dialog box for the entry of text into the form field.

The solution to this problem is to add an explicit `onchange` handler to the text input itself, to make sure our button is turned on when text is entered into the field. Here are the lines in the `enableScreenReaderFeatures` method:

File: **applogin.js** (excerpt)

```
    self.form.insertBefore(checkboxDiv, fieldDiv);
    self.form.Pass.onchange = self.evalFormFieldState;
};
```

**Figure 4.10. Text Entry mode in IBM Home Page Reader**

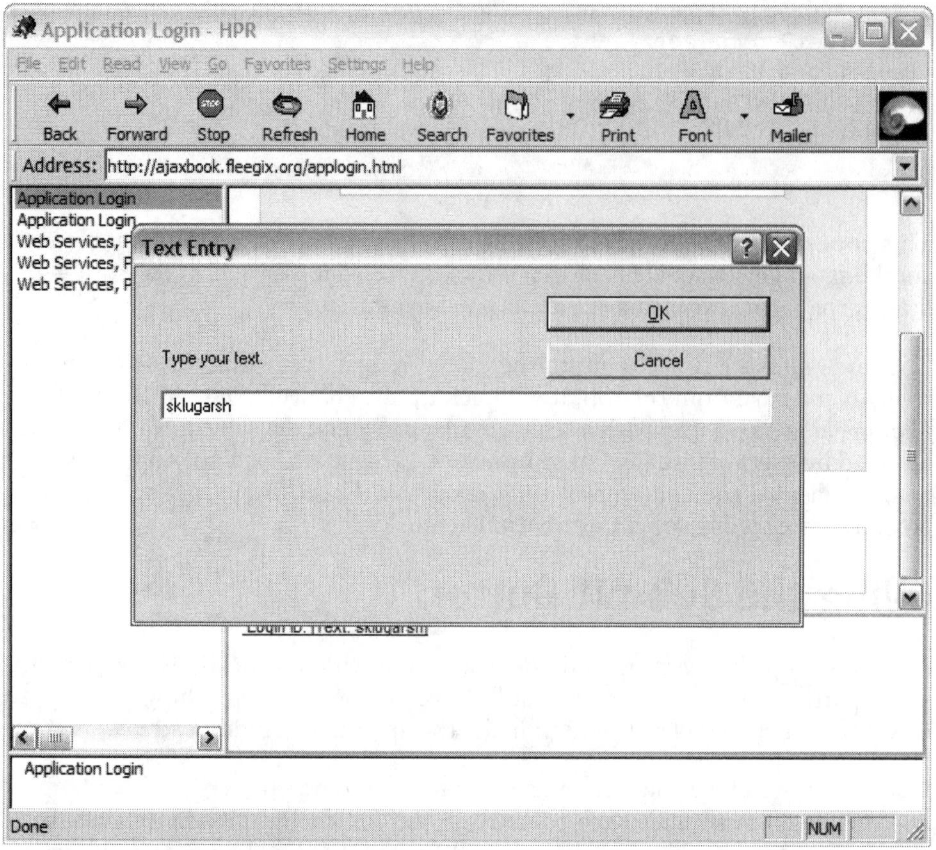

It's only a single line of code, but without it, this form is completely unusable for people with screen readers.

# Adding Instructions to a Form Element

Lastly, we need to add code to `enableScreenReaderFeatures` to give screen reader users some extra instructions about using the form. Since the form starts off with a disabled Submit button, users with screen readers might be a bit puzzled about how they are supposed to submit it. They don't receive visual feedback, so they can't see the Submit button change to an enabled state as they type into the form fields.

The solution is simply to add to the password `input` element a `title` attribute that tells screen reader users that filling in that field will activate the Submit button. Here's the code:

File: **applogin.js (excerpt)**

```
self.form.insertBefore(checkboxDiv, fieldDiv);
self.form.Pass.onchange = self.evalFormFieldState;
self.form.Pass.title = 'Password. Enter text to ' +
    'activate the Submit button.';
};
```

The screen reader will read that `title` as it reads through the information for each of the form elements, and users with screen readers will know what they need to do to activate the Submit button.

# Further Reading

Here are some online resources for learning more about the techniques and concepts we've covered in this chapter.

**http://www.webaim.org/**
WebAIM is a non-profit organization within the Center for Persons with Disabilities at Utah State University.

**http://www.w3.org/WAI/**
The World Wide Web Consortium's Web Accessibility Initiative works with organizations around the world to develop strategies, guidelines, and resources to help make the Web accessible to people with disabilities.

**http://www.section508.gov/**
This site is maintained by the US Government General Services Administration to provide information about Section 508 of the Rehabilitation Act, which mandates minimum information-technology accessibility requirements for US government agencies and the companies that do business with them.

**http://joeclark.org/book/sashay/serialization/**
*Building Accessible Websites*, by Joe Clark, is available online. Published in 2002, it was updated in 2005.

# Summary

The AJAX-ified login code in this chapter provides good examples of the ways in which you can use AJAX to improve the usability of your application while still accommodating screen readers and browsers with limited or no JavaScript support.

Tasks that would normally necessitate trips to multiple pages of the app can now be done with AJAX in a single, nicely formatted page. `POST`ing form data with AJAX is actually pretty painless—and with attention to details like keyboard input, status messages, and animations, and some basic testing in screen reader programs, you can use AJAX to craft an accessible user interface that still gives your users a very "application-like" experience.

# 5

# Broader AJAX with Edit-in-place

*You keep using that word—I do not think it means what you think it means.*
—Inigo Montoya, *The Princess Bride*

Here comes the fun part! It's now time to get into some of the territory encompassed by the broader meaning of "AJAX." Some of the more dogmatic folks in the web development and JavaScript communities will jump up and down and shout that it's not AJAX if it doesn't use `XMLHttpRequest`, but this is pure silliness. Take, for example, one of the "poster child" applications of AJAX, Google Maps.[1] This service uses an old-school hidden `iframe` to pull content from the server—not `XMLHttpRequest` at all.

So, we'll just accept that the term "AJAX" can refer more generally to next-generation web applications that boast much richer interactivity and responsiveness than traditional web apps. Within this broader definition, AJAX can significantly improve the usability of your web application by allowing users to interact with data more easily, and making the application's behavior much more obvious to users.

One fantastic usability feature that's particularly handy for users dealing with text is **edit-in-place** (also called "typeover text"), which allows users to click or double-click on areas of text on a page, edit that text content inline, and save

---

[1] http://maps.google.com/

their changes. Edit-in-place makes changing a page's text content extremely convenient, as users don't have to pop up a separate window or go to a whole new page just to change one snippet of text. Figure 5.1 shows an example of edit-in-place functionality in action in an AJAX-powered blog.

**Figure 5.1. A blog page on which edit-in-place is activated**

A blog is often made up of a number of short chunks of text, so it's a perfect candidate for the deployment of edit-in-place functionality. In this chapter, we'll create a blog page that uses this functionality; with edit-in-place, you'll be able to add new entries to the page, and double-click on any existing entry to edit it. The application will also include an animation effect that will indicate when the server is saving a change.

# Page Markup

Figure 5.2 shows what the blog page should look like when you first load it in your browser.

## Figure 5.2. The blog page display on initial page load

There's not really a lot happening here. You can see how little markup this page uses:

File: **blog.html**

```
<!DOCTYPE html PUBLIC "-//W3C//DTD XHTML 1.0 Strict//EN"
    "http://www.w3.org/TR/xhtml1/DTD/xhtml1-strict.dtd">
<html xmlns="http://www.w3.org/1999/xhtml">
  <head>
    <meta http-equiv="Content-Type"
        content="text/html; charset=iso-8859-1" />
    <title>Blog</title>
    <script type="text/javascript" src="ajax.js"></script>
    <script type="text/javascript"
        src="formdata2querystring.js"></script>
    <script type="text/javascript" src="blog.js"></script>
    <link rel="stylesheet" href="blog.css" type="text/css"/>
  </head>
  <body>
    <form id="blogForm" method="post" action="">
      <div>
        <input type="hidden" id="editEntryId" name="editEntryId"
            value="" />
        <div id="colDiv">
          <div id="promptDiv">(Double-click any entry to
              edit)</div>
          <div id="newEntryButtonDiv">
            <input type="button" id="newEntryButton"
                name="newEntryButton" class="inputButton"
                value="New Entry" />
          </div>
          <div class="clearBoth"></div>
          <div id="allEntryDiv"></div>
        </div>
      </div>
    </form>
  </body>
</html>
```

### CSS is Available for Download

We won't be discussing the CSS for this application in depth. The CSS file is available in the code archive, which can be downloaded from this book's web site.

This page contains a `form` that holds all of our form elements, a prompt that provides the user with some instructions, a New Entry button, and a `div` with the ID `allEntryDiv`, which will contain all of our blog entries.

When loaded with entries, the `allEntryDiv` div contains the following markup:

```
<div id="allEntryDiv">
  <div id="main1">
    <div id="title1" class="entryTitle">Stargate
        SG-1</div>
    <div id="body1" class="entryBody"><p>Is that
        actually sci-fi? Or just a bunch of guys in Army
        uniforms?</p></div>
  </div>
  <div id="main2">
    <div id="title2" class="entryTitle">Luxan or
        Klingon?</div>
    <div id="body2" class="entryBody"><p>Who would win
        in a fight between Farscape's Ka D'Argo and Star Trek
        TNG's Worf?</p>
        <p>They both seem like pretty tough guys.</p></div>
  </div>
</div>
```

Each entry is surrounded by a `div` with an ID of `mainn`, where *n* is the entry's ID. This entry ID is repeated in the entry's title and body `div`s; it's used by the script to access the elements of each entry quickly and easily.

# Accessibility and Backward Compatibility

Note that the application we're building here will not work in older browsers, mobile devices, or with some screen readers.

To support non-JavaScript browsers and provide better accessibility, you could take one of two approaches. You could build a separate, non-JavaScript version of the page that provided equivalent functionality, or you could branch your code in certain spots using a server-side scripting language like PHP.

In the case of our New Entry button, we might provide one code branch that includes the JavaScript-driven button; for non-JavaScript clients, we could provide a different branch that included a normal hyperlink to a non-AJAX web form with which the blogger could create new blog entries. The code might look like this:

```
<div id="newEntryButtonDiv">
  <?php
    if ($javaScriptBrowser) {
      print('<input type="button" id="newEntryButton" '.
        'name="newEntryButton" class="inputButton" '.
        'value="New Entry"/>');
    }
    else {
      print('<a href="new_blog_entry.php">New Entry</a>');
    }
  ?>
</div>
```

The approach you choose will depend on factors such as the complexity of your client-side code, the kinds of development resources you have available, and the types of clients your applications need to support.

# The Blog Class

Once again, we'll organize our code by making a `Blog` class that's a singleton. By using a singleton class, we take care of the loss-of-scope problem we saw in previous chapters when we used `setTimeout`.

Here's the initial setup for our `Blog` class:

File: **blog.js (excerpt)**

```
var Blog = new function() {
  this.ajax = null;
  this.form = null;
  this.proc = 'ready'; // 'ready', 'proc' or 'done'
  this.fadeIncr = 0;
  this.statusInterval = null;
  this.isInputDisabled = false;
  this.editId = '';
  this.saveId = '';
  this.origTitle = '';
  this.origBody = '';
};
```

First, we declare some properties: `ajax` for the instance of the `Ajax` class that will talk to the app's back end; `statusInterval` for the status animation interval ID; `isInputDisabled`, which will serve as a flag that disables user input; and `editId` and `saveId`, which will store the IDs of the blog entries we're saving or editing. We also have `origTitle` and `origBody`: two properties that will store a backup of the edited blog entry content, so we can back out of changes if need be.

# The `init` Method

The `Blog` object has an `init` method, which will be triggered by the `window.on-load` event handler. It looks like this:

File: **blog.js (excerpt)**

```
this.init = function() {
  var self = Blog;
  self.ajax = new Ajax();
  self.form = document.getElementById('blogForm');
  self.form.newEntryButton.onclick = self.addNewEntry;
};
```

This method performs some basic application setup. It creates an instance of our `Ajax` class for submitting data to the server, sets a shortcut reference to the `form` on the page, and adds an `onclick` event handler to the New Entry button.

### Event Handlers in the Markup

You can certainly attach event handlers to elements within the markup, but markup generally looks a lot cleaner when it doesn't contain JavaScript code.

To trigger this method, attach it to the `window.onload` event at the end of `blog.js`:

File: **blog.js (excerpt)**

```
window.onload = Blog.init;
```

# Edit-in-place

### Editing Entries and Creating Entries

The process of creating new entries in this blog application leverages much of the code that controls the app's editing capabilities. The process of creating a new entry will make a lot more sense if you understand the process of editing, so we'll jump ahead to discuss edit-in-place now. A little later, we'll come back to discuss how we'll use that same code to create new entries.

Edit-in-place is the ability to make changes to text directly on the page, rather than having to load a new page or open some sort of pop-up window. This technique is being used increasingly in AJAX applications, as it makes it very easy for site owners to implement quick changes to text, and takes full advantage of AJAX's ability to update page content in small sections.

Note that being able to type and make changes to text right on the page is still very new to a lot of people, so it's a good idea to make really clear exactly how the feature works. Some sites change the color of editable text on mouseover to indicate what content uses edit-in-place, but I prefer a really explicit approach: to display a prompt that tells people what they can do. So I'm going to display a prompt that says "Double-click any entry to edit" at the top of the page in our demo app.

We'll start with a page to which some dummy entries have already been saved. Add the following markup to the page:

File: **blog.html (excerpt)**

```
<div id="allEntryDiv">
  <div id="main1">
    <div id="title1" class="entryTitle">Stargate SG-1</div>
    <div id="body1" class="entryBody"><p>Is that actually sci-fi?
        Or just a bunch of guys in Army uniforms?</p></div>
  </div>
  <div id="main2">
    <div id="title2" class="entryTitle">Luxan or Klingon?</div>
    <div id="body2" class="entryBody"><p>Who would win in a fight
        between Farscape's Ka D'Argo and Star Trek TNG's Worf?</p>
        <p>They both seem like pretty tough guys.</p></div>
  </div>
</div>
```

## Figure 5.3. The blog page to which some entries have been saved

Figure 5.3 shows the page display.

As a temporary measure, we'll attach event handlers to the `ondblclick` events of these two entries in the `init` method of our `Blog` class:

File: **blog.js (excerpt)**

```
this.init = function() {
  var self = Blog;
  self.ajax = new Ajax();
  self.form = document.getElementById('blogForm');
  self.form.newEntryButton.onclick = self.addNewEntry;
  var entry1 = document.getElementById('main1');
  var entry2 = document.getElementById('main2');
  entry1.ondblclick = self.toggleEditInPlace;
  entry2.ondblclick = self.toggleEditInPlace;
};
```

We'll replace this code later, but it will serve our current development purposes just fine.

If you double-click on any of these entries, you'll activate the edit-in-place functionality—this swaps the text on the page for editable form elements that contain the same text. The title becomes a text input, and the body becomes a `textarea`.

# Editing an Entry

By double-clicking an entry, we activate the `toggleEditInPlace` method; as its name suggests, this method toggles between the two states of a blog entry: the edit-in-place state and its natural display state. When you're in edit-in-place mode, clicking the Cancel button will toggle the entry's state back to the display state.

Here's the code for the `toggleEditInPlace` method:

File: **blog.js (excerpt)**

```
this.toggleEditInPlace = function(e) {
  var self = Blog;
  var elem = null;
  if (!e) {
    e = window.event;
  }
  elem = self.getSrcElem(e);
  id = elem.id.replace(/main|title|body/, '');
  if (id != 'editCancel' && !self.isInputDisabled) {
    self.editId = id;
    self.editInPlaceOn();
    self.disableEnableMainWinInput(false);
  }
  else if (id == 'editCancel') {
    if (self.editId == 'NewEntryTemp') {
      self.removeEntryDiv();
    }
    else {
      self.editInPlaceOff(false);
    }
    self.editId = '';
    self.disableEnableMainWinInput(true);
  }
};
```

This code achieves quite a lot, so let's take a look at it piece by piece.

Here's the first half:

File: **blog.js (excerpt)**

```
this.toggleEditInPlace = function(e) {
  var self = Blog;
  var elem = null;
  if (!e) {
    e = window.event;
  }
  elem = self.getSrcElem(e);
```

These first few lines access an object, stored as e, that holds information about the event that triggered the call to this method. In Firefox, Safari, and Opera, this object is passed to an event handler as its first parameter; in Internet Explorer, the same information can be accessed via window.event. The getSrcElem method uses this object to gain access to the event's source element.

## The getSrcElem Method

The task of identifying the source element of an event requires a little browser-specific code, so let's wrap this into a utility function called getSrcElem:

File: **blog.js (excerpt)**

```
this.getSrcElem = function(e) {
  var ret = null;
  if (e.srcElement) {
    ret = e.srcElement;
  }
  else if (e.target) {
    ret = e.target;
  }
  while (!ret.id && ret) {
    ret = ret.parentNode;
  }
  return ret;
};
```

The first part of this method gets a reference to the node that triggered the event; it obtains this reference either through the srcElement property or the target property, depending on which browser is executing the code. Internet Explorer supports the srcElement property, Firefox supports target, and Safari and Opera support both.

Next, there's a `while` loop, which ensures that we're returning the element we expect. Despite the fact that we've attached the event handler to the entry's main `div`, the `srcElement` or `target` property will contain a reference to the actual element on which the user clicked. For example, consider the following markup. If the user clicks on the text in the paragraph, the `p` element will be returned—not the `main1` div you might have expected.

```
<div id="main1">
  <div id="title1" class="entryTitle">
    Stargate SG-1
  </div>
  <div id="body1" class="entryBody">
    <p>Is that actually sci-fi? Or just a bunch of guys in Army
        uniforms?</p>
  </div>
</div>
```

To get around this behavior, we inspect the innermost element to see if it has an `id` attribute. If it doesn't, we check its parent, and if its parent doesn't, we check *its* parent, and so on. The first element we find with an `id` attribute should be the main, title, or body `div`, any of which will be just fine for our purposes in `toggleEditInPlace`.

# Getting the Entry's ID

Now that we have one of the entry's `div`s in `toggleEditInPlace`, we use the `id` of the returned element to work out the ID of the entry to edit:

File: **blog.js** (excerpt)

```
elem = self.getSrcElem(e);
id = elem.id.replace(/main|title|body/, '');
```

This code pulls out the ID of the entry from the `id` of the `div`. To do so, the code uses `replace` to strip the `main`, `title`, or `body` prefix from the ID of the `div` element, which leaves us with the entry's ID.

This technique of using event listeners, and taking specific actions according to the ID of the clicked interface element, is a very powerful one. We'll expand on it further a little later in the book.

# Changing the State

The last chunk of `toggleEditInPlace` is the part that actually turns the editable state on and off. The code looks like this:

File: **blog.js (excerpt)**

```
if (id != 'editCancel' && !self.isInputDisabled) {
  self.editId = id;
  self.editInPlaceOn();
  self.disableEnableMainWinInput(false);
}
else if (id == 'editCancel') {
  if (self.editId == 'NewEntryTemp') {
    self.removeEntryDiv();
  }
  else {
    self.editInPlaceOff(false);
  }
  self.editId = '';
  self.disableEnableMainWinInput(true);
}
```

The `if` clause switches the entry to edit-in-place mode. It saves to `editId` the ID value of the entry we want to edit, and activates the editable state for that double-clicked blog entry. It then uses the `disableEnableMainWinInput` method to disable the New Entry button, so the user can't try to add a new entry while they're editing an existing one.

The `else` clause is executed when the user clicks an entry's Cancel button while in edit-in-place mode. You'll see where the Cancel button comes from in just a moment. If you hit Cancel while creating a new entry, you'll remove that new entry completely. If you hit Cancel while you're working with an already-saved entry, the code switches the entry back to a non-editable state by calling `editInPlaceOff` with a parameter of `false`. This call ensures that the entry will revert to its original state. `toggleEditInPlace` then clears out the saved ID value for the entry we were editing, and re-enables the New Entry button, again using the `disableEnableMainWinInput` method.

# Turning on Editable State

Actually making the entry editable is a fairly easy process. Here's how we do it:

1.  Store the text in the title and body `div` elements for the entry.

2.  Replace the text in the `div` elements with form fields.

3.  Set the values of the form fields to the saved text.

We use DOM methods (with just a pinch of `innerHTML`) to achieve all this, which makes the code a little verbose. However, if you break it into chunks, you'll find that it's still fairly manageable.

File: **blog.js (excerpt)**

```
this.editInPlaceOn = function(id) {
  var self = Blog;
  var id = self.editId;
  var entryDiv = null;
  var titleDiv = null;
  var bodyDiv = null;
  var titleInput = null;
  var bodyArea = null;
  var cancelButton = null;
  var saveButton = null;
  var leftButtonDiv = null;
  var rightButtonDiv = null;
  var clearBothDiv = null;
  entryDiv = document.getElementById('main' + id);
  titleDiv = document.getElementById('title' + id);
  bodyDiv = document.getElementById('body' + id);
  self.origTitle = titleDiv.innerHTML;
  self.origBody = bodyDiv.innerHTML;
  while(titleDiv.firstChild) {
    titleDiv.removeChild(titleDiv.firstChild);
  }
  while(bodyDiv.firstChild) {
    bodyDiv.removeChild(bodyDiv.firstChild);
  }
  titleInput = document.createElement('input');
  bodyArea = document.createElement('textarea');
  titleInput.id = 'titleText';
  titleInput.name = 'titleText';
  bodyArea.id = 'bodyText';
  bodyArea.name = 'bodyText';
  bodyArea.cols = "36";
  bodyArea.rows = "8";
  titleInput.className = 'titleInput';
  bodyArea.className = 'bodyArea';
  titleDiv.appendChild(titleInput);
```

```
  bodyDiv.appendChild(bodyArea);
  titleInput.value = self.origTitle;
  bodyArea.value = self.origBody;
  cancelButton = document.createElement('input');
  saveButton = document.createElement('input');
  leftButtonDiv = document.createElement('div');
  rightButtonDiv = document.createElement('div');
  clearBothDiv = document.createElement('div');
  leftButtonDiv.className = 'leftButton';
  rightButtonDiv.className = 'rightButton';
  clearBothDiv.className = 'clearBoth';
  clearBothDiv.style.paddingBottom = '12px';
  cancelButton.type = 'button';
  cancelButton.className = 'inputButton';
  cancelButton.id = 'editCancel';
  cancelButton.onclick = self.toggleEditInPlace;
  cancelButton.value = 'Cancel';
  saveButton.type = 'button';
  saveButton.className = 'inputButton';
  saveButton.id = 'updateSave';
  saveButton.onclick = self.doSave;
  saveButton.value = 'Save';
  entryDiv.appendChild(leftButtonDiv);
  leftButtonDiv.appendChild(cancelButton);
  entryDiv.appendChild(rightButtonDiv);
  rightButtonDiv.appendChild(saveButton);
  entryDiv.appendChild(clearBothDiv);
};
```

Well, I did say it was verbose! Let's break it down and examine what's going on here.

Here's the first chunk, which comes just after our variables are declared and initialized:

File: **blog.js (excerpt)**

```
entryDiv = document.getElementById('main' + id);
titleDiv = document.getElementById('title' + id);
bodyDiv = document.getElementById('body' + id);
self.origTitle = titleDiv.innerHTML;
self.origBody = bodyDiv.innerHTML;
while(titleDiv.firstChild) {
  titleDiv.removeChild(titleDiv.firstChild);
}
while(bodyDiv.firstChild) {
```

```
  bodyDiv.removeChild(bodyDiv.firstChild);
}
```

The first three lines simply get references to the div elements we want to swap out for editable form elements. Next, we grab the title and body text from those divs. Here, we're using innerHTML instead of DOM methods so that we can include markup along with the text to preserve our links, paragraphs, and other nice formatting (DOM methods would treat all of these as separate elements). We then strip all text and other DOM nodes from the title and body divs using removeChild with a while loop.

Now we're ready to add the form elements:

File: **blog.js (excerpt)**

```
titleInput = document.createElement('input');
bodyArea = document.createElement('textarea');
titleInput.id = 'titleText';
titleInput.name = 'titleText';
bodyArea.id = 'bodyText';
bodyArea.name = 'bodyText';
bodyArea.cols = "36";
bodyArea.rows = "8";
titleInput.className = 'titleInput';
bodyArea.className = 'bodyArea';
titleDiv.appendChild(titleInput);
bodyDiv.appendChild(bodyArea);
titleInput.value = self.origTitle;
bodyArea.value = self.origBody;
```

As we've seen before, adding elements to a document takes three steps: first, we create the elements using createElement; then, we set all the element properties and styles; finally, we stick them into an appropriate place in the document using appendChild. Once the form elements are there on the page, we can set their values using the values we recorded before.

We end up with the equivalent of the following markup, the new parts of which are emphasized in bold:

```
<div id="main1">
  <div id="title1" class="entryTitle">
    <input id="titleText" name="titletext" class="titleInput"
        value="Stargate SG-1" />
  </div>
  <div id="body1" class="entryBody">
    <textarea id="bodyText" name="bodyText" cols="36" rows="8"
```

```
          class="bodyArea"><p>Is that actually sci-fi? Or just a
          bunch of guys in Army uniforms?</p></textarea>
   </div>
</div>
```

Now we have our edit-in-place form fields on the page, and set with the original title and body text of that entry. This is nice, but we also need to provide some way for users to save their changes, or to forget them and leave the entry the way it was. We need to add some buttons beneath the form fields. We'll use DOM methods to add those buttons inside div elements floated left and right, giving us a proper form layout for the editable entry:

File: **blog.js (excerpt)**

```
cancelButton = document.createElement('input');
saveButton = document.createElement('input');
leftButtonDiv = document.createElement('div');
rightButtonDiv = document.createElement('div');
clearBothDiv = document.createElement('div');
leftButtonDiv.className = 'leftButton';
rightButtonDiv.className = 'rightButton';
clearBothDiv.className = 'clearBoth';
clearBothDiv.style.paddingBottom = '12px';
cancelButton.type = 'button';
cancelButton.className = 'inputButton';
cancelButton.id = 'editCancel';
cancelButton.onclick = self.toggleEditInPlace;
cancelButton.value = 'Cancel';
saveButton.type = 'button';
saveButton.className = 'inputButton';
saveButton.id = 'updateSave';
saveButton.onclick = self.doSave;
saveButton.value = 'Save';
entryDiv.appendChild(leftButtonDiv);
leftButtonDiv.appendChild(cancelButton);
entryDiv.appendChild(rightButtonDiv);
rightButtonDiv.appendChild(saveButton);
entryDiv.appendChild(clearBothDiv);
```

Again, adding the div elements and buttons with DOM methods is a three-step process. In effect, you'll end up with the following document:

```
<div id="main1">
  <div id="title1" class="entryTitle">
    <input id="titleText" name="titletext" class="titleInput"
        value="Stargate SG-1" />
```

```
    </div>
    <div id="body1" class="entryBody">
      <textarea id="bodyText" name="bodyText" cols="36" rows="8"
          class="bodyArea"><p>Is that actually sci-fi? Or just a
          bunch of guys in Army uniforms?</p></textarea>
    </div>
</div>
```

Note that the CSS declaration `clear: both;` has been applied to the final `div` we added, to clear the left and right button `div`s.

The Cancel button is assigned an `onclick` event handler tied to the `toggleEditInPlace` method, which reverts the text, putting it back into a normal state on the page. The Save button's `onclick` event handler points to `doSave`, which submits the changed text to the server for "saving," and kicks off the processing animation.

# Enabling and Disabling Other Input

Our `Blog` class is capable of keeping track of only a single editable entry at any one time. It would be possible to design this application to allow multiple entries to be edited simultaneously, but this would blow out the complexity of the code, so, for now, we'll keep it simple. Once an entry is being edited, we don't want the user to be able to edit any other entries, so we need to temporarily disable the double-click event handler's functionality on all other entries. Similarly, we don't want the user to be able to add any entries while they're in edit mode, so we need to disable the New Entry button as well. Once the entry returns to its natural state, these handlers need to be reinstated.

Enabling and disabling these handlers is the responsibility of `disableEnableMainWinInput`:

File: **blog.js** (excerpt)

```
this.disableEnableMainWinInput = function(enable) {
  var self = Blog;
  var but = document.getElementById('newEntryButton');
  self.isInputDisabled = !enable;
  if (enable) {
    but.onclick = self.addNewEntry;
    but.disabled = false;
  }
  else {
    but.onclick = null;
```

```
      but.disabled = true;
   }
};
```

After declaring and initializing some variables, this method sets the `isInputDisabled` flag, which is checked in `toggleEditInPlace` before an entry can be switched to its editable state. If this flag is set to `true`, `toggleEditInPlace` will not allow the entry to be switched.

Next, this method deals with the New Entry button. If `enabled` is set to `true`, the `onclick` event handler is set and the button is enabled. If `enabled` is false, the `onclick` event handler is removed and the button is disabled.

All this code works together to create a nice, editable form for the editable state of the blog entry. Once you have it all working, the effect you see when you double-click on a blog entry is great—it morphs quickly into a little form that you can edit. This is a huge improvement over having to launch another window or navigate to some other location to change a small scrap of text. Figure 5.4 shows an entry toggled into its editable state.

# Returning to Display State

You can return an entry to its normal state in two ways: by saving a change, or by canceling a change. The only difference between these two actions is in deciding whether to use the new text, or to revert back to the original text that was displayed previously.

The `editInPlaceOff` method changes an entry back to its normal, un-editable state. It takes one parameter: *acceptChanges*, which tells the method whether we're saving or canceling the changes. Here's the code for this method:

File: **blog.js (excerpt)**

```
this.editInPlaceOff = function(acceptChanges) {
  var self = Blog;
  var id = self.editId;
  var entryDiv = null;
  var titleDiv = null;
  var bodyDiv = null;
  var t = null;
  var b = null;
  entryDiv = document.getElementById('main' + id);
  titleDiv = document.getElementById('title' + id);
  bodyDiv = document.getElementById('body' + id);
```

## Figure 5.4. Blog entry toggled to editable state

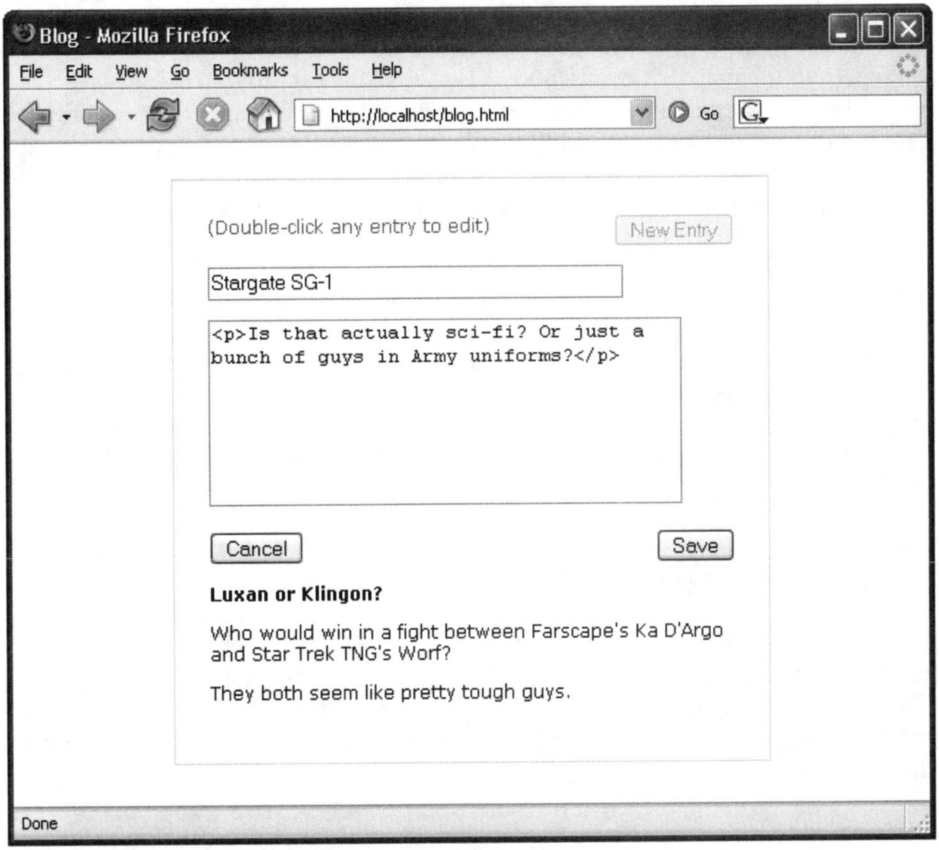

```
entryDiv.removeChild(entryDiv.lastChild);
entryDiv.removeChild(entryDiv.lastChild);
entryDiv.removeChild(entryDiv.lastChild);
if (acceptChanges) {
  t = titleDiv.firstChild.value;
  b = bodyDiv.firstChild.value;
}
else {
  t = self.origTitle;
  b = self.origBody;
}
titleDiv.removeChild(titleDiv.firstChild);
bodyDiv.removeChild(bodyDiv.firstChild);
titleDiv.innerHTML = t;
```

```
bodyDiv.innerHTML = b;
};
```

After declaring and initializing the variables used in this method, and getting references to the main, title, and body `divs`, `editInPlaceOff` strips the last three elements from the main `div`. Those three elements are the `divs` that contain the Cancel and Save buttons and the float-clearing `div`. These `div` elements are appended to the end of the main `div`, so we know that they come last. We strip the last element from the list of children by running `removeChild`; we run the method repeatedly to strip all the elements from the list.

Next, the code uses the *acceptChanges* parameter to decide which text it will use to replace each form element. If the changes are being saved, the code uses the changed text in the form fields. If the changes are being canceled, it reverts to the values stored in `origTitle` and `origBody`. Once it knows which text to use, it removes the form elements from the title and body `div` elements using `removeChild`, and uses `innerHTML` to replace those elements with the appropriate text.

# Saving Changes

When you click the Save button, you should return to the entry's display state and see some kind of notification that indicates that the changes you made to the entry are being submitted to the server. It's with the `doSave` method that we submit the changes and start up a "processing" animation to notify the user that the save is in progress:

File: **blog.js (excerpt)**

```
this.doSave = function() {
  var self = Blog;
  var postData = '';
  self.form.editEntryId.value = self.editId;
  postData = formData2QueryString(self.form);
  self.ajax.doPost('/blog_process.php', postData, self.handleSave);
  self.editInPlaceOff(true);
  self.proc = 'proc';
  self.startStatusAnim();
};
```

Since there are only a couple of elements in our form, it would be fairly easy to pull the data out of the form elements manually and format it for submission, but it's even easier to pull data from the form using the `formData2QueryString` function we saw in the last chapter. That function automatically grabs the data out of the form and formats it into the query string style that we need for POSTing the data.

Note that just before getting the data from the form, we're setting the hidden input, `editEntryId`, to the value of `editId`. This is how we place the ID of the entry that's being saved into the form data.

Once we have the form data in `postData`, we send the changes to the server by calling `doPost` and passing it the address of the page to `POST` to, the data, and the handler `handleSave`, which will be called when the response is received.

After submitting the changes to the server, we restore the entry to its display state using the `editInPlaceOff` method we saw above. We pass it a `true` value to tell it that we're keeping the changes the user has made.

Lastly, the code starts up the animation that indicates the server is busy saving the changes. It also sets the `proc` property to `proc` to indicate that the app is in processing state. We'll also be using this value to control the animation.

Let's take a look at how that status animation works before we move on to discuss the "saving" process and explore the task of handling the response from the server.

# The Status Animation

As we've already discussed, it's really important to let the user know what the application is doing. An AJAX application gives users new ways to interact with the app—ways that are different from what users might expect from an old-fashioned web application. Those new interactions may be somewhat confusing to users, so it's vital that you take the necessary steps to give them good feedback, and make them feel that the application is responding to them.

This animation works very similarly to the ones we saw in previous chapters, with a couple of exceptions. First, rather than changing opacity or appending dots to a string, this animation changes the CSS background color of a `div`.

The other big difference is that we won't always animate the same `div`. We could animate a `div` for any of the entries on the page, including a new entry.

# Starting the Animation

We start the animation by initializing an incrementing variable, performing the first step of the animation, and kicking off a `setInterval` process:

File: **blog.js (excerpt)**

```
this.startStatusAnim = function() {
  var self = Blog;
  self.fadeIncr = 0;
  self.doStatusAnim();
  self.statusInterval = setInterval(self.doStatusAnim, 200);
};
```

The `setInterval` process calls `doStatusAnim` once every 200 milliseconds until the server finishes processing the submission. As before, we save the interval ID in a property—called `statusInterval`—so we can stop the process later.

The animation process works by setting the CSS background color of the animation `div` with integer RGB values instead of the usual hexadecimal values. The syntax for this is a bit different from the normal pound-sign-plus-six-character string you may be used to seeing in web programming—it's set using `rgb` and three numbers between 0 and 255, which occur in parentheses. These numbers represent values for the red, green, and blue colors, respectively, which will be used in the animated background.

Table 5.1 a few examples in both RGB and hex values:

## Table 5.1. Examples of colors in both RGB and hexadecimal notation

| | | |
|---|---|---|
| Red | `rgb(256, 0, 0)` | `#ff0000` |
| Light Blue | `rgb(200, 200, 255)` | `#c8c8ff` |
| Gray | `rgb(128, 128, 128)` | `#808080` |

I decided to use a nice blue for this animation. One way to achieve a fading blue color is to set the blue value to the maximum of 255, set both red and green to a lower number (in this case I used 235), and to increase the red and green values together in increments of five until each value reaches 255. As the red and green values get closer to 255 (the maximum value), the blue color grows lighter and lighter, until it's completely white. Repeating this process over and over in a tight loop creates a nice fading color effect. Figure 5.5 shows, step by step, what this effect looks like.

## Figure 5.5. Creating animation that uses a CSS color fade

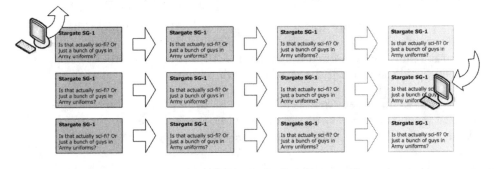

# The doStatusAnim Method

Here's the doStatusAnim method that executes the color change:

File: **blog.js (excerpt)**

```
this.doStatusAnim = function() {
  var self = Blog;
  var r = 235;
  var g = 235;
  var fadeDiv = null;
  fadeDiv = document.getElementById('main' + self.editId);
  if (self.fadeIncr < 20) {
    self.fadeIncr += 5;
  }
  else {
    if (self.proc == 'proc') {
      self.fadeIncr = 0;
    }
    else {
      self.fadeIncr = 20;
      self.stopReset();
    }
  }
  r += self.fadeIncr;
  g += self.fadeIncr;
  fadeDiv.style.background = 'rgb(' + r + ', ' + g + ', 255)';
};
```

The top part of the code retrieves a reference to the `div` that we're going to animate so that we can manipulate that `div`'s properties. The `editId` property will either have as its value an ID number (for existing entries), or `NewEntryTemp` (for new entries). We'll discuss the use of `NewEntryTemp` as a placeholder for the entry ID in more detail later, when we talk about creating new entries.

Once we have a reference to the `div` to be animated, we calculate the value of `fadeIncr`, which controls the value of the red and green components of the `div`'s color. `fadeIncr` cycles through the values 0, 5, 10, and 20 each time `doStatusAnim` is called, until the value of the `proc` property is changed.

Finally, the value of `fadeIncr` is added to `235` to produce the value of both the red and green components of the `div`'s color; this value is then applied to the div using the CSS `rgb(`*`red`*`, `*`green`*`, `*`blue`*`)` syntax.

# The Fake Back-end Page

In most blog applications, new entries, or changes to existing entries, are posted to some processing code that saves your text on the back end (often in a database such as MySQL or PostgreSQL). For the purposes of our simple blog page, we're going to use a fake back-end page called `blog_process.php`. Though it doesn't really save anything, it does return to the browser the same kind of data that a real page would return after any content changes were saved.

## Using YAML

Since we're using the same page to handle both new entries and edits to existing ones, the response from the page will need to be a bit more complicated than the plain text response we've seen in previous chapters.

Our needs are still not complex enough to need all the extra overhead of XML, though, so for this page I chose a structured data format called **YAML** (this stands for YAML Ain't Markup Language, and rhymes with "camel"), which is simple, easily parsed, and human-readable.

Here's an example of some YAML data—the summary information for an episode of the sci-fi TV show *Farscape*:

```
---
title: Throne for a Loss
order: season 1, episode 2
airdate: 1999-04-09
```

```
actors:
  - name: Ben Browder
    character: John Crichton
  - name: Claudia Black
    character: Aeryn Sun
  - name: Anthony Simcoe
    character: Ka D'Argo
synopsis: >
  Rygel is abducted by Tavleks, aggressive soldiers with
  gauntlet weapons on their forearms that inject them full of
  stimulants.
quote: >
  That's your plan? Wile E. Coyote would come up with a better
  plan than that!
...
```

Read more about YAML's syntax rules on the YAML web site.[2]

You can see how easy it is to read, and how little "ink" it uses on the page. Compare it with the XML markup for the same data, which uses more characters and is less readable than it's YAML counterpart:

```
<episode>
  <title>Throne for a Loss</title>
  <order>season 1, episode 2</order>
  <airdate>1999-04-09</airdate>
  <actors>
    <actor>
      <name>Ben Browder</name>
      <character>John Crichton</character>
    </actor>
    <actor>
      <name>Claudia Black</name>
      <character>Aeryn Sun</character>
    </actor>
    <actor>
      <name>Anthony Simcoe</name>
      <character>Ka D'Argo</character>
    </actor>
  </actors>
  <synopsis><![CDATA[Rygel is abducted by Tavleks, aggressive
      soldiers with gauntlet weapons on their forearms that
      inject them full of stimulants.]]></synopsis>
  <quote><![CDATA[That's your plan? Wile E. Coyote would come up
```

---

[2] http://www.yaml.org/

```
      with a better plan than that!]]></quote>
</episode>
```

# The PHP Code

Here's the code for the back-end page:

File: **blog_process.php (excerpt)**

```
<?php
$editEntryId = $_POST["editEntryId"];
sleep(3);
header("Content-Type: text/plain");
print "---\n";
print "status: success\n";
if ($editEntryId == "NewEntryTemp") {
  print "type: new\n";
  print "id: " . time() . "\n";
}
else {
  print "type: edit\n";
  print "id: " . $editEntryId . "\n";
}
print "...";
?>
```

This fairly short chunk of PHP basically does the same thing whether you're saving a new entry or editing an existing one.

In both cases, it returns the ID of the entry—either the ID for an edited entry that's passed in from the browser, or a pretend ID that's generated by the PHP `time` function to mimic the value that would be returned if this code were actually saving something to a database (like a MySQL `auto_increment` field, or a PostgreSQL `serial`). The main difference is whether the `type` is set to `new` or `edit`.

# Response Examples

Here's an example of the response for a newly-created entry:

```
---
status: success
type: new
id: 1138946552
...
```

And an example of a response for an edit:

```
---
status: success
type: edit
id: 1138946597
...
```

These plain text results are handed back to the response handler function, `handleSave`, for parsing.

# Parsing YAML in JavaScript

The first thing we'll need to do in our AJAX app is parse the YAML result text into a form that JavaScript can use. We could use a parsing library like YAML JavaScript[3] to take care of this step for us, but in this case, the returned result is very simple—it doesn't seem to make much sense to include an entire library just for that!

Instead, we'll just write a small method, `parseYamlResult`, which will parse into an associative array the name-value pair results that appear in the returned text:

File: **blog.js (excerpt)**

```
this.parseYamlResult = function(str) {
  var arr = [];
  var res = [];
  var pat = /(\S+): (\S+)\n/g;
  while (arr = pat.exec(str)) {
    res[arr[1]] = arr[2];
  }
  return res;
};
```

`parseYamlResult` receives the YAML document as a string in the *str* parameter.

Since we know our result string contains only the header and footer lines, and a few lines of name-value pairs separated by a colon and a space, it's pretty easy to parse it into an associative array using the **exec** method of a regular expression and two sets of capturing parentheses. The keys of the hash will be the names that start each line of the result, and the values will be the values that appear after the colon. For example, `type: new` will result in an array item `res['type']` with a value of `new`.

---

[3] http://sourceforge.net/projects/yaml-javascript

If you use the g flag with the regular expression, you can use `exec` multiple times on a string to find all the matches of a certain pattern. Each time you call `exec`, it starts its search immediately after the position of the last match (which is stored in the `lastIndex` property of the regular expression object). Doing this in a `while` loop lets you pull out all the matches for your desired pattern.

# Handling the Response

Because so much of the code is the same whether you're adding a new entry or editing an existing entry, we'll use the same method, `handleSave`, to deal with the server response in both cases.

Here's the code for `handleSave`:

File: **blog.js (excerpt)**

```
this.handleSave = function(str) {
  var self = Blog;
  var res = [];
  var err = '';
  res = self.parseYamlResult(str);
  switch (res['type']) {
    case 'new':
      if (res['status'] != 'success') {
        err = 'Could not save the new entry.';
      }
      else {
        self.saveId = res['id'];
      }
      break;
    case 'edit':
      if (res['status'] != 'success') {
        err = 'Could not save changes to entry.';
      }
      break;
    default:
      err = 'Unknown error.';
      break;
  }
  self.proc = 'done';
  if (err) {
    alert(err);
  }
};
```

The *str* parameter is the result that's passed back to our page from the server; we pass it straight to `parseYamlResult` for parsing into an associative array.

Next, we handle the different response types using a `switch` statement. When `type` has a value of `new` and the response's `status` property is `success`, we record the new entry's ID in the `saveId` property, which we can use to replace the placeholder ID we set originally. You'll see more about how this works when we talk about creating a new entry. However, if an error is returned from the server, or the value of `type` is unrecognized or missing, we record an error message and move on.

Next, we disable the processing notification animation by setting `proc` to `done`, then display any error that was recorded in a simple `alert` box. If this were a real application, you'd want to present the error in a more attractive and helpful way, for instance, writing it out to a specially formatted `div` element on the page.

# Stopping the Status Animation

Once the edits have been saved on the server, it's time to stop the status animation. The process works much the same as the status animation code we saw in previous chapters.

Just as before, our application checks the processing status of the request between each completed cycle of the animation by looking at one of the object's properties—in this case, the `proc` property. Having the animation check status between cycles like this ensures that it ends smoothly after a request completes, instead of cutting suddenly, mid-fade.

Once the request comes back from the server, and `proc` is set to `done`, `doStatusAnim` will call `stopReset`, which will stop the animation, and perform some other cleanup that's needed after a request completes.

## Cleaning Up with `stopReset`

Here's the code for `stopReset`:

File: **blog.js (excerpt)**

```
this.stopReset = function() {
  var self = Blog;
  clearInterval(self.statusInterval);
  self.disableEnableMainWinInput(true);
  self.editId = '';
```

```
    self.proc = 'ready';
    if (self.saveId) {
      self.setNewEntryRealId();
    }
};
```

The first thing on the agenda for this method is to kill the processing animation, which it does by calling `clearInterval` on the interval ID stored in `statusInterval`. Making sure this is called at the end of an animation cycle, when the color of the animated `div` is completely white, ensures the animation appears to stop smoothly.

Once the animation has stopped, we need to re-enable user input in the main window; we do so with a call to `disableEnableMainWinInput`. This enables the New Entry button at the exact moment at which the animation stops.

Next, this method performs some final cleanup, clearing out the value for `editId`, and setting the `proc` property back to `ready`, which tells us that the app is not processing any requests and the processing animation has stopped.

For new entries, it also calls `setNewEntryRealId`, which changes the placeholder `div`s' IDs to their permanent values. We'll see how this works in the next section.

# Adding a New Entry

As I mentioned at the beginning of this chapter, the code we'll use to add a new blog entry leverages much of the code we use to editing existing entries, with just a few differences:

❑ The code must add the `div` elements for the new entry.

❑ The `div` elements must be removed if the user cancels the new entry's addition.

❑ The `div` elements use a placeholder ID until they receive a real ID from the server.

Clicking the New Entry button calls the `addNewEntry` method. That code takes care of two tasks: it adds the `div` elements for the new entry and toggles the entry to edit-in-place mode. Here's the code:

File: **blog.js (excerpt)**

```
this.addNewEntry = function() {
  var self = Blog;
```

```
  if (self.insertEntryDiv()) {
    self.editId = 'NewEntryTemp';
    self.editInPlaceOn();
    self.disableEnableMainWinInput(false);
  }
};
```

After calling insertEntryDiv to add the new div elements to the page, the method sets editId to NewEntryTemp—a placeholder value for the ID. When this new entry is submitted back to the server, the server will use that placeholder value to identify the submission as a brand-new blog entry, rather than an edit to an existing entry.

Next, addNewEntry goes through the steps we saw in the toggleEditInPlace method: it calls editInPlaceOn to make the entry editable, and disableEnableMainWinInput to disable the New Entry button.

# Adding the New Entry divs

The insertEntryDiv method puts the div elements for the new entry onto the page. As it uses DOM methods to add the divs, it's quite verbose, but despite its length, it's fairly simple. Here's the code:

File: **blog.js (excerpt)**

```
this.insertEntryDiv = function() {
  var self = Blog;
  var allEntryDiv = null;
  var entryFirst = null;
  var newEntryDiv = null;
  var titleDiv = null;
  var bodyDiv = null;
  allEntryDiv = document.getElementById('allEntryDiv');
  newEntryDiv = document.createElement('div');
  titleDiv = document.createElement('div');
  bodyDiv = document.createElement('div');
  newEntryDiv.id = 'mainNewEntryTemp';
  titleDiv.id = 'titleNewEntryTemp';
  bodyDiv.id = 'bodyNewEntryTemp';
  titleDiv.className = 'entryTitle';
  bodyDiv.className = 'entryBody';
  titleDiv.appendChild(document.createTextNode('New entry'));
  bodyDiv.appendChild(
      document.createTextNode('Type body here ...'));
  newEntryDiv.appendChild(titleDiv);
```

```
  newEntryDiv.appendChild(bodyDiv);
  entryFirst = allEntryDiv.firstChild;
  if (entryFirst) {
    allEntryDiv.insertBefore(newEntryDiv, entryFirst);
  }
  else {
    allEntryDiv.appendChild(newEntryDiv);
  }
  return true;
};
```

The bulk of this code sets up all the `div` elements we need to add to the page for a new blog entry. Note that all three of the `div` elements' `ids` end in `NewEntryTemp`—the placeholder we're using instead of an actual ID number. When the server "saves" an entry, it will pass back an actual ID for that entry; we'll use this ID to replace the placeholder.

Once we've created the elements, we use DOM methods to add the placeholder text that you'll see when you create a new blog entry. We'll use `(New entry)` for the title placeholder text and `Type body here ...` for the body placeholder. Figure 5.6 shows what a brand-new blog entry looks like.

Next, the code adds the title and body `div`s as children of the new entry's main `div`.

We want new entries to appear at the top of the page, so we can't use the `appendChild` DOM method to add the main `div` to the page: this approach would add the new entry to the end of the list of child nodes, making it appear at the bottom of the page. If entries already exist on the page, our code uses `insertBefore` to place the new `div` in front of the existing first entry. If there are no `div`s inside the `allEntryDiv` div, we can simply append our new main `div` as a child of the `allEntryDiv` div.

Once the new `div` is in place, the rest of the editing process is exactly the same as that for editing an existing blog entry, with one exception: the process for canceling a new entry is different from canceling an edit.

## Figure 5.6. Entering a new blog entry

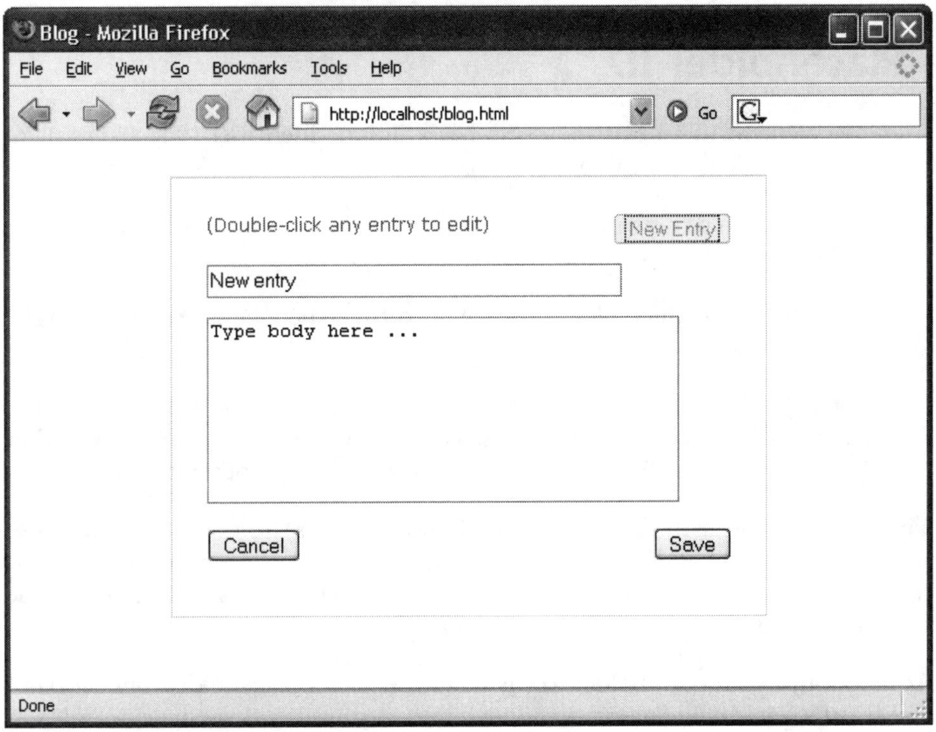

# Canceling the New Entry

When you cancel a new entry, the only sensible thing to do is to make that new entry disappear—there's no "previous state" to which the entry can revert. When you click the Cancel button after you start to create a new entry, the removeEntryDiv method is called:

File: **blog.js** (excerpt)

```
this.removeEntryDiv = function() {
  var self = Blog;
  var allEntryDiv = document.getElementById('allEntryDiv');
  var entryDiv = document.getElementById('main' + self.editId);
  allEntryDiv.removeChild(entryDiv);
};
```

It's very simple. You can see it in action by clicking the Cancel button on a new entry and watching it vanish.

# The Placeholder ID

Each `div` element in an existing entry has a unique identifier that allows us to edit it. This ID does two things for us:

❑ It tells us which `div` elements we're working with when we toggle edit-in-place and display the status animation.

❑ It tells the server which blog entry we're editing when we save changes to the app's back end.

However, in the case of new entries, there's one tiny problem with this scenario. A newly-created entry has no ID. But, once it's been saved, we want the `div` that contains the entry to be linked to a unique ID, as are all the other existing entries.

The solution is actually fairly simple. When we first create the placeholder `div`, we give it a placeholder ID. And, when the server returns a response that contains the ID of the newly-saved entry, we just replace that entry's placeholder value with the real one.

At that point, your placeholder `div` is no longer just a placeholder: once it has a real ID, it's a normal blog entry `div` among the other existing entries.

## Be Careful Messing with the `id` Attribute

Be aware that changing the `id` of a DOM element has the potential to cause problems with code that assumes that the ID will never change. Some external JavaScript libraries might not deal with changing IDs very well, so exercise some care and judgement when messing with a DOM element's `id`.

## The `setNewEntryRealId` Method

The `setNewEntryRealId` method that switches the ID is pretty straightforward:

File: blog.js (excerpt)

```
this.setNewEntryRealId = function() {
  var self = Blog;
  var entryDiv = null;
  var titleDiv = null;
  var bodyDiv = null;
```

```
entryDiv = document.getElementById('mainNewEntryTemp');
titleDiv = document.getElementById('titleNewEntryTemp');
bodyDiv = document.getElementById('bodyNewEntryTemp');
entryDiv.id = 'main' + self.saveId;
titleDiv.id = 'title' + self.saveId;
bodyDiv.id = 'body' + self.saveId;
entryDiv.ondblclick = self.toggleEditInPlace;
self.saveId = '';
};
```

This method grabs references to the `div` elements to which we need to make changes, then resets their `id`s based on the ID values that are passed back from the server and stored in `saveId`. Once the `div` elements have their permanent `id` values, the method clears out `saveId`.

### Timing the ID Change

Changing the `id` this way is really easy; however, we can't just make this change as soon as the new entry is saved. (Remember how I said you have to be careful when you do this?)

The status animation in the new entry `div` is likely to be in progress when the result comes back from the server. We've chosen to let the animation turn itself off when it's finished the current fade cycle, to avoid an abrupt cutoff of the fade effect; this means that the animation may continue for a few more rounds after the result comes back.

The animation code is pointed at the `div`'s original placeholder ID, and if you change the ID while the animation is in the middle of a cycle, your code will break. Thus, we perform the ID switch last, after all the other cleanup in the `stopReset` method has taken place.

# Future Enhancements

This is a pretty basic, bare-bones blog page. The edit-in-place functionality works pretty well, but there are countless other enhancements you could add to make this a fully-fledged working application.

## Loading Existing Entries

If you were storing real blog entries, you'd want them to load from the application's back end as the page loaded in users' browsers. You'd need some kind of paging model as well, so that you didn't get all possible entries for all timeframes on a single page. There are two different approaches you could take to the question of pagination.

You could load the entries inline, building them into the page markup on the server, to be served as a normal part of the web page. This is the original, old-fashioned way to build a page, and is more compatible with older browsers.

Alternatively, you could serve a page with a `body` that contained nothing but an empty `div` to hold the content, and use AJAX to load the text for specific entries from the server in some sort of structured data format, such as YAML, XML, or JSON (which we'll be having a look at later), inserting those entries into the content area on the page.

This approach has the advantage of being less cumbersome and a little faster, since you only load the actual text for each page of entries—you don't have to rebuild the entire page every time you add or edit an entry.

Your code might also be more reusable in this case than in the first solution: you could, potentially, use the same code to serve the structured data content to all devices, instead of coding up a separate version for each one. Of course, you'd still have to have client-side code that rendered the document into something that each device could display.

# Concurrency and Locking

Editing content in small chunks like this using AJAX makes the application feel a lot speedier, and as the improved performance begins to make your blog feel more and more like a desktop app, you may have to work to remind people that the content they're editing doesn't live on their local machines.

This becomes a real problem if multiple people can log into your app and make changes to the content simultaneously. This problem is one of **concurrency**—the issue of multiple things or people wanting simultaneous access to a single resource. If more than one person can access and change your blog's content, you'll need to create some way to lock the content that's being edited so that you don't have different users overwriting each other's edits.

A good way to achieve this is to mark the entries as read-only, or to lock out access to an entire page of text entries when one of the entries is being edited. In such a system, it can be helpful to indicate who has caused the content to be locked, so that others know who to badger if they can't make changes to content because of a lock.

Note that this problem is not specific to AJAX applications. Any web app that provides multiple people with access to the same data will experience concurrency issues, but using AJAX may magnify its effects in your users' eyes.

## Errors and Timeouts

In the case of an error or timeout—a case in which the changes to the text aren't actually saved on the server (not the process of reporting an error to the user)—it's a good idea to revert the text to its original state, so the user has an accurate picture of the content's state on the server.

This is a bigger issue with AJAX applications than it is with old-fashioned web apps, because AJAX applications make changes to data in small pieces. Often, the process of saving a change can occur in the background while the user continues to perform other work in the app.

If the application does not save that change successfully, you need to alert the user that there was a problem, and return the application to a state that accurately reflects the "reality" on the server.

# Summary

Often, when people use the term AJAX, they're referring broadly to super-interactive, next-generation web applications built with XHTML, JavaScript, CSS, and the DOM. Edit-in-place is a perfect example of the kind of feature that you can add to your web app using AJAX-style development in an effort to improve the user experience. Of course, given the increased performance and interactivity of your AJAX application, you have to do more work in the UI, including items such as clear prompts that make it obvious how users can interact with your app, and animations that make the state of the data clear to users.

If they're used in the right places within your application—and in the right way—AJAX features like edit-in-place can give your users a greatly improved online experience.

# 6

# Web Services and Slide-and-hide

*I could never understand, The wind at all, Was like a ball of love, And when I'm sad, I slide*
—T-Rex, *The Slider*

In the brave new AJAX world, everything is supposed to be connected to everything else. Apps that only talk back to their own server are *so* Web 1.0.

Within the past couple of years, a surprising number of the large web companies like Google, Amazon, eBay, and Yahoo! have found that providing outside developers access to their services gives them a real competitive advantage. People who sell things online through Amazon's affiliate program, for example, can keep track of their sales using Amazon's E-Commerce Service. There is also an entire cottage industry made up of people who run businesses through eBay—and the eBay Platform provides those people with a way to automate their sales, inventory, and shipping.

Even more buttoned-down business like banks and auto manufacturers are reaping the benefits of giving their suppliers, partners, and customers easier access to company data.

Web services provide a standardized way to deliver that access, whether it's for some sort of automated back-end process running between two businesses, or a web "mashup" that displays the location of the best real estate deals in your town with Google Maps.

# Slide-and-hide Window

In this chapter, we'll learn, first-hand, how to access Amazon's web services as we embed into a web page a scrollable window that displays a rotating set of searches of Amazon books.

As each search completes, the new set of results will slide on-screen, hiding the previous set. Figure 6.1 shows the slide-and-hide effect in action, with the results for a search on "Ruby programming" replacing those for "PostgreSQL."

## Figure 6.1. Amazon book search with slide-and-hide

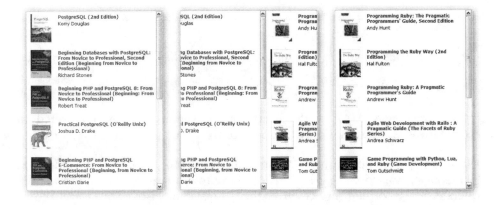

The slide-and-hide is a neat visual effect, but to implement this embedded search window, we need to get some search results to display. We'll start with a quick overview of web services, to make sure you understand what we're actually using to get the results to display on the page.

# Web Services: an Overview

If you ask a dozen IT professionals to define web services, you'd likely get a dozen different answers. The definition is kind of vague, and descriptions might involve everything from specific technologies like Java to a barrage of acronyms like SOAP, XML-RPC, and WSDL. The reality is not that difficult, though. The term "web services" generally just refers to an application that is available over the Internet and uses open standards to exchange data.

More and more applications have this kind of open access built in, and the popularity of this approach to developing apps has given rise to the name **service-oriented architecture** (SOA). This term refers to apps that allow other applications to access their functionality across the network in a standardized way.

# APIs and Protocols

Companies that have opened up their services to outside access provide a standard way of requesting information, and also define a standard way in which the requested information will be returned. This is called an **API** (application programming interface), and makes it really simple for developers to take advantage of the services the API providers offer.

Once a company decides on an API for the web service that they want to offer, they have to decide which protocols they want to support to give users access to them. The big names in web services protocols are **XML-RPC** and **SOAP** (it wouldn't be much of a technology without a bunch of fun acronyms to remember, would it?). There's also **REST**, which is simpler than the other two, and isn't really a protocol at all—it's built directly on the HTTP protocol.

## REST

REST is the simplest method for accessing a web service's API. It stands for Representational State Transfer. It's a very fancy name for the simple idea that everything out there on the Web—pages, images, Flash movies, PDFs—are just resources that are available to us.

The idea of REST is that each these resources can be accessed over HTTP, with each different HTTP request method giving us the ability to do something different to that resource. For example, we might use a GET HTTP request to download the resource, a PUT or POST to make changes to it, and DELETE to remove it. In REST jargon, these request methods are called verbs, since they're actions you can perform on different items out there on the Web.

According to REST, you locate these things using a **URI** (Universal Resource Identifier), which can be acted on by these standard HTTP verbs. In the web services world, this would be the URI that a company (like Google or Amazon) publishes to allow people access to their service.

## Google Search Example

A good example of REST in action is the Google search page. Do a quick Google search on any topic, and as you do so, have a look in your browser's location bar. When you submit your search, you're performing a GET request of the search page URI. Here's an example:

http://www.google.com/search?q=*logan%27s+run*

The search page's URI is `http://www.google.com/search`. Performing a GET request with the *q* parameter for the search term allows you to download the resource—in this case, a bunch of links about a really cheesy sci-fi movie from the 1970s.

APIs that provide access using REST methods are often described as being RESTful.

# XML-RPC

XML-RPC stands for XML Remote Procedure Call. It's a very simple protocol that allows a computer to call functions on a cooperating machine over a network. XML-RPC uses HTTP requests (usually POST) to send XML-encoded commands and responses back and forth between the client and server.

Many web service APIs include support for XML-RPC, and the XML-RPC web site[1] offers a long list of open-source and commercial implementations in a variety of languages and environments—everything from Perl, Python, Java, and C to Lisp, PHP, and .NET. XML-RPC is the ancestor of SOAP, and was developed cooperatively between UserLand Software and Microsoft in 1995.

The idea of XML-RPC is that your code can call functions on another machine, and get the result back just as if it were calling code inside your own application. The function calls and results are automatically packaged up as XML and sent back and forth without your code needing to know anything about it.

---

[1] http://www.xml-rpc.com/

# SOAP

SOAP (which originally stood for Simple Object Access Protocol[2]) is an XML-based protocol with roots in XML-RPC. As with plain XML-RPC, SOAP relies on libraries of code to create and decode the XML commands that magically allow your code to call code on the remote machine.

In theory, you should never have to deal with the complexity of SOAP—your chosen library should take care of it all for you. However, in reality, getting to a point where you can actually work with SOAP—getting a library in place, figuring out its API, and deciphering the cryptic error messages that appear when something unexpected happens—can prove to be fairly complex and frustrating in its own right.

## WSDL

WSDL (Web Services Description Language) reduces the complexity of SOAP by providing a description of the web service that your code can use in setting up its SOAP client. It includes information such as the URI that should be used to make queries, and the functions and datatypes the service supports.

A WSDL file is an XML-based document that acts something like a remote config file for your SOAP client. Ideally, you should be able just to pass your SOAP client the URI of the WSDL file, and have it figure out how to use the service. Using WSDL with PHP's SOAP extension looks something like this:

```
$soapClient =
    new SoapClient("http://badscifi.com/api/MovieSearch.wsdl");
$result = $soapClient->doMovieSearch($key, $movieTitle);
```

It should be as simple as that—once you get your library set up and figured out, that is.

# Network-centric vs Application-centric

REST is a network-centric protocol, meaning that it was designed with the idea of making network communication easier, without a heavy focus on the applications that have to work with it.

---

[2]The SOAP acronym was officially changed by the W3C in version 1.2 of the specification, when it was realized it wasn't simple at all. SOAP now stands for ... SOAP.

The pieces of your app are expected to comprise a "resource" with a URI, and to respond to HTTP request "verbs" like GET, POST, and PUT. This makes the process simple from the network communication side of things, but forces your server-side code to figure out what all these simple "verbs" mean to your specific application. Ultimately, you have to map your app to the network and its communication.

XML-RPC and SOAP take the opposite approach. They are application-centric, mapping the actual logic of the application into the communication process. The HTTP request type makes no difference (although POST is most common), and all the information about how to interact with your server-side code is written out in the XML data used in the communication process.

This makes things much easier for the application logic, but more difficult for communication, since the XML needed to transmit all the data is a lot more verbose and complicated.

In this chapter, we'll learn how to access web services with REST. We'll look at example code that uses XML-RPC and SOAP in the next chapter.

# Amazon Web Services Client

Our project for this chapter will be an AJAX client that accesses one of Amazon's web services. Our AJAX client will pull down the results of several different product-listing searches on a rotation, and insert the result into a web page. Figure 6.2 shows an example of the search results the client gets for the search "Ruby programming."

## Figure 6.2. Amazon web services client showing a set of search results

**Programming Ruby: The Pragmatic Programmers' Guide, Second Edition**
Andy Hunt

**Programming the Ruby Way (2nd Edition)**
Hal Fulton

**Programming Ruby: A Pragmatic Programmer's Guide**
Andrew Hunt

**Game Programming with Python, Lua, and Ruby (Game Development)**
Tom Gutschmidt

**Agile Web Development with Rails : A Pragmatic Guide (The Facets of Ruby Series)**
Andrea Schwarz

# Amazon Web Services Accounts

To use this service, you'll need to have an Amazon Web Services (AWS) account. This will give you an Access Key ID, which you'll need in order to make queries using the service. Many of the large technology companies that offer web services require you to have this kind of key or token to access their services. This is only natural—they want good data about who's using their service, and how they're using it. These keys are usually free to set up and use, although sometimes they may limit the number of queries you can perform per day for free.

Amazon displays a very obvious link on the AWS home page[3] (shown in Figure 6.3) to the information that explains how to create a free AWS account. Once you have your account set up, and your Access Key ID has been emailed to you, you'll be all ready to get started.

## Figure 6.3. The link for creating a free AWS account

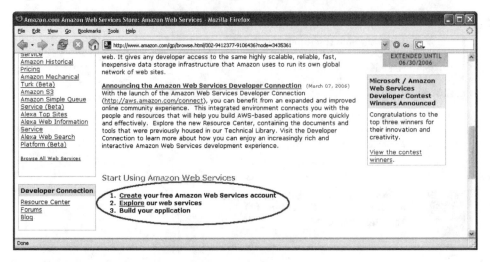

# Amazon E-Commerce Service

We will be using Amazon's E-Commerce Service (ECS), one of Amazon's web services, which provides access to product data and ecommerce functions. This gives you access to the full range of search functionality that's available from Amazon's main site. Excellent documentation is available on the Amazon web services site, although it does take a bit of surfing around to find the bits of information you need.

The first thing for us to do is to pick the method we want to use to access the ECS web service. Amazon offers access via SOAP and REST. Since our needs are modest, we'll go with the REST method, so we can get right to work performing a search and pulling down some results. With REST access to Amazon ECS, we'll be sending AJAX-style `GET` requests to perform searches. The search details will be specified on the query string.

---

[3] http://www.amazon.com/aws/

To make sure the results we receive are easy to parse and work with, Amazon returns its search results as XML. This will be our first foray into the process of consuming XML, and you'll find that, initially, it can be tricky to get it to work. On the other hand, the nice thing about XML is that it's very predictable, so once you get the results you want, it's fairly easy to make adjustments without breaking things.

# The `Client` Class

For lack of a better term, we'll call our client class `Client`. It's not terribly inspired, but it is accurate: it's a web service client. To keep our rotating searches ticking over we'll be using `setTimeout` and, predictably, we'll make the class a singleton so that we don't have to worry about loss of scope. Here's the initial code:

File: **webservice1.js (excerpt)**

```
var SEARCH_TERMS = ['ajax', 'postgresql', 'ruby programming',
    'php', 'javascript'];
var ACCESS_KEY = 'Access Key ID';

var Client = new function() {
  this.SEARCH_TERMS = null;
  this.ACCESS_KEY = null;
  this.ajax = null;
  this.incr = 0;
  this.containerDiv = null;
  this.currDiv = null;
  this.newDiv = null;
  this.slideInterval = null;
  this.slideIncr = 380;
};

window.onload = Client.init;
```

At the start of this file, we declare a couple of constants for the application. These are included so that a webmaster could set up and configure this code without having to know anything about how it works (in theory, at least). `SEARCH_TERMS` is an array of search phrases through which the app will cycle. `ACCESS_KEY` is your AWS Access Key ID.

## What's the Value of ACCESS_KEY?

Note that the value of ACCESS_KEY is not set in the sample code provided with this book—you'll have to sign up for an AWS account and obtain an access key of your own if you want to see this code in action.

The ajax property is an instance of our familiar Ajax class, which we'll use to make the HTTP requests to the Amazon service. The incr property is used to remember our position within the list of search terms. The rest of the properties are used in the fancy slide-and-hide effect to show the search results.

# Initial Setup

The init method takes care of some setup, then starts up the lookup process:

File: **webservice1.js (excerpt)**

```
this.init = function() {
  var self = Client;
  self.ajax = new Ajax();
  self.containerDiv = document.getElementById('containerDiv');
  self.SEARCH_TERMS = SEARCH_TERMS;
  self.ACCESS_KEY = ACCESS_KEY;
  if (!self.ACCESS_KEY) {
    alert('Amazon Web Services Access Key ID is not set. ' +
      'This code will not work without a key.\n' +
      'Sign up for a free key at http://www.amazon.com/aws/.');
  }
  else {
    self.doLookup();
  }
};
```

This method instantiates the Ajax class for making requests to the AWS service, sets up a convenient reference to the div element we'll be using for the slide-and-hide effect, then initializes the list of search phrases through which the page will cycle, and the AWS Access Key ID that will be used.

Next, the init method checks to make sure the ACCESS_KEY property is set before it tries to access the service. Making sure that the value is a valid key is far beyond the scope of what we're trying to do here, but at least we can make sure that if someone fires up this app without setting an AWS key, they know that a key is needed, and where to go to get one.

Lastly, our code calls doLookup to start the search process.

# Cross-site AJAX

Up to this point, all of our AJAX pages have talked back to the same server from which they were served—a very Web 1.0-style approach to development. As AJAX increases the power of browsers as a platform for application development, web application developers can get in on the action of accessing content from multiple locations and mixing it together in interesting ways.

A popular source of data for these web apps—which are referred to as "mashups"—is Google Maps, where users have their own data applied on top of a map. A classic example of this kind of application is the range of maps available at chicagocrime.org,[4] which shows reported crime incidents in Chicago overlaid on a map of the city.

## XMLHttpRequest and Security

There's one small hurdle that we'll have to deal with before our AJAX app can join the great interconnectedness party—browser security. Due to the very real problem of malicious code usage—yes, sometimes it's even JavaScript!—browsers will not allow `XMLHttpRequest` to send requests to any domain other than the one from which the page originated. This is called a **cross-site request**, and means that if you serve your AJAX application page from `www.example.com`, requests made from `XMLHttpRequest` to any other domain will result in an error.

As an example, you can take the simple monitoring app from Chapter 3, and change its `TARGET_URL` to something like `http://www.yahoo.com/` or `http://maps.google.com/`. When you hit that Start button, your request will fail with a "permission denied" error. Figure 6.4 shows the resulting error as it displays in the JavaScript console (which is part of the Web Developer Toolbar Firefox extension).

---

[4] http://www.chicagocrime.org/map/

## Figure 6.4. A cross-site security exception thrown by XMLHttpRequest

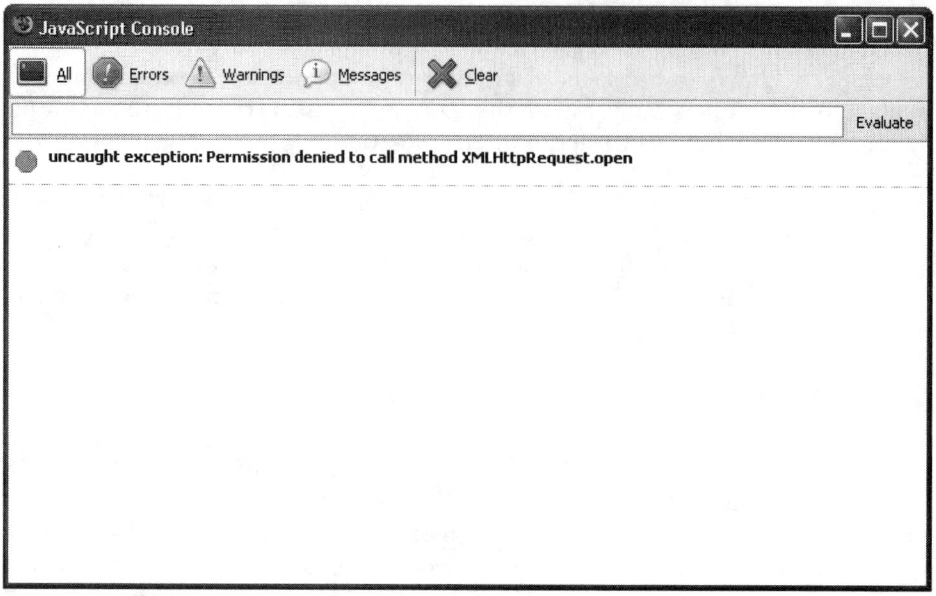

This is a reasonable security precaution. Cross-site scripting exploits are among the most common browser security problems, and giving people a scripted way to make HTTP requests is something that could be abused very easily.

# An AJAX Relay

There is a fairly easy solution to this problem. Your browser can't make AJAX requests directly to another site, but it's very easy to set up a simple proxy script that runs on your server and relays requests from your browser to those other sites. A proxy is simply a go-between—a piece of code or a process that relays information between two things that can't interact directly.

In this case, the proxy script on your server will receive the cross-site HTTP requests from the AJAX code in the browser, and pass those requests along to the desired destination. When that other server hands back a response to your server, your server will pass it back to the browser as-is. Figure 6.5 shows how this communication works.

## Figure 6.5. Cross-site AJAX communication with proxy scripts

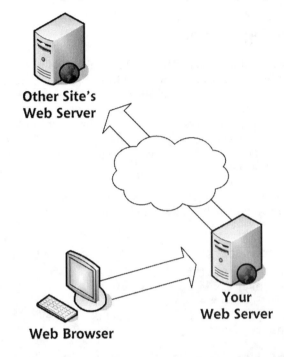

To the browser, it looks a lot like we're making requests directly to the other site; all your server has to do is relay the requests and responses back and forth.

All communication between your browser and the other site occurs through your server. This means that sometimes, although the AJAX code that's running in the browser may be able to reach your server, for some reason your server may not be able to reach the other site's server. For cases like this, in which requests relayed from your server to the other site time out or fail, you need to build in some kind of decent fallback mechanism; for instance, you may have your proxy script return an error code or message that your client-side AJAX script is equipped to address. For our web service client, we're going to use the most basic proxy script possible. This exercise in intended to show you how this process works, so we're not building in any fancy error-handling or fallback here.

# The Proxy Script

We're going to use the excellent `HTTP_Request` package available from the PHP Extension and Application Repository (PEAR) for our proxy. The `HTTP_Request` package is a bundle of code that makes it really easy to make HTTP requests using PHP.

**IMPORTANT**

## Installing HTTP_Request

This isn't a tutorial on PHP or PEAR, but the process of installing HTTP_Request on most Unix-like systems with an up-to-date PHP installation should be as simple as running **pear install HTTP_Request** from the command line. If you're using Windows, or running pear install doesn't do the trick for you on a Unix-like system (including Mac OS X), there are literally dozens of places online at which you can find help. Check out the Support section of the PEAR web site for info about mailing lists, tutorials, and the IRC channel for PEAR.

Assuming you have PEAR and get HTTP_Request installed, the following code is all you need to run the most basic server-side proxy script:

File: **ecs_proxy.php**

```php
<?php
require_once "HTTP/Request.php";
$uri = "http://webservices.amazon.com/onca/xml" .
    "?Service=AWSECommerceService" .
    "&AWSAccessKeyId=" . urlencode($_REQUEST["key"]) .
    "&Operation=ItemSearch" .
    "&SearchIndex=Books" .
    "&Keywords=" . urlencode($_REQUEST["search"]) .
    "&Sort=relevancerank";
$req =& new HTTP_Request($uri);
if (!PEAR::isError($req->sendRequest())) {
  header("Content-Type: text/xml");
  print $req->getResponseBody();
}
?>
```

Note that this page sets the response's Content-Type header to text/xml, as we know that the response from Amazon is going to be in XML. Issues can arise on the client side if these headers aren't set properly—we'll look at that in detail later.

As I said, this is a really basic proxy—it reads the *key* and *search* parameters from the query string, constructs a URI to access Amazon's E-Commerce Service, then spits out whatever response the other site's server sends back. You can test this by loading the page in your browser and supplying the required parameters manually. For example, you could use the following URL:

http://localhost/ecs_proxy.php?key=*AccessKeyID*&search=*ajax*

ecs_proxy.php then forwards this request to Amazon and, provided everything works as expected, the following XML is returned:

```
<?xml version="1.0" encoding="UTF-8"?>
<ItemSearchResponse xmlns="http://webservices.amazon.com/
    AWSECommerceService/2005-10-05">
  <OperationRequest>
    <HTTPHeaders>
      <Header Name="UserAgent" Value="PEAR HTTP_Request class
          ( http://pear.php.net/ )"></Header>
    </HTTPHeaders>
    <RequestId>ReturnedRequestID</RequestId>
    <Arguments>
      <Argument Name="Keywords" Value="ajax"></Argument>
      <Argument Name="Operation" Value="ItemSearch"></Argument>
      <Argument Name="Service"
          Value="AWSECommerceService"></Argument>
      <Argument Name="AWSAccessKeyId"
          Value="AccessKeyID"></Argument>
      <Argument Name="SearchIndex" Value="Books"></Argument>
      <Argument Name="Sort" Value="relevancerank"></Argument>
    </Arguments>
    <RequestProcessingTime>0.21</RequestProcessingTime>
  </OperationRequest>
  <Items>
    <Request>
      <IsValid>True</IsValid>
      <ItemSearchRequest>
        <Keywords>ajax</Keywords>
        <SearchIndex>Books</SearchIndex>
        <Sort>relevancerank</Sort>
      </ItemSearchRequest>
    </Request>
    <TotalResults>155</TotalResults>
    <TotalPages>16</TotalPages>
    <Item>
      <ASIN>1234567890</ASIN>
      <DetailPageURL>http://www.amazon.com/…</DetailPageURL>
      <ItemAttributes>
        <Author>Arthur Frayn</Author>
        <ProductGroup>Book</ProductGroup>
        <Title>Xtreme AJAX to the Max</Title>
      </ItemAttributes>
    </Item>
```

```
        ⋮
    </Items>
</ItemSearchResponse>
```

In a few moments we'll take this raw XML output, pull out the pieces we want, then format it and insert it into a web page.

# Sending the Request to Amazon Web Services

Now that we've set up our proxy middleman, we're ready to make some web service requests, and perform some searches. Here's the doLookup method that sends the search request:

File: **webservice1.js (excerpt)**

```
this.doLookup = function() {
  var self = Client;
  var searchStr = '';
  var uri = '';
  var dt = new Date();
  searchStr = self.getSearchItem();
  uri = '/ecs_proxy.php?key=' + escape(self.ACCESS_KEY) +
      '&search=' + escape(searchStr) +
      '&d=' + escape(dt.getTime());
  self.ajax.doGet(uri, self.handleResp, 'xml');
};
this.doLookupDelay = function() {
  var self = Client;
  setTimeout(self.doLookup, 10000);
};
```

There's not a lot going on here until the point at which we get the search term for this request from the getSearchItem method, and the part where we append the current date to the query string. The date is appended to the query string to keep Internet Explorer's implementation of XMLHttpRequest from caching the result. By constantly changing the value on the query string, Internet Exploreris forced always to grab a new version of the page.

Just after doLookup is doLookupDelay, which simply calls setTimeout to schedule another call to doLookup in ten seconds. As we won't be canceling this call, there's no need to keep track of its interval ID.

# Getting the Search Text

The `getSearchItem` method is a small chunk of code that pulls an item out of the array of search terms, then increments the counter so that we know which one to get the next time:

File: **webservice1.js (excerpt)**

```
this.getSearchItem = function() {
  var self = Client;
  var str = self.SEARCH_TERMS[self.incr];
  self.incr++;
  if (self.incr >= self.SEARCH_TERMS.length) {
    self.incr = 0;
  }
  return str;
};
```

We use `incr` to keep track of the next search phrase that's to be returned. If `incr` reaches the end of the array of search phrases, it's reset to `0`, which makes the search rotate continuously through the list of search terms.

# Sending the Request

The last step of the `doLookup` method uses our instance of the `Ajax` class to send the request through our proxy script.

The call to `Ajax`'s `doGet` method should be familiar from previous chapters, but in addition to the two normal parameters of the target page and response handler function, there's a third parameter, `xml`. Adding that parameter indicates that we want to get the results back from the `XMLHttpRequest` object as an XML document object, instead of the normal text. You'll see how we parse this different type of result in the next section.

## XML Results and `Content-Type`

XML has some definite advantages, but compared to plain text, it can be a bit finicky. As such, we generally have to be a bit more careful when working with XML.

Remember that if the `Content-Type` of the response is not `text/xml` or `application/xml`, the `responseXML` property of the `XMLHttpRequest` object will be set to `null`, even if the response contains a valid XML document. Firefox and Safari offer the `overrideMimeType` method, which you can call to force the browser to recognize the results as XML, but if you need to support more than these two browsers, you're out of luck.

Fortunately, we can control the `Content-Type` of our response by inserting the following line into `ecs_proxy.php`:

File: **ecs_proxy.php (excerpt)**

```
header("Content-Type: text/xml");
```

# Handling the Results from Amazon

Once we have the XML document element back from Amazon, we hand it off to the `handleResp` method to be parsed, formatted, and inserted into the web page:

File: **webservice1.js (excerpt)**

```
this.handleResp = function(xml) {
  var self = Client;
  var res = [];
  var mainDiv = document.getElementById('mainDiv');
  var resultsDiv = null;
  var itemDiv = null;
  var imageDiv = null;
  var titleDiv = null;
  var authorDiv = null;
  var clearBoth = null;
  var im = '';
  var ti = '';
  var au = '';
  var bookImg = null;
  res = XMLParse.xml2ObjArray(xml, 'Item');
  resultsDiv = document.createElement('div');
  resultsDiv.className = 'resultsDiv';
  for (var i = 0; i < res.length; i++) {
    itemDiv = document.createElement('div');
    imageDiv = document.createElement('div');
    titleDiv = document.createElement('div');
    authorDiv = document.createElement('div');
    clearBoth = document.createElement('div');
    itemDiv.className = 'itemDiv';
    imageDiv.className = 'imageDiv';
    titleDiv.className = 'titleDiv';
    authorDiv.className = 'authorDiv';
```

```
    clearBoth.className = 'clearBoth';
    as = res[i].ASIN;
    ti = res[i].ItemAttributes.Title;
    au = res[i].ItemAttributes.Author;
    bookImg = document.createElement('img');
    bookImg.src = 'http://images.amazon.com/images/P/' + as +
        '.01.THUMBZZZ.jpg';
    imageDiv.appendChild(bookImg);
    titleDiv.appendChild(document.createTextNode(ti));
    authorDiv.appendChild(document.createTextNode(au));
    itemDiv.appendChild(imageDiv);
    itemDiv.appendChild(titleDiv);
    itemDiv.appendChild(authorDiv);
    itemDiv.appendChild(clearBoth);
    resultsDiv.appendChild(itemDiv);
  }
  if (!self.currDiv) {
    self.containerDiv.appendChild(resultsDiv);
    self.currDiv = resultsDiv;
    self.doLookupDelay();
  }
  else {
    self.newDiv = resultsDiv;
    self.slideAndHide();
  }
};
```

As you can see, this is a pretty long method, so we'll discuss it piece by piece.

After declaring and initializing the variables we'll be using, there's a deceptively simple-looking call to XMLParse.xml2ObjArray:

File: **webservice1.js (excerpt)**

```
res = XMLParse.xml2ObjArray(xml, 'Item');
```

XMLParse is a library of functions available under the Apache License, Version 2.0, at http://www.fleegix.org/downloads/xmlparse.js.

# Using xml2ObjArray

The xml2ObjArray method **deserializes** the XML, which means that it transforms the XML into data structures that a programming language can use easily—in this case, it's transforming the XML into an array of JavaScript objects.

The xml2ObjArray method does the hard parsing work for you, but to be able to work with the results, you'll need to know what's in the array it returns. Let's have a look at what happens when we pass in the search result XML that's returned by Amazon.

## Example XML Document

We've already seen what the XML returned by Amazon looks like: a bunch of data about the search appears at the top, followed by all of the search result items, each of which is wrapped inside <Item> and </Item> tags. Here's an example of what the XML for one item might look like:

```
<Item>
  <ASIN>1234567890</ASIN>
  <DetailPageURL>http://www.amazon.com/…</DetailPageURL>
  <ItemAttributes>
    <Author>Arthur Frayn</Author>
    <ProductGroup>Book</ProductGroup>
    <Title>Xtreme AJAX to the Max</Title>
  </ItemAttributes>
</Item>
```

The document has one of these Item elements for each result that's returned. By default, Amazon limits pages of results to ten items, so you'll never have to worry about being inundated with a huge list of results.

The xml2ObjArray method takes two parameters—the XML document element, and the tag name it should use to create its objects. In this case, we're telling it to make an object out of each Item element. The code creates a generic JavaScript Object for each item. It gives the object a property for each element it finds inside each item, and assigns the property the value that's found between the tags.

## Example Object

So, if we took the Object that was created from the previous scrap of XML, and decided to print out all its properties and their values, we'd end up with something like this:

```
res[0].ASIN: 1234567890
res[0].DetailPageURL: http://www.amazon.com/…
res[0].ItemAttributes.Author: Arthur Frayn
res[0].ItemAttributes.ProductGroup: Book
res[0].ItemAttributes.Title: Xtreme AJAX to the Max
```

It helps to look back and forth between the XML and the `Object` to see what went where.

Notice that the `ItemAttributes` property itself is actually an `Object`, with its own properties. That's because `Author`, `ProductGroup`, and `Title` are all XML elements that are nested inside `ItemAttributes`. The `xml2ObjArray` function walks through the XML document tree recursively, creating new `Object` properties that correspond to any tags it finds that have subtags.

### note

### `xml2ObjArray` Alternatives

`xml2ObjArray` is a very simple nonvalidating parser, which means that it makes no attempt to verify the validity of the XML you load into it. If you have a need to do something fancier, larger libraries of code, such as Sarissa[5] or XML for Script,[6] are available online. They offer features such as proper XML parsing, XSLT, and XPath queries. However, for any kind of serializing or deserializing that's more complicated than what we're doing here, using a native JavaScript data-exchange format like JavaScript Object Notation (JSON) will likely make more sense. We'll be using JSON in a later chapter.

# Formatting the Results

Now that we have the results from Amazon in an array, it's time to make them look good and insert them into a web page. This is the next part of the `handleResp` method. We'll use DOM manipulation methods for this, so again, the code is a bit verbose, but it's likely to be cleaner and more readable than equivalent code that used `innerHTML`.

File: **webservice1.js (excerpt)**

```
resultsDiv = document.createElement('div');
resultsDiv.className = 'resultsDiv';
for (var i = 0; i < res.length; i++) {
  itemDiv = document.createElement('div');
  imageDiv = document.createElement('div');
  titleDiv = document.createElement('div');
  authorDiv = document.createElement('div');
  clearBoth = document.createElement('div');
  itemDiv.className = 'itemDiv';
  imageDiv.className = 'imageDiv';
  titleDiv.className = 'titleDiv';
  authorDiv.className = 'authorDiv';
```

---

[5] http://sarissa.sourceforge.net/
[6] http://xmljs.sourceforge.net/

```
clearBoth.className = 'clearBoth';
as = res[i].ASIN;
ti = res[i].ItemAttributes.Title;
au = res[i].ItemAttributes.Author;
bookImg = document.createElement('img');
bookImg.src = 'http://images.amazon.com/images/P/' + as +
    '.01.THUMBZZZ.jpg';
imageDiv.appendChild(bookImg);
titleDiv.appendChild(document.createTextNode(ti));
authorDiv.appendChild(document.createTextNode(au));
itemDiv.appendChild(imageDiv);
itemDiv.appendChild(titleDiv);
itemDiv.appendChild(authorDiv);
itemDiv.appendChild(clearBoth);
resultsDiv.appendChild(itemDiv);
}
```

Basically, the code starts off by creating a main `div`, with the class `resultsDiv`, into which all the results will be placed. It follows that with a really long "for" loop that creates the markup for each entry and appends it to the main `div`. Within each iteration of the loop, `res[i]` is one of the `Objects` created from the Amazon search results XML.

This code follows the same pattern we've seen in previous chapters—we create the elements, set properties, then add content to them. Once we have the `div` elements assembled and the content inserted, we need to append them to the `div` with the ID `resultsDiv`. The only thing that's a little unusual in this section of code is the creation of an `img` element. We use the ASIN (Amazon Standard Identification Number) to calculate where each item's thumbnail image is. We then set the `img` element's `src` attribute to this value, and append it to one of the `div`s that make up the item's display.

# Performing the Slide-and-hide

Once we have populated `resultsDiv` with all the items that were returned in the search, it's finally time to insert the `div` into the main page and begin the slide-and-hide process. The very simple markup for our page is as follows:

File: **webservice1.html (excerpt)**

```
<!DOCTYPE html PUBLIC "-//W3C//DTD XHTML 1.0 Strict//EN"
    "http://www.w3.org/TR/xhtml1/DTD/xhtml1-strict.dtd">
<html xmlns="http://www.w3.org/1999/xhtml">
  <head>
```

```
    <meta http-equiv="Content-Type"
        content="text/html; charset=iso-8859-1" />
    <title>Web Services, Part 1</title>
    <script type="text/javascript" src="ajax.js"></script>
    <script type="text/javascript" src="xmlparse.js"></script>
    <script type="text/javascript" src="webservice1.js"></script>
    <link rel="stylesheet" href="webservice1.css"
        type="text/css" />
  </head>
  <body>
    <div id="mainDiv">
      <div id="containerDiv"></div>
    </div>
  </body>
</html>
```

Looking at the markup for the page, you'll notice that the only thing that appears in the body of the page is a couple of nested div elements. handleResp will put the initial set of search results into the inner div element:

File: **webservice1.js (excerpt)**

```
if (!self.currDiv) {
   self.containerDiv.appendChild(resultsDiv);
   self.currDiv = resultsDiv;
   self.doLookupDelay();
else {
   self.newDiv = resultsDiv;
   self.slideAndHide();
}
};
```

If currDiv has not been defined, this code uses appendChild to stick the results div into the container div we set up in the markup. The code then saves a reference to the results div element in currDiv, and starts the setTimeout process for the new search using doLookupDelay.

The next time this code is executed, currDiv would have been defined, and it's time to slide in the new results. We save a reference to the second set of search results in newDiv, and then, given two sets of results to work with, we slide the new result in and hide the old one with the slideAndHide method.

# The Slide-and-hide Effect

The slide-and-hide effect takes place in two steps: the list of results is loaded "off-camera," to the right-hand side of the container `div`, then we slide the list of search results into view by changing its position using `setInterval`. Here's the code that sets this up:

File: **webservice1.js** (excerpt)

```
this.slideAndHide = function(elem) {
  var self = Client;
  self.newDiv.style.left = '380px';
  self.containerDiv.appendChild(self.newDiv);
  self.slideInterval = setInterval(self.doSlide, 50);
};
this.doSlide = function() {
  var self = Client;
  if (self.slideIncr > 0) {
    self.slideIncr -= 10;
    self.newDiv.style.left = self.slideIncr + 'px';
    self.currDiv.style.left = (self.slideIncr - 380) + 'px';
  }
  else {
    self.slideIncr = 380;
    self.containerDiv.removeChild(self.containerDiv.firstChild);
    self.currDiv = self.containerDiv.firstChild;
    clearInterval(self.slideInterval);
    self.doLookupDelay();
  }
};
```

Within `slideAndHide`, we stick the new `div` into the container with its far left edge at a position of 380 pixels. That's the same as the width of the container, so initially, the new `div` will not actually be visible. Once the new `div` is in place, we can call the `doSlide` method every 50 milliseconds with `setInterval`. Each time it's called, this method will move both the current and new `div`s a little further to the left. The `slideInterval` property holds a reference to the interval ID for the `setInterval` that we'll use to stop the slide when it's done.

The `doSlide` method performs the slide, and keeps track of the slide's progress using the `slideIncr` property. Because we're moving the two `div`s to the left, we have to make the `div`s' `left` property progressively smaller. So, with each call to this method, we drop the value of `slideIncr` by 10. As long as this number is greater than zero, we just keep using it to set the positions of the two `div` elements relative to one another. This creates the nice slide-to-the-left effect that we want.

As soon as the counter variable hits zero, we're done sliding; it's time to reset everything to get ready for the next slide, and start the process over. After resetting the counter, we throw away the original `div` that contains the old results, and update the `currDiv` property to point to the new results that just finished sliding in.

The code stops the slide process by calling `clearInterval` on the interval ID that's stored in the `slideInterval` property, then starts the entire search process over again from the beginning by calling `doLookupDelay` to perform another search after a brief delay.

# AJAX Fat-client Code

The slide-and-hide code provides a good opportunity to talk about a big issue associated with AJAX development. With AJAX techniques, increasing amounts of application code and logic end up living on the client, and more and more of the user interface is built on the client. As I mentioned previously, in many AJAX apps, markup for whole sections of the page is created dynamically by JavaScript. This can cause serious problems for the end user, not just in terms of older browsers and accessibility, but also with the app's usability, since these more complicated "fat-client" AJAX applications can make the browser act in ways that users don't expect. The good news is that if you're careful about how and where you use AJAX in your web application, you can minimize these problems.

## Legacy Browsers and Accessibility

This fat-client approach to web app development can cause serious problems for users with older browsers and screen readers. It's vital when you're developing an application to consider the target audience, and ensure that you make accommodations for the parts of your user-base with legacy browsers or special needs.

If you are designing for backward compatibility and accessibility, it might not be feasible to build your entire app using the latest bleeding-edge AJAX techniques. By the same token, it may not be possible to provide precisely the same user experience to all of your users. The key is making sure that equivalent functionality is available to all of them.

## Degrading the Search Results

One possible solution we could use to replace the fancy DHTML slide-and-hide effect in this chapter would be to do more of the work on the server-side, and pick a random search to display statically in each served page. This approach requires server-side code that processes the XML results from Amazon and embeds the result as XHTML markup in a normal web page. Each page reload in a non-JavaScript-capable browser would then display a different set of results. I'll be showing an example of this approach in the next chapter.

# Usability: the Back Button Problem

Now that you've seen a few AJAX applications at work, you might have an idea of another potential problem with AJAX-style web applications: the process of making updates to a web page in small pieces breaks the mental model that most people use to navigate around web sites or web applications. This is typically referred to as the AJAX Back button problem, because the Back button is the most obvious example of a point at which users become confused while using AJAX applications. For example, after watching the search results change on the page, users may assume that clicking their browsers' Back button will take them back to the previous list of search results. Clicking the browser's Back button and ending up in an unexpected place is an experience shared by many, many people who have used AJAX applications. Your goal as an AJAX application developer should be to eliminate that possibility by using AJAX only in situations in which it's unlikely to confuse users. You shouldn't use AJAX just for the sake of it—and you should absolutely avoid it in cases where normal page navigation would be more natural.

## Using Warnings as a Safety Net

Granted, the cases in which AJAX should be used aren't always 100% cut-and-dried, and there may be some cases where your use of AJAX could cause your users some confusion. In those cases, you should provide your users with the bare minimum form of a safety net—some sort of warning that is displayed when they hit the Back button. Ideally the alert would warn them they'll be leaving your application, and gives them the opportunity to cancel their action.

You can provide such alerts in browsers that support the `onbeforeunload` event listener. Point this to a function that returns the message you want your users to see, and it will be displayed in a dialog that asks users if they want to navigate away from the page.

Add the event listener like so:

```
window.onbeforeunload = function() {
    alert('You will actually go somewhere else. ' +
      'You will not go back to the previous search results.');
};
```

Figure 6.6 shows what this message will look like to users leaving the page.

## Figure 6.6. Warning users before they leave the page

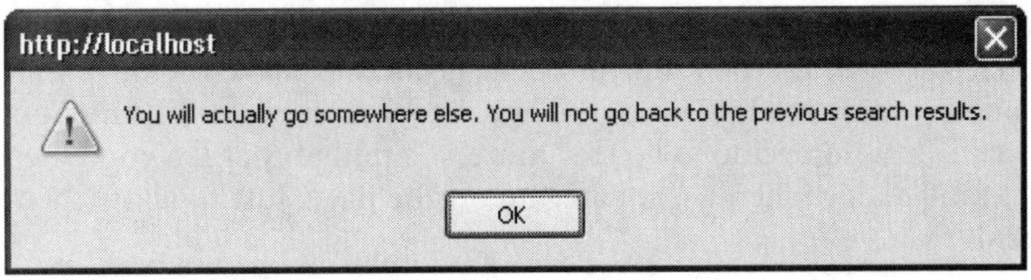

This strategy should, of course, be used as a last resort. You should avoid using AJAX in ways that make navigation weird or ambiguous. Above all, avoid using AJAX just because you can. AJAX functionality should always be something that you add to your application to improve the end user experience.

# Fixing the Browser Back Button?

This problem with the Back button is a longstanding issue for AJAX development, and a lot of very smart people have come up with solutions that may work very well for you, depending on the situation at hand. One good example is the code implemented in the Dojo JavaScript toolkit[7] to make the browser Back button behave in a normal way even with page updates that are made using XMLHttpRequest.

Your decision to use something like this might depend on the browsers you have to support (it doesn't work at all in Safari, for example), and your tolerance for hacks in the code you use. According to the Dojo docs, this Back button work-around contains "a lot of black magic, browser-specific foo, and general hackery" to make it work.

If you want the browser Back button to work, and don't mind code that uses an iframe and even document.write, the above code may represent a viable solution

---

[7] http://dojotoolkit.org/

for you. We'll see an implementation of a similar fix for the browser's Back button in the next chapter.

## Replacing the Back Button

Another potential solution is to code a Back button replacement right into your application. If you make your application's navigation intuitive and obvious, you may be able to avoid problems with the browser's Back button by keeping your users away from it completely.

If it's implemented properly, this can be a better alternative to the previous fix, because it allows you to avoid the kinds of hacks needed to make the browser's Back button function more-or-less properly, and lets you support all browsers equally. However, if you do decide to go this route, it's probably still a good idea to include a warning dialog when users navigate off the page, just to allow them to verify their intent.

We'll also be implementing a Back button replacement like this in the code for the next chapter, to allow you to see both approaches—using a bit of hackery to make the browser's buttons work correctly, and the cleaner approach that creates navigation buttons right in the app.

## Asking the Right Question

With the sorts of gymnastics required to code around the Back button, you can see that the problem with the Back button is a really good justification for taking the approach I mentioned in the first chapter: before you start asking the question, "How can I do this with AJAX?" you should be asking the question, "Should I be doing this with AJAX?" This approach can help you avoid at least some of the usability issues right up-front, rather than waiting until it becomes a problem that you have to deal with in a potentially ad hoc, hacked fashion.

# Debugging Client-side AJAX

Complicated client-side code can also create serious headaches for developers. Many web developers are not well trained in things like application design and architecture, and the tools for doing this kind of work are still fairly new.

So the first line of defense for you as an AJAX developer is to make sure that you use AJAX in the right places in your app—points at which it makes your application easier and better to use. As you've seen, putting more of your code on the client side creates an application that's far more responsive and dynamic than apps in which everything is done on the server.

Yet complex client-side JavaScript code is notoriously difficult to debug. And when things go wrong, you may find yourself scratching your head trying to figure out what particular piece of your whizzy, new, fat-client AJAX code is failing on you.

AJAX-style development with `XMLHttpRequest` is still fairly new, so JavaScript coders don't have access to the same wide range of debuggers, IDEs, and refactoring tools that developers using other languages have at their disposal. People moving to JavaScript from other languages are often shocked by how primitive the tools are.

Fortunately, the increasing popularity of AJAX has encouraged a sort of renaissance in JavaScript development, and the quality of available tools is improving rapidly. Here are some highlights:

**Log4JS**[8]

This is a JavaScript class that allows the customized logging of error messages for debugging JavaScript.

**Venkman**[9]

This full-featured JavaScript debugger for Mozilla-based browsers includes sophisticated features such as breakpoint management, call stack inspection, and variable/object inspection. The console also allows the execution of JavaScript code in the current window. Venkman is the oldest of these tools—it's been around since 2001.

**LiveHTTPHeaders**[10]

This tool displays HTTP headers in real time. It also allows you to edit headers and record and replay header traffic between the browser and the server.

**FireBug**[11]

A relatively new tool for Firefox (requires version 1.5), FireBug is actually several tools combined into one: the original JavaScript console from Mozilla-based browsers, a DOM inspector, a logging tool, and a command-line

---

[8] http://log4js.sourceforge.net/
[9] http://developer.mozilla.org/en/docs/Venkman/
[10] http://livehttpheaders.mozdev.org/
[11] http://www.joehewitt.com/software/firebug/

JavaScript interpreter that lets you execute JavaScript code in the current window. It also includes XMLHttpRequest Spy, a tool that logs `XMLHttpRequest` requests to the console, and allows you to inspect its response as text or XML.

Using these tools will boost your debugging ability dramatically, and you'll go from peppering your code with annoying `alert` boxes, or keeping special debug `div` sections in your UI, to completing proper logging, inspecting objects in your code, and watching the real-time flow of data between your browser and the server.

Given the complexity of all the technologies that work together in an AJAX application, it's inevitable that things will break. When that happens, the key to keeping your sanity is having the ability to see reliably what's going on at any point in the round-trip of communication between your client-side code and the server.

# Further Reading

Here are some online resources for learning more about the techniques and concepts we've discussed in this chapter.

## Cross-site Scripting (XSS)

**The Cross Site Scripting FAQ**[12]
This FAQ was written to provide a better understanding of the threat of XSS, and to give guidance on detection and prevention.

**HTML Code Injection and Cross-site scripting**[13]
This paper by Gunter Ollman discusses the cause and effect of CSS (XSS) vulnerabilities.

**XSS Cheat Sheet**[14]
The cheat sheet is ideal for people who already have grasped the basics of XSS attacks, but want a deeper understanding of the nuances of filter evasion.

---

[12] http://www.cgisecurity.com/articles/xss-faq.shtml
[13] http://www.technicalinfo.net/papers/CSS.html
[14] http://ha.ckers.org/xss.html

# Mashups

**Programmable Web**[15]
> This site offers news, information, and resources for developing applications and mashups using the Web 2.0 APIs.

**Google Maps Mania**[16]
> This unofficial Google Maps blog tracks the web sites, mashups and tools being influenced by Google Maps.

# Summary

In this chapter, we took a quick look at web services and the different ways in which we can access them, and also showed a slick slide-and-hide effect that embeds different sets of search data into a web page. We worked through the browser security issues associated with making cross-site requests to access web services data, and showed how a simple proxy script can provide a relay over which your browser-based application can talk to those web services.

---

[15] http://www.programmableweb.com/
[16] http://googlemapsmania.blogspot.com/

# 7

## More Web Services and a Back Button

*You go back Jack do it again, Wheel turnin' 'round and 'round, You go back Jack do it again*
—Steely Dan, *Do It Again*

In the previous chapter, we had a look a working with web services, and built a sample application that sent AJAX requests through a proxy page to access Amazon's E-Commerce web service. The application used simple REST-style GET requests to access the service, and inserted the results into a web page.

One of the great things about web services in general is that they provide easy and open access to the data offered by different sources, so in this next chapter, we'll work on tying our application to multiple services. We'll be building a search application that accesses the Google API, eBay's web services, and Amazon using REST, XML-RPC and SOAP. Figure 7.1 shows the search application in action.

This search application returns sets of results much like a regular search engine, so it also provides a nice opportunity to demonstrate a fix for a well-known issue with AJAX—the Back button problem.

## Figure 7.1. The search application with a set of results

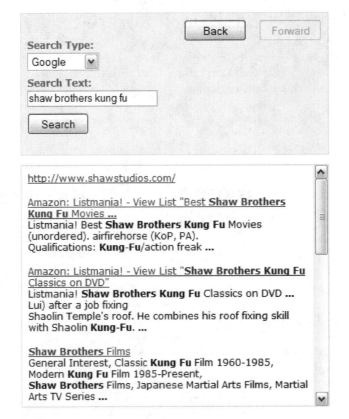

# The Search Application

This multi-source search application will let the user search a number of different online sources for a desired term or terms. It will have a select box that lets users choose the service to search, and a text input in which users can enter their search strings. The application will be able to search the following services:

❏ Amazon

❏ eBay

❏ Google

It will also be very easy to add new services to this list.

# Accessibility and Backward Compatibility

It's important to know up-front which types of users you intend your app to support, so that you can make sure it's accessible to all those users, and provide equivalent non-JavaScript functionality for your AJAX code where it's needed.

As you saw back in Chapter 4, supporting screen readers doesn't mean you can't use JavaScript. Screen readers work along with a browser, so they're dependent on the browser for their JavaScript support. If you design your code carefully, you can build your application so that users with screen readers can take advantage of your AJAX code.

On the other hand, there are clients that have limited or no JavaScript support. In some of these cases, you'll be able to use progressive enhancement in your code so that it degrades gracefully; in others, you may have to build and maintain a separate, simplified version of your app.

In this chapter, we'll be applying the principle of progressive enhancement to build the accessibility features and a fallback for non-JavaScript browsers right into the main code of our application.

# Fixing the Back Button

In our sample app, we'll demonstrate two different ways of dealing with the classic AJAX Back button problem.

One approach is to build history navigation right into your application interface. The challenge is to make the navigation so obvious that users are more inclined to use it than they are to use the browser's built-in Back button. The advantage of this approach is that it uses clean, standards-compliant code, and plays nicely with screen reader software.

The other method we'll be looking at is very similar to the solution that some JavaScript and AJAX toolkits use: actually "fixing" the browser's built-in Back button to work as users expect. This has the huge advantage of making your application behave the way users expect a browser-based app to behave, but this solution relies on ugly, inefficient, browser-specific hacks and does not work well with screen reader software.

We'll be using a constant value of BROWSER_BACK to branch the code in the few places it's necessary, so it should be very obvious where we're adding the stuff for the Back-button fix.

# Setting Up the Search Class

As we've done in previous chapters, I'm going to create Search as a JavaScript singleton class because we only need one copy of the object, and creating a singleton makes it easy for us to deal with the loss-of-scope issues we experience when using callback functions. Here's the setup for the Search object:

File: **webservices2.js (excerpt)**

```
var Search = new function() {
  this.ajax = null;
  this.form = null;
  this.service = '';
  this.searchText = '';
  this.hist = [];
  this.histIndex = -1;
  this.hand = [];
};
```

Most of the properties of the Search object will look fairly familiar to you if you've read the previous chapters.

The properties hist and histIndex come into play when we implement the search history and Back button functionality. We'll see the hand property in use in the next section, in the init method.

# The init Method

We start the application up with an init method that's tied to the window's onload event listener:

File: **webservices2.js (excerpt)**

```
window.onload = Search.init;
```

Here's the first chunk of the init method's code:

File: **webservices2.js (excerpt)**

```
this.init = function() {
  var self = Search;
```

```
var enable = false;
self.ajax = new Ajax();
self.form = document.getElementById('searchForm');
document.getElementById('resultsDiv').style.display = 'block';
self.form.onsubmit = function() { return false; };
self.hand['searchButton'] = self.submitSearch;
self.evalSearchTextState();
```

The init method starts off by doing all your normal app initialization stuff—it creates the Ajax object for submitting searches and sets up a reference to the web form.

Next, it "turns on" the results section of the UI. A CSS declaration of display: none is associated with the div that has the ID resultsDiv; as such, non-JavaScript browsers won't see the div, but browsers that do support JavaScript will. This is the div that will contain our AJAX-powered UI. As part of this application, we'll be looking at how we could build an alternate UI for non-JavaScript browsers that will POST to a different page.

Next, init sets up an event handler for the form's Submit button. We're using an input type="submit" element for this button, which allows the form to work for non-JavaScript-capable clients too. We don't want our JavaScript clients to submit the actual form because we're making our requests with AJAX; thus, we have to suppress form submission.

Then, the method places a reference to what will become the Submit button's onclick event handler into the hand property—an associative array with the button ID as key.

Then, the method places into the hand property an associative array with the button ID as its key. The method places into hand a reference to the method that will become the Submit button's onclick event handler.

This gives us a convenient way to store all the onclick handlers for the buttons so we can turn buttons on and off at will. We'll see how this works in the next section.

Next is a call to evalSearchTextState, which looks at the SearchText field, and either enables or disables the Search button based on whether or not it contains any text. Here's the code for evalSearchTextState:

File: **webservices2.js** (excerpt)

```
this.evalSearchTextState = function() {
  var self = Search;
  var enableState = 'off';
  if (self.form.SearchText.value.length > 0) {
    enableState = 'on';
  }
  self.setButtonState(self.form.searchButton, enableState);
};
```

This method prevents users from trying to submit a search without entering any search terms.

The middle chunk of the `init` method deals with the Back button code:

File: **webservices2.js** (excerpt)

```
if (BROWSER_BACK) {
  self.startHist();
}
else {
  self.addHistoryNav();
}
```

The first part of the if-else branch is for the browser Back button fix. It fires up some code that watches for changes to the browser history and the location bar—we'll be covering how this works in the section devoted to the browser Back button fix. The other branch sets up an application navigation panel that has both Back and Forward buttons. You'll see how all this works in the section that explains how to build your own Back button.

The final chunk of code turns on these features for users with screen readers:

File: **webservices2.js** (excerpt)

```
  self.enableScreenReaderFeatures();
};
```

This method is almost identical to the method with the same name that was part of our login application in Chapter 4. There are a few tweaks that need to be made to the screen reader code that's specific to this app. We'll be going over these in the section on screen reader code near the end of the chapter.

# Disabling and Enabling Buttons

We saw above that the `evalSearchTextState` method called from `init` prevents users from submitting searches with no search text. It does so by calling `setButtonState` to enable or disable the Submit button according to whether or not the `SearchText` field has a value.

Here's the code for `setButtonState`:

File: **webservices2.js (excerpt)**

```
this.setButtonState = function(buttonRef, enableState) {
  var self = Search;
  if (enableState == 'on') {
    buttonRef.disabled = false;
    buttonRef.onclick = self.hand[buttonRef.id];
  }
  else {
    buttonRef.disabled = true;
    buttonRef.onclick = null;
  }
};
```

The method takes two parameters — *buttonRef*, a reference to the button to be toggled on and off, and *enable*, a boolean that says whether we're turning the button on or off.

Enabling the button sets its `disabled` property to `false`. The code then looks at the associative array of handler methods stored in `hand`, and uses the button's ID as a key to figure out which method should be attached to that button.

Disabling the button is simple—we just set its `disabled` property to `true` so that it appears properly dimmed out, and set the button's `onclick` event handler to `null` so that clicking the button will have no effect.

# Enabling Search

Now that we've got the UI all set up, it's time to perform some searches. Initially, the Search button is disabled, because the search text box is empty. This approach, which is similar to what we did with the application login in Chapter 4, represents a proactive approach to validating input. In this way, we prevent users from making mistakes, rather than waiting until they've taken some action before we tell them "sorry, that was wrong." When the button is disabled, it's impossible for legitimate users to submit an empty search.

Once the user has typed something into the text field, we need to enable the Search button. We do this in the same way we enabled the Search button in Chapter 4—via a method attached to the `document.onkeyup` event for the page:

File: **webservices2.js (excerpt)**

```
document.onkeyup = Search.keyup;
```

That method will fire each time users hit a key, and will check to see whether or not they're typing into the search text box. Here's the code for `keyup`:

File: **webservices2.js (excerpt)**

```
this.keyup = function(e) {
  var self = Search;
  e = e || window.event;
  if (e.keyCode == 13) {
    if (!self.form.searchButton.disabled) {
      self.submitSearch();
    }
  }
  else {
    self.evalSearchTextState();
  }
};
```

Note that since all keyboard input goes through this method, we're also using it to submit the search when the user hits the **Enter** key (which has a `keyCode` of 13). If the pressed key was the **Enter** key, it will submit the search—but only if the Search button has been enabled.

# The `submitSearch` Method

Once users have typed something into the search text box, and the Search button is enabled, they can either click the Search button or hit **Enter** to perform the search. Both options call the `submitSearch` method. Here's the first chunk of the code for `submitSearch`:

File: **webservices2.js (excerpt)**

```
this.submitSearch = function() {
  var self = Search;
  var service = '';
```

```
var searchText = '';
var proxyURI = '';
var dt = new Date();
service = self.form.SearchService.value;
searchText = self.form.SearchText.value;
if (service != self.service || searchText != self.searchText) {
  self.service = service;
  self.searchText = searchText;
  self.setButtonState(self.form.searchButton, 'off');
```

This code is fairly straightforward. It pulls the form values into some local variables (`service` for the web service to use for the search, and `searchText` for the string of text to search on), then checks that this isn't the user's previous search by comparing `service` and `searchText` against properties of the same names. Provided at least one of these doesn't match, we disable the Search button and store `service` and `searchText` in these properties. This stops an impatient user from repeating the same search over and over again. The `service` and `searchText` properties will be used later as we navigate the user's search history with the Back button.

# Passing to the Proxy Script

The next chunk of the code looks like this:

File: **webservices2.js** (excerpt)

```
proxyURI = '/webservices2_proxy.php' +
    '?search=' + escape(self.searchText) +
    '&service=' + self.service +
    '&dt=' + dt.getTime;
```

As in the previous chapter, this application will use a proxy script to relay our AJAX requests to URIs on a server that's different from the one on which our AJAX app lives. Browser security prevents us from making requests directly to those other servers, so we go through a proxy script on our own server. Note that we need to `escape` the service and search terms in order to pass them along on the query string.

# Submitting the Search

Here's the last chunk of code for the `submitSearch` method:

File: **webservices2.js** (excerpt)

```
    document.getElementById('resultsDiv').innerHTML =
      '<div class="resultsPaneDiv">Processing ...</div>';
    self.ajax.doGet(proxyURI, self.handleResp, 'xml');
  }
};
```

The code clears out the `div` used to display search results, and sets its displayed text to "Processing ... ."

That's right, folks: for this application we're going to take a break from fancy animated status animations, and just use a plain text notification to let the user know that the app is busy performing the search. If you have seen the animations in our other demo applications, you may be surprised to see how effective static text can be. The really important thing, in any case, is to give your users clear cues about what the app is doing.

The other thing to notice is the method we're using to set the processing status text—the dreaded `innerHTML` property. Despite the fact that it may make some of the more dogmatic developers among us hyperventilate, in this app, there are good reasons to use `innerHTML`. I'll explain more about why we're using it a little later, in the section that talks about processing the response from the web service.

Finally, we pass the request to the proxy page using the `doGet` method of our `Ajax` object, passing `xml` as the last parameter so that we get the results back as an XML document.

You may remember from this chapter's introduction that this application is supposed to work with web services by sending XML-RPC and SOAP requests; XML-RPC and SOAP rely on `POST` requests that send XML back to the server. You might be wondering how we're going to do all that with this simple `GET` request and a couple of variables on the query string. Well, sending the `POST` request will be a job for our proxy script.

# The Proxy Script

Dealing with all the different web services that we want to use for searches is going to require more complicated server-side code than what we saw in the last chapter. After all, we're not just sending simple REST requests with `GET` any more—some of these web services use XML-RPC; others use SOAP. As such, we'll need to use different libraries of code to talk to the different web services.

The proxy script for this application is `webservices2_proxy.php`. We're developing it in PHP, but you could easily use another language, such as Ruby, Python, Perl, ASP, or Java.

To make things as clear and easy as possible to follow, I've arranged the code as a bunch of `case` statements—one for each web service. All the web services we're using in our example code return the result as an XML document; we then return this document to our client-side JavaScript code for parsing and display.

# Requirements

Just like with the simple web services example we saw in the last chapter, we're using the PHP PEAR module `HTTP_Request` to perform the HTTP requests in this app's proxy script. These code examples will not work unless you have the `HTTP_Request` package installed.

Additionally, the SOAP calls to the Google Web APIs will require that you either use the PEAR SOAP package,[1] or that your PHP installation is compiled with `--enable-soap`.

# Initial Setup

Here's how the code for the proxy script starts:

File: **webservices2_proxy.php** (excerpt)

```php
<?php
require_once "HTTP/Request.php";
var $searchText = $_REQUEST['search'];
var $service = $_REQUEST['service'];
var $uri = '';
var $key = null;
var $userToken = '';
var $xml = '';
switch ($service) {
```

After including the `HTTP_Request` package, we make some variable declarations. The first two variables are the inputs passed on the query string—`$service`, the web service we want to use to perform the search, and `$searchText`, the text for which we're searching.

---

[1] http://pear.php.net/package/SOAP/

## Validate Input from the Client

Because this is only a demonstration app, we're not doing anything special to validate the input from the browser. However, if this were a production application, you would absolutely want to take steps to make sure that the data coming from the browser was safe before you used it in your code.

The other variables will contain some fairly basic pieces of information that we need for the request, such as the URI, access keys, and `$xml`, the variable into which we're going to put the response from the server.

In the last line of this code snippet, we start a `switch` statement that will contain a `case` for each of the services that our application can access.

# Amazon Web Services

We'll start with Amazon's E-Commerce Service, the service we accessed in the last chapter. Here's the code we'll use in our new proxy script to set up a search with the Amazon E-Commerce Service:

File: **webservices2_proxy.php (excerpt)**

```
case 'amazon':
  $key = 'Access Key ID';
  $uri = 'http://webservices.amazon.com/onca/xml'.
      '?Service=AWSECommerceService' .
      '&AWSAccessKeyId=' . urlencode($key) .
      '&Operation=ItemSearch' .
      '&SearchIndex=Books' .
      '&Keywords=' . urlencode($searchText) .
      '&Sort=relevancerank';
  var $req =& new HTTP_Request($uri);
  var $result = $req->sendRequest();
  if (PEAR::isError($result)) {
    die($result->getMessage());
  }
  else {
    $xml = $req->getResponseBody();
  }
  break;
```

This looks very similar to the code we saw in the last chapter. We set the access key, then add it to the query string along with our search term. Be sure to URL-encode the term.

We then use the `HTTP_Request` module to make the request and put the result in the `$xml` variable.

# Printing the Response

The code for printing out the result lives at the very bottom of the page, outside the `switch` statement.

File: **webservices2_proxy.php (excerpt)**

```
}
header('Content-Type: text/xml');
print($xml);
?>
```

This very simple scrap of code sets the `Content-Type` header for the response to `text/xml`, and prints the result into `$xml`. Once executed, the code for each web service puts its results into `$xml`, which is then returned to our AJAX client.

# Google Web APIs

Next, we'll have a look at how to perform a search using Google's web service APIs. To access the Google Web APIs, you need an access key, as was the case with Amazon Web Services. You can sign up for an account and get your free key from the Google Web APIs site.[2]

Unlike Amazon, Google's web services limit you to 1000 requests per day. If you attempt to make more than 1000 queries in a day, Google's server will respond with a SOAP fault stating that you have exceeded the maximum number of queries allowed. The Google Web APIs FAQ suggests that in such cases "you might want to get some sleep and start querying again tomorrow."

## Using a SOAP Library

Google's web services use SOAP, which we mentioned briefly in the overview of web services in the previous chapter. The idea with SOAP is that you should be able to use a library to make simple calls to the service as if you were calling methods on an object in your own code.

---

[2] http://www.google.com/apis/

However, sometimes getting your library set up and working properly can be a bit of a challenge. PHP provides SOAP support via an extension, but to use it you have to compile PHP with the --enable-soap option. The alternative is to use the SOAP module from PHP's PEAR repository.[3] Since that module is officially still in beta at the time of writing, installation using the command-line pear command will not work—you'll need to download the package, unzip it, and place the SOAP directory in a place where the webservices2_proxy.php page can find it.

Here's the first part of our Google code:

File: **webservices2_proxy.php** (excerpt)

```
case 'google':
  var $wsdlURI = 'http://api.google.com/GoogleSearch.wsdl';
  $key = 'Licence Key';
```

This section sets up your licence key and the location of the WSDL document for Google's web service.

We talked about WSDL a little bit in last chapter's introduction to web services. A WSDL document provides a description of a SOAP web server. Our SOAP library uses it kind of like a remote configuration file to set itself up to perform calls to the Google service.

## Code for the SOAP Extension

First comes the section of code that works with the SOAP extension that you made available by compiling PHP with the --enable-soap option:

File: **webservices2_proxy.php** (excerpt)

```
if (extension_loaded('soap')) {
  $soapClient = new SoapClient($wsdlURI, array('trace' => 1));
  $result = $soapClient->doGoogleSearch($key, $searchText, 0, 10,
    false, '', false, '', 'latin', 'latin');
  if (is_soap_fault($result)) {
    trigger_error("SOAP Fault: (faultcode: {$result->faultcode},
        faultstring: {$result->faultstring})", E_ERROR);
  }
  else {
    $xml = $soapClient->__getLastResponse();
  }
}
```

---

[3] http://pear.php.net/package/SOAP/

The code sets up a SOAP client using Google's WSDL document, makes the call to doGoogleSearch, and receives the raw XML output of the request.

You'll notice the call to the doGoogleSearch method is very simple—it looks just like you're calling any other normal method in your code, even though it's actually making a call to Google's servers. This is the power of SOAP—once you actually set everything up so that SOAP can work, the function call is very simple.

The WSDL file describes the methods that the web service offers so the SOAP client can expose them as if it was just another method of the class. For example, Google's WSDL file includes the following description of the doGoogleSearch method:

```
<message name="doGoogleSearch">
  <part name="key" type="xsd:string"/>
  <part name="q" type="xsd:string"/>
  <part name="start" type="xsd:int"/>
  <part name="maxResults" type="xsd:int"/>
  <part name="filter" type="xsd:boolean"/>
  <part name="restrict" type="xsd:string"/>
  <part name="safeSearch" type="xsd:boolean"/>
  <part name="lr" type="xsd:string"/>
  <part name="ie" type="xsd:string"/>
  <part name="oe" type="xsd:string"/>
</message>
```

Here, the parameters for the doGoogleSearch method are defined, including the Google Web APIs license key, the actual search terms, and so on. What these parameters actually do is documented on the Google Web APIs site.[4] If you're interested in learning more about WSDL, the Further Reading section at the end of this chapter offers some links to get you started.

When you create the SoapClient using the SOAP PHP extension, the second parameter is an associative array of options for the SOAP client. One option that we must turn on in order to get access to the response XML is trace. When this has been set to 1, we can get access to the raw XML response using the __getLastResponse method.

## Code for the PEAR SOAP Module

Here's the code that uses the PEAR SOAP client module to access Google's web service:

---

[4] http://www.google.com/apis/

File: **webservices2_proxy.php (excerpt)**

```
else {
  require_once 'SOAP/Client.php';
  $wsdl = new SOAP_WSDL($wsdlURI);
  $soapClient = $wsdl->getProxy();
  $result = $soapClient->doGoogleSearch($key, $searchText, 0, 10,
    false, '', false, '', 'latin', 'latin');
  if (PEAR::isError($result)) {
    die($result->getMessage());
  }
  else {
    $xml = $soapClient->xml;
  }
}
break;
```

This code is pretty similar to the code for the compiled-in extension. After the `require` statement for the SOAP client module, the code sets up the SOAP client, makes the call to `doGoogleSearch`, then gets the raw XML output of the response.

Again, once everything is in place, making the call to `doGoogleSearch` is super-simple. In fact, the call is exactly the same for both the extension and the PEAR-module clients, thanks to the WSDL definition.

The PEAR module makes it a bit easier to get the XML from the response. It provides a built-in `xml` property for the client object that contains the actual XML response from the server.

Remember that once we break from this `case`, the content of `$xml` will be printed out, so we're all done with our Google proxy!

# The eBay Platform

eBay also provides a set of web services to application developers.[5] It offers a wide range of ways to access the service, including REST, SOAP, and plain XML. Since we've already seen examples of REST and SOAP, we'll use XML-RPC to access eBay's web services.

---

[5] http://developer.ebay.com/

# A Few Hurdles

Since eBay provides full access to buying and selling functions through its web services, there are a few extra security hurdles you'll need to jump in order to get eBay web services working. eBay requires us to use SSL encryption when communicating with the server, three separate keys (as opposed to Amazon and Google, which require just one), and a user token that represents the user performing the transaction. As we'll only be performing searches, we'll just set up a single user and use the same token for every query.

### SSL Encryption

Communicating with eBay requires SSL encryption, so please note that the example code we'll use to work with the eBay service will only work if your server can send HTTPS requests. To find out if your server supports SSL, ask your system administrator. PHP users can run `phpinfo` and look for OpenSSL. If OpenSSL is present, you shouldn't have a problem.

## Access Keys and User Tokens

Instead of the single key we've used with other web services, eBay requires us to use three keys, plus a user token, to access the service. You receive the three access keys when you sign up for the Developers' Program, but you'll need to go through a separate process to obtain the user token. The three keys are:

**AppID**  the unique identifier for the application

**DevID**  the developer's unique identifier

**CertID**  an authentication certificate that ensures the application really is what it says it is

To get your own keys, you'll need to sign up on eBay's Developers' Program web site.[6] Once you've signed up, instructions on how to get your keys will be emailed to you.

Once you have your keys, it's time to create a user token in the eBay Sandbox.

---

[6] http://developer.ebay.com/

## The Sandbox

Your eBay developer account gives you unlimited access to the eBay Sandbox,[7] and the opportunity to self-certify your application to gain limited free access to the eBay production environment. The eBay Sandbox is a mockup of the real eBay environment that contains realistic "dummy" data. It gives you a chance to play around with realistic data without worrying that you might wreak havoc with actual customer information. Our test code performs its searches using the Sandbox, which means we won't be displaying the same results we'd receive from a search on the actual eBay site.

To create a user in the Sandbox environment, sign in to eBay's developer program web site, then click the Sandbox User Registration link to register a dummy user. Once you've registered your dummy user, click the link to generate an authentication and authorization token. You'll need to sign in as the dummy user as part of this process, and eventually you'll be presented with a user token—a rather lengthy string of characters.

# The Code

Here's the section of code that creates the request for eBay:

File: **webservices2_proxy.php (excerpt)**

```
case 'ebay':
  require_once "eBayXMLRPC.php";
  $key['devID'] = 'Your DevID';
  $key['appID'] = 'Your AppID';
  $key['certID'] = 'Your CertID';
  $userToken = 'Your User Token';
  $xmlRPC = new eBayXMLRPC();
  $xmlRPC->createSession($key, 'GetSearchResults');
  $xml = $xmlRPC->GetSearchResults($userToken, $searchText);
  break;
```

This code uses a small helper library, eBayXMLRPC.php, which contains a class for making XML-RPC requests to eBay. The library takes care of creating the XML message for your search, and sets the eBay-specific HTTP request headers that set up your eBay session. The library is included in the code archive, so have a look at it if you're interested in what XML-RPC is doing behind the scenes.

---

[7] http://sandbox.ebay.com/

Our proxy script simply uses the library to create an instance of **eBayXMLRPC**, an XML-RPC client for the eBay Platform. Then, it creates a session and performs the search. As before, we're sticking the result into $xml so that we can print it out later.

# Testing the Proxy Script

A very simple way to test the proxy code is to enter the proxy page's address into your browser's location bar manually, along with the query string that the client-side JavaScript would add, and view the results directly in the browser window. For example, if you were to search Amazon for a certain famous kung fu movie studio, you might enter an address like this:

http://.../webservices2_proxy.php?search=shaw%20brothers&service=amazon

The browser will display the XML data response inline, without any styling. It's a fairly ugly response, but at least you can see what it is. Figure 7.2 shows how the result from that search will display in the browser.

## Figure 7.2. Displaying search results as plain XML in the browser

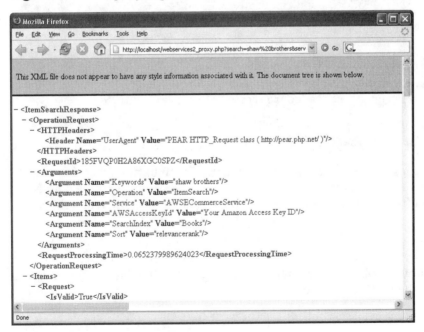

# Handling the Results

Now that we're receiving XML results from a few different web services through our proxy script, it's time to hop back over to the client side and insert those results—formatted nicely, of course—into a web page.

We made the original request to the proxy page with this call to our `ajax` object:

File: **webservices2.js (excerpt)**

```
self.ajax.doGet(proxyURI, self.handleResp, 'xml');
```

In this case, the handler function for the response is the intuitively named `handleResp`, and the `xml` flag that's passed last indicates that we're expecting the results to come back as XML.

The code for `handleResp` is broken up into a number of `case` statements inside one large `switch` statement, like the one we used in the proxy script:

File: **webservices2.js (excerpt)**

```
this.handleResp = function(xml) {
  var self = Search;
  var res = [];
  var item = '';
  var str = '';
  self.setButtonState(self.form.searchButton, 'on');
  if (!xml) {
    str += '<div class="resultsPaneDiv">' +
        '(Error or no response from the server)</div>';
  }
  else {
    switch (self.service) {
```

The first thing we need to do is to re-enable the Search button to let the user run more searches. Then, after a cursory check to make sure we received an XML result from the server, the code goes on to the `case`s for each different web service.

## Amazon

Let's start by handling responses from Amazon; the code below is very similar to that from the previous chapter:

```
case 'amazon':
  res = XMLParse.xml2ObjArray(xml, 'Item');
  str += self.noResultsCheck(res.length);
  for (var i = 0; i < res.length; i++) {
    item = '<div class="itemDiv">';
    item += '<div><a' +
        ' href="http://www.amazon.com/exec/obidos/tg/detail/-/'
        + res[i].ASIN + '">' +
      res[i].ItemAttributes.Title + '</a></div>';
    if (res[i].ItemAttributes.Author) {
      item += '<div>' + res[i].ItemAttributes.Author + '</div>';
    }
    item += '</div>';
    str += item;
  }
  break;
```

The first step in the process for the Amazon service is to get an array of JavaScript objects from the XML response returned by the server.

The XMLParse library makes this fairly easy—we just call the XMLParse.xml2ObjArray method, passing it the XML document and the name of the element in that document that we want transformed. xml2ObjArray returns an array of JavaScript Objects. In the case of Amazon, we pass xml2ObjArray Item, because each of the items is in an Item element.

If you're adding your own services later, note that this parameter is case-sensitive.

Next, we use the noResultsCheck method to make sure we have some results. This method simply sets the string to display a "no results" message if the returned array is empty:

```
this.noResultsCheck = function(len) {
  str = '';
  if (len == 0) {
    str = '<div class="resultsPaneDiv">(No results returned)' +
        '</div>';
  }
  return str;
};
```

If there are any JavaScript Objects in the res array, the code proceeds to jump through that array, creating a string of markup that we can display in the results pane. We'll be displaying the results with innerHTML in this application; you'll see the reason why in the next section.

# Google

Displaying Google's results is a bit trickier than the process for Amazon's results. Let's take a look:

File: **webservices2.js (excerpt)**

```
case 'google':
  var resultsArr = xml.getElementsByTagName('resultElements');
  xml = resultsArr[0];
  res = XMLParse.xml2ObjArray(xml, 'item');
  str += self.noResultsCheck(res.length);
  for (var i = 0; i < res.length; i++) {
    item = '<div class="itemDiv">';
    item += '<div>';
    item += '<a href="' + res[i].URL + '">';
    if (res[i].title) {
      item += res[i].title;
    }
    else {
      item += res[i].URL;
    }
    item += '</a></div>';
    if (res[i].snippet) {
      item += '<div>' + res[i].snippet + '</div>';
    }
    item += '</div>';
    str += item;
  }
  break;
```

Google makes it a bit harder on us. In the XML document that Google returns, there are actually two different sets of elements called item. Figure 7.3 shows these two different sections within the results.

We're only interested in the items inside resultElements.

# Figure 7.3. Google results with two sections of `item` elements

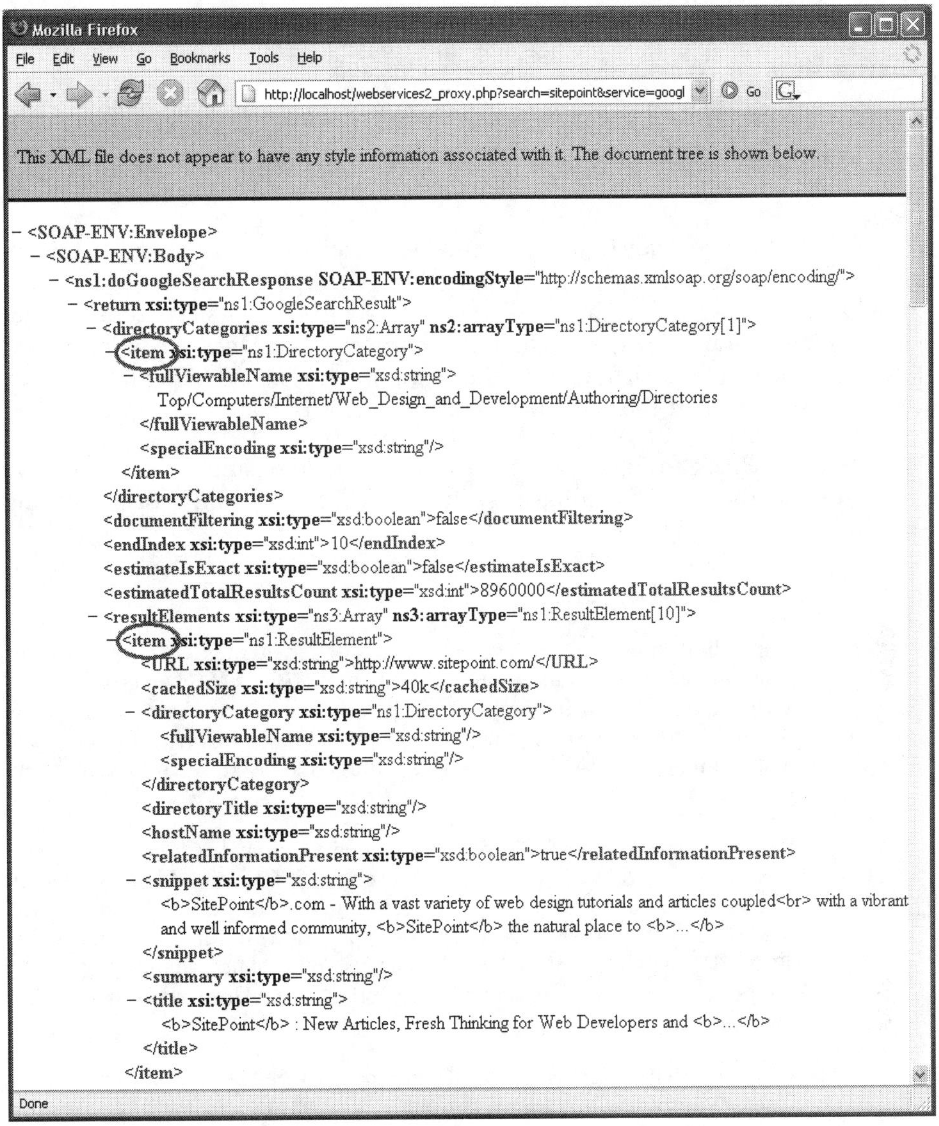

# Getting the `resultElements` XML

Here, DOM methods save the day, letting us get our hands on the list of `item` elements we want. We do so with these two lines:

File: **webservices2.js** (excerpt)
```
var resultsArr = xml.getElementsByTagName('resultElements');
xml = resultsArr[0];
```

We use the `getElementsByTagName` method to get an array of all the `resultElements` in our XML response. In this case, there's only the one, so the returned array has only a single item in it. We then set `xml` to that `resultElements` element, which contains all the `items` we're interested in. Once we've narrowed down our document to the element that contains the `item` elements we want, we can parse our result the normal way using `xml2ObjArray`.

After that, we check to make sure that there are some results in `res`, then we jump through the array, building a string of HTML that we'll display using `innerHTML`.

## Is innerHTML Evil?

Depending on which web developers you talk to, you might get very different reactions when you talk about using `innerHTML`. This property is not a W3C standard, and it's seen as being somewhat "less clean" than DOM methods; indeed, putting long strings of markup in your JavaScript code can make things very sloppy. However, `innerHTML` is fully supported in all modern browsers.

Practically speaking, despite the fact that it gives some developers conniption fits, the question of whether or not to use `innerHTML` should be decided on a case-by-case basis, and often is purely a matter of personal taste. In the case of this web service-based search application, it turns out that using `innerHTML` to display our results makes more sense than using DOM methods, as Google returns formatted HTML (that is, markup such as `<b>` tags) in its results.

If we were to insist on using DOM methods like `createTextNode` to display Google's response, we'd have to strip all of the markup out of the results, which would mean more development work, and see us lose a lot of presentation information simply because we want to avoid `innerHTML`.

A good rule thumb for deciding whether to use `innerHTML` or DOM methods is this: *if you're dealing with content that contains a lot of HTML or XHTML markup, using `innerHTML` is likely the way to go.*

# eBay

After our battle with Google, parsing the results from eBay seems a breeze. Here's the code:

File: **webservices2.js** (excerpt)

```
case 'ebay':
  res = XMLParse.xml2ObjArray(xml, 'Item');
  str += self.noResultsCheck(res.length);
  for (var i = 0; i < res.length; i++) {
    item = '<div class="itemDiv">';
    item += '<div><a href="' +
        res[i].ListingDetails.ViewItemURL + '">' +
        res[i].Title + '</a></div>';
    item += '<div>Started: ' +
        res[i].ListingDetails.StartTime + '</div>';
    item += '<div>End: ' +
        res[i].ListingDetails.EndTime + '</div>';
    item += '<div>Current Bids: ' +
        res[i].SellingStatus.BidCount + '</div>';
    item += '<div>Current Price: ' +
        res[i].SellingStatus.CurrentPrice + '</div>';
    item += '</div>';
    str += item;
  }
  break;
```

# Displaying the Results

Now that we have our search results in an HTML string, displaying the results is easy—we just set the innerHTML of the results div element to the content string str that we built for the specific service we used to search:

File: **webservices2.js** (excerpt)

```
    }
  }
  document.getElementById('resultsDiv').innerHTML = str;
};
```

# Fallback for Non-JavaScript Browsers

To provide a fallback for browsers that don't support JavaScript, we have set up our page to work as an old-fashioned web form that submits directly to a page with server-side code that's similar to our client-side AJAX code. Here's an example of how we could display results from eBay in PHP (this code assumes that we've already loaded the search result XML into a variable called $xml):

```php
header('Content-Type: text/html');
$resp = new DomDocument();
$resp->loadXML($xml);
print("<!DOCTYPE html PUBLIC \"-//W3C//DTD XHTML 1.0 Strict//EN" .
    "\" \"http://www.w3.org/TR/xhtml1/DTD/xhtml1-strict.dtd\"" .
    ">\n");
  print("<html xmlns=\"http://www.w3.org/1999/xhtml\">\n");
  print("<head>\n");
  print("<title>Search Results</title>\n");
  print("</head>\n");
  print("<body>\n");
  switch ($service) {
    case "ebay":
      $items = $resp->getElementsByTagName("Item");
      if ($items->length > 0) {
        foreach($items as $item) {
          $title = $item->getElementsByTagName("Title");
          $url = $item->getElementsByTagName("ViewItemURL");
          $startTime = $item->getElementsByTagName("StartTime");
          $endTime = $item->getElementsByTagName("EndTime");
          $bidCount = $item->getElementsByTagName("BidCount");
          $currPrice = $item->getElementsByTagName(
              "CurrentPrice");
          print("<div class=\"itemDiv\">\n");
          print("<div><a href=\"" . $url->item(0)->nodeValue .
              "\">" . $title->item(0)->nodeValue .
              "</a></div>\n");
          print("<div>Started: " .
              $startTime->item(0)->nodeValue . "</div>\n");
          print("<div>End: " . $endTime->item(0)->nodeValue .
              "</div>\n");
          print("<div>Current Bids: " .
              $bidCount->item(0)->nodeValue . "</div>\n");
          print("<div>Current Price: " .
              $currPrice->item(0)->nodeValue . "</div>\n");
          print("</div>\n");
        }
      }
      break;
    // Cases for other web services would go here
  }
}
```

Once you get the values of the properties for each item, it's fairly easy to display. The section that prints out the result here is basically a PHP clone of the JavaScript code in the AJAX version.

# Screen Reader Code

As you may remember from the login code in Chapter 4, screen readers are capable of dealing with DHTML content in the browser—you simply have to observe some basic principles that allow screen readers to take advantage of your AJAX code.

Much of the screen reader code for this application is identical to the code we saw in Chapter 4. There are just a few specific tweaks we need to make for the code to work with this search app.

File: **webservices2.js (excerpt)**

```
this.enableScreenReaderFeatures = function() {
  var self = Search;
  var appendDiv = document.getElementById('searchForm');
  var beforeDiv = document.getElementById('searchTypeTitleDiv');
  var msg = '';
  var readerDiv = null;
  var innerDiv = null;
  var resultsA = null;
  var changeCheck = null;
  msg = 'This Web page uses dynamic content. Page content may' +
      ' change without a page refresh. Check the following' +
      ' checkbox if you would like an alert dialog to inform' +
      ' you of page content changes.';
  readerDiv = document.createElement('div');
  readerDiv.className = 'screenReader';
  readerDiv.appendChild(document.createTextNode(msg));
  appendDiv.insertBefore(readerDiv, beforeDiv);
  readerDiv = document.createElement('div');
  readerDiv.className = 'screenReader';
  innerDiv = document.createElement('div');
  innerDiv.appendChild(
      document.createTextNode('Content Change Alert'));
  readerDiv.appendChild(innerDiv);
  innerDiv = document.createElement('div');
  changeCheck = document.createElement('input');
  changeCheck.type = 'checkbox';
  changeCheck.id = 'ChangeAlert';
  changeCheck.name = 'ChangeAlert';
```

```
    changeCheck.value = 'true';
    changeCheck.title = 'Content Change Alert';
    innerDiv.appendChild(changeCheck);
    readerDiv.appendChild(innerDiv);
    appendDiv.insertBefore(readerDiv, beforeDiv);
    appendDiv = document.getElementById('pageTopDiv');
    resultsA = document.createElement('a');
    resultsA.href = '#searchResults';
    resultsA.appendChild(document.createTextNode(
        'Skip to search results'));
    appendDiv.appendChild(resultsA);
    self.form.SearchText.onchange = self.evalSearchTextState;
    self.form.SearchText.title = 'Search Text. Enter text' +
        ' to activate Search button.';
};
```

The difference between this and the code that we saw in Chapter 4 is that here, we've added a link that can be used to jump straight to the top of the search results—the link points to a named anchor within the page. We'll insert this anchor into the page in handleResp, just after the switch statement, as shown in bold below:

File: **webservices2.js (excerpt)**

```
    str = '<div class="screenReader"><a id="searchResults" ' +
        'name="searchResults"></a>Search results for: ' +
        self.searchText + ' on ' + self.service + '</div>' + str;
    document.getElementById('resultsDiv').innerHTML = str;
};
```

We've also added a prompt just before the results to indicate the terms for which the user searched, since users with screen readers can't quickly scan the form to find this information. This is particularly useful for users who have performed a number of searches, and begin to page back and forth through their search history.

# Alerting Users to Page Changes

The biggest problem that screen reader users experience with AJAX is that if the whole web page doesn't refresh, users will remain unaware that the page content has changed. In this application, we're using the same strategy we used in Chapter 4 to let screen reader users know that a partial page refresh has occurred: we provide the user with a checkbox that gives them the option to receive an alert dialog box when the page content changes. This checkbox is hidden from users of regular browsers.

The main difference in this particular case is that rather than placing the changed content into the `alert` box, we let the users know the search has completed, and tell them where on the page they can find the search results. To do this, we add to the `handleResp` method some extra code that parses the results from the server and inserts the content into the page:

File: **webservices2.js (excerpt)**

```
document.getElementById('resultsDiv').innerHTML = str;
if (self.form.ChangeAlert.checked) {
  alert('Search completed. Results are on the page ' +
    'below the search form.');
}
};
```

This is fairly straightforward. The `alert` box tells our screen reader users that the search is done, and where they can go to find the updated content. Users of screen reader software will easily be able to find the search results, thanks to the Skip to search results link.

# The Back Button Problem

Users who aren't used to AJAX-style web applications may not be aware that it is possible for part of a page to update, so when they see a piece of a web page change, they may think they have navigated to a new page. They may then try to click the browser's Back button to get back to the previous state of the page. Needless to say, it confuses and frustrates users when they click on the Back button and end up in a completely unexpected place.

## The Two Options

In this section, I'm going to demonstrate two different approaches to fixing the Back button problem. One method encourages users to avoid the Back button in favor of Back and Forward buttons we'll build right into the app, while the other attempts to coerce the browser's built-in Back and Forward buttons to work as the user would expect.

Both options have their pros and cons:

### Option 1: building your own **Back** button

Pros:    ❏ works in all browsers, including Safari

❏ uses standards-compliant code

❏ works well with screen readers

**Cons:** ❏ potentially confusing to users

❏ Back button is still "broken"

### Option 2: "fixing" the **Back** button

**Pros:** ❏ browser behaves as users may expect

**Cons:** ❏ only works in Firefox and IE

❏ uses ugly browser-specific hacks and "dummy" requests to the server

❏ requires "Transitional" markup

❏ doesn't work well with screen readers

To switch between the two options in this application, you'll only need to change the value of the BACK_BUTTON constant: a value of `false` will tell the code to use the build-your-own Back button method, but if we change BACK_BUTTON to `true`, the code will "fix" the browser's Back button.

For both of these solutions, we'll store the page state in a class called SearchHistory. The only difference between the two methods is the way in which the user calls up the history entries to be displayed. First, we'll look at the shared SearchHistory code; then, we'll break down the two different methods we can plug into it.

# SearchHistory Class

The first thing we need to do is decide what information we want to keep in the history when users perform a search. Ideally, when users try to access search results from their history, you'd like to display every aspect of the UI in the state that it was in when the user performed that search. This is easy for us, since our search application is fairly simple. To present the results of a prior search, all we need are:

❏ the web service that was used for the search

❑ the search terms

❑ the formatted search results

We need somewhere to store this information, so we'll create class for it, called `SearchHistory`:

File: **webservices2.js (excerpt)**
```
function SearchHistory(service, search, results) {
  this.service = service;
  this.search = search;
  this.results = results;
};
```

The `hist` property of our `Search` class will contain an array of these `SearchHistory` objects, each one holding one of the searches that the user has performed.

# Adding to the History

At the end of the `handleResp` method, after displaying the search results, we use the following call to add a new entry for each search that's performed into the history:

File: **webservices2.js (excerpt)**
```
document.getElementById('resultsDiv').innerHTML = str;
self.updateHistory(str);
if (self.form.ChangeAlert.checked) {
```

The `updateHistory` method adds each new search to the history list, and performs a few other tasks to make the history work identically to the browser's Back button. Here's the code:

File: **webservices2.js (excerpt)**
```
this.updateHistory = function(str) {
  var self = Search;
  var maxLength = self.histIndex + 1;
  var newHist = null;
  while (self.hist.length > maxLength) {
    self.hist.pop();
  }
  newHist = new SearchHistory(self.service, self.searchText, str);
  self.hist.push(newHist);
```

```
  self.histIndex++;
  if (BROWSER_BACK) {
    self.setHash(self.histIndex);
  }
  else {
    if (self.hist.length > 1) {
      self.setButtonState(self.form.backButton, 'on');
    }
    self.setButtonState(self.form.forwardButton, 'off');
  }
};
```

After declaring and initializing a few variables, the code enters a while loop. This loop only comes into effect if users run a new search while looking at an entry somewhere in the middle of the history list. In that case, the new search should be the new end of the search history, so all entries after that position must be erased.

This is exactly how the normal browser history works—you can see it in action yourself. Open a browser window and click a few links from your bookmarks list to give yourself a history. Then, click the browser's Back button a few times to surf back through the history by a few entries. You should see that both the Back and Forward buttons are active. Now, click another link in your bookmarks list, and you'll see that the Forward button becomes disabled. The history list we stored in the hist array should work in exactly the same way.

Next, we actually update the history list. We create a SearchHistory object, passing in to the SearchHistory constructor the service and searchText properties of the Search object, along with the HTML used to display the search results.

Next, updateHistory adds that SearchHistory object to the hist array, which holds the search history list, and increments histIndex to show that the new entry has been added.

The final part of updateHistory is specific to the two different Back button implementations. If BROWSER_BACK is true, we call setHash to "fix" the browser's Back button. We'll go over setHash in detail in a moment

The build-your-own buttons code is a bit simpler—it simply toggles the Back and Forward buttons on and off appropriately, making them behave in the same way that the browser's buttons would when you hit a new location in your browser.

# Navigating the History

Navigating back and forth through the history is pretty easy—it works just like the normal history functionality in your browser. Whether you're using the build-your-own option or "fixing" the browser's Back button, once there are at least two searches in the history, the Back button becomes active.

Regardless of the method we choose to use, clicking the Back button calls the goBack method:

File: **webservices2.js (excerpt)**

```
this.goBack = function() {
  var self = Search;
  self.histIndex--;
  self.showHistory();
  if (!BROWSER_BACK) {
    self.setButtonState(self.form.forwardButton, 'on');
    if (self.histIndex == 0) {
      self.setButtonState(self.form.backButton, 'off');
    }
  }
};
```

The Forward button calls the goForward method:

File: **webservices2.js (excerpt)**

```
this.goForward = function() {
  var self = Search;
  self.histIndex++;
  self.showHistory();
  if (!BROWSER_BACK) {
    self.setButtonState(self.form.backButton, 'on');
    if (self.histIndex == (self.hist.length - 1)) {
      self.setButtonState(self.form.forwardButton, 'off');
    }
  }
};
```

If you've decided to build your own Back and Forward button, the goBack and goForward methods are called directly as a result of the onclick events. The event handlers are attached to the buttons when we enable them. Using the browser's built-in buttons requires us to use something of a roundabout approach to call goBack and goForward, but the end result is the same—Back calls goBack, and Forward calls goForward.

The two methods work pretty similarly, either incrementing or decrementing `histIndex`, which tells us the position of the search we're viewing within the history list, and calling `showHistory` to show that stored search.

With the build-your-own option, these methods perform an additional task: they always toggle the opposite button on (going forward should always toggle the Back button on, and going back should toggle the Forward button on), and disable the Back or Forward buttons if we're at the end of the list. Clicking back and forth through the history after you perform a couple of searches should give you a feel for how this works.

# Displaying the History Entry

Showing the saved search from the history is simplicity itself. You just pull the web service, search terms, and formatted results text out of the `SearchHistory` object that corresponds to the desired position in the `hist` array, and use that data to update the search box and results areas in the UI:

File: **webservices2.js (excerpt)**

```
this.showHistory = function() {
  var self = Search;
  var currHist = null;
  var serviceElem = self.form.SearchService;
  displayHist = self.hist[self.histIndex];
  self.form.SearchText.value = displayHist.search;
  for (var i = 0; i < serviceElem.options.length; i++) {
    if (serviceElem.options[i].value == displayHist.service) {
      serviceElem.selectedIndex = i;
      break;
    }
  }
  document.getElementById('resultsDiv').innerHTML =
      displayHist.results;
};
```

Navigating back and forth through the history sets the value of the `histIndex` property, which tells us which instance of the `SearchHistory` class we should be displaying. The `hist` property is our array of `SearchHistory` objects, so we just look up the desired entry using `self.hist[self.histIndex]`.

Once we know which entry we want to display, we update the search box form elements to display the web service and the search terms for that search, and update the results area with our stored, formatted results. This is another case in which using innerHTML simplifies things for us—we use just one line of code to show those stored results.

Now it's time to take a look at the two different ways of hooking into the SearchHistory to go back and forth through the search history.

# Building your own Back Button

The most straightforward way to solve the Back button problem is to add your own navigation right into the application—to put your own Back and Forward buttons onto the page, and have the goBack and goForward methods handle the buttons' onclick events. The only thing that's remotely tricky about the code for this option is the task of disabling and re-enabling the buttons at the appropriate times, and you've actually already seen all of that code in the explanation of the SearchHistory class above.

This solution uses clean, standards-compliant code that will work in all modern browsers (including Safari), and plays nicely with assistive technology like screen readers.

Of course, the downside is that the browser's built-in buttons still don't work as users expect, and the extra navigation may initially confuse users. We need to provide a safety net for those users who reflexively move their cursor up and click on the browser's own Back button.

## Adding the Buttons

We don't want these navigation buttons to display in browsers that can't handle JavaScript, so we'll insert them into the page in the init method by calling addHistoryNav. This approach gives the AJAX functionality to the people who can use it, and allows us to serve a plain old web form to everyone else. Here's the code:

File: **webservices2.js (excerpt)**

```
this.addHistoryNav = function() {
  var self = Search;
  var searchForm = document.getElementById('searchForm');
  var historyNavDiv = document.createElement('div');
  var btn = null;
  historyNavDiv.id = 'historyNavDiv';
  btn = document.createElement('input');
  btn.type = 'button';
```

```
  btn.id = 'backButton';
  btn.name = 'backButton';
  btn.value = 'Back';
  btn.title = 'Back button for search history';
  btn.className = 'inputButtonDisabled';
  historyNavDiv.appendChild(btn);
  historyNavDiv.appendChild(
    document.createTextNode('\u00A0'));
  historyNavDiv.appendChild(
    document.createTextNode('\u00A0'));
  btn = document.createElement('input');
  btn.type = 'button';
  btn.id = 'forwardButton';
  btn.name = 'forwardButton';
  btn.value = 'Forward';
  btn.title = 'Forward button for search history';
  btn.className = 'inputButtonDisabled';
  historyNavDiv.appendChild(btn);
  searchForm.appendChild(historyNavDiv);
  self.hand['forwardButton'] = self.goForward;
  self.hand['backButton'] = self.goBack;
  self.setButtonState(self.form.forwardButton, 'off');
  self.setButtonState(self.form.backButton, 'off');
};
```

Most of the code in this method comprises calls to DOM methods that add the buttons to the form. In the final few lines, addHistoryNav stores the onclick handlers for those buttons in the hand array, then disables both buttons.

Obviously, users can't use the Back and Forward buttons to go back and forth through their history if they haven't performed any searches, so we disable these buttons by default. We'll enable the buttons when users can actually use them.

# Using the Browser's Back Button

Our other option is a fix that allows the browser's built-in Back button to behave as users may expect. This is the fix that you may have seen in JavaScript toolkits such as Dojo and Really Simple History.[8]

This solution has the huge advantage of making the browser behave the way users expect. However, as you'll see, it comes at a pretty significant price in terms of

---

[8] http://codinginparadise.org/projects/dhtml_history/

the solution's "hackishness." The end result will not work well with assistive technology like screen readers, and won't work in Safari at all.

In short, the fix works like this:

❑ Store the history position in the page's address after the hash that's usually reserved for internal page navigation (e.g., `mypage.html#section1`).

❑ Run a process on a timer that synchronizes the page state with what it sees in the page address.

### The Hash

The part of a web address that appears after the pound or hash sign is known by many names. Here, we'll refer to it as the hash.

# Using the Location Hash

This solution works because the browser history tracks all changes to the page address, including changes to the hash. So if you set it up right, as you run your searches, the page URI displayed in the location bar will change like so:

webservices2.html
webservices2.html#0
webservices2.html#1
webservices2.html#2
webservices2.html#3

This allows users to click back and forth in the normal browser history and pull up the appropriate search history entry.

### Breaking Accessibility

Because this fix co-opts the internal navigation hash to store the search-history position, internal links such as skip navigation links will break this technique.

# Setting Up the Fix

Way back when we added the `init` method to our `Search` class, we set it up to call `startHist` when `BROWSER_BACK` was set to `true`. This `startHist` method sets up some of the IE-specific stuff for us, and activates the process we'll be using to synchronize the history state to the one that's indicated in the browser's location bar. Here's the code:

File: **webservices2.js (excerpt)**

```
this.startHist = function() {
  var self = Search;
  var href = '';
  var ifr = null;
  if (document.all) {
    ifr = document.createElement('iframe');
    ifr.name = 'historyFrame';
    ifr.id = 'historyFrame';
    ifr.src = '';
    ifr.style.display = 'none';
    document.body.appendChild(ifr);
  }
  if (location.hash) {
    href = location.href.split('#')[0];
    location = href;
  }
  setInterval(self.watchHist, 100);
};
```

The first big chunk of code uses DOM methods to create the `iframe` that allows this hack to work in IE. Note that this means that our page must be declared as XHTML 1.0 (or HTML 4.01) Transitional, since `iframe` is not supported in Strict.

*Tip*

### Supporting Older Versions of IE

If you want this solution to support versions of Internet Explorer that are older than version 6, you'll either have to include your `iframe` in the initial markup for the page, or use `document.write` to insert it. This would mean sticking with HTML 4.01, since XHTML throws out support for `document.write`.

I'll explain more about why this `iframe` is necessary in the next section.

Next, `startHist` removes any hash that appears in the page's address, then uses `setInterval` to start up the process that synchronizes the page state with what's reported in the page address.

# Setting the Hash

Next, we need some code that will set the hash in the page address for each new search entry. Adding the hash to the page address creates the history trail through which users can page back and forth using the browser's built-in Back and Forward buttons.

In `updateHistory`, there's a call to a method named `setHash`, which we use to append the search history index to the hash in the location. The code for `setHash` looks like this:

File: **webservices2.js** (excerpt)

```
this.setHash = function(val) {
  if (val == 0) {
    location.replace('#' + val);
  }
  else {
    location = '#' + val;
  }
  if (document.all) {
    document.getElementById('historyFrame').src = 'blank.txt?'
        + val;
  }
};
```

In the top part of this code, you can see that it adds the new hash onto the current location. It's just as if the user were clicking an internal navigation link on a web page, except that, in this case, instead of setting the location to something like `#searchResults`, we're just setting it to a number, such as #2 or #37, to indicate the search history entry we're looking at.

## The `iframe` Hack for IE

Unfortunately, IE doesn't make history entries for locations that reflect the page's internal navigation, so although you can change the page's address by adding a hash, IE won't keep track of these changes in its history. To get this solution to work in IE, we need to resort to a hack.

This is where things get a little ugly. It turns out that you can trick IE into making history entries by creating an invisible `iframe` andhaving it make requests to a dummy placeholder page. You stick the history index value onto the query string of the requested page (in this case, a blank text file) and use this, when you're paging through the history, to know which entry to display.

As you perform searches, the following addresses will be loaded into the `iframe`:

blank.txt?0
blank.txt?1
blank.txt?2
blank.txt?3

So, for IE, you're making the actual AJAX request to the server to get the data, and, at the same time, you're making a bogus request to a blank document on the server in order to have the browser store a history entry for that search.

# Watching the Hash

At the very beginning of this solution, we started up a process with `setInterval` that calls the `watchHist` method in a tight loop; this method watches for changes in the location hash as the user clicks Back or Forward, and displays whatever search history entry the user has selected.

The first half of the method contains all of the IE-specific code that pulls the history index out of the location in the `iframe`:

File: **webservices2.js (excerpt)**

```
this.watchHist = function() {
  var self = Search;
  var href = '';
  var index = 0;
  var hash = '';
  if (document.all) {
    href = frames['historyFrame'].document.location.href;
    hash = href.split('?')[1];
    if (hash) {
      hash = '#' + hash;
    }
    else {
      hash = '';
    }
    if (hash && location.hash && (hash != location.hash)) {
      location.replace(hash);
    }
  }
}
```

The `location` of the `iframe` will change as users click back and forth through the history. The code looks at the current location of the `iframe`, pulls the number from the query string, and then compares it to the value on the hash in the location bar. If there's been any change—that is, if the user has clicked Back or Forward since the last cycle through this method—the code synchronizes the hash in the location bar with the query string value using location.replace.

Now that we have the correct history position loaded in the hash in the location bar, the code is the same for both browsers from this point forward:

File: **webservices2.js** (excerpt)

```
if (location.hash) {
   index = parseInt(location.hash.substr(1));
}
else {
   index = -1;
}
if (index != self.histIndex) {
   self.goHistoryEntry(index);
}
};
```

This code pulls the search history index off the hash, and compares it with the value that's set in the histIndex property of the Search object. Any time there's a change—when the user clicks forward or backward through the history—it calls the goHistoryEntry method to go to that specific entry.

# Displaying the Entry

The goHistoryEntry code looks like this:

File: **webservices2.js** (excerpt)

```
this.goHistoryEntry = function(val) {
  var self = Search;
  self.histIndex = val;
  self.showHistory();
};
```

This code is pretty simple—it just sets the histIndex property to the value that was passed in, then calls the showHistory method. At this point, we're finally hooked into the normal code for displaying search-history entries. The rest of the history navigation process works exactly the same way

# Decisions, Decisions

It *is* pretty cool to click the built-in Back and Forward buttons in your browser, and see your AJAX application change state to match, just as a normal series of web pages would. However, the weird coding acrobatics needed to produce this happy state of affairs definitely hark back to the bad old days before we had widespread support for web standards or AJAX; of course, the solution also isn't cross-browser compatible and breaks screen reader support.

Your decision about whether to work around the AJAX Back button problem by implementing your own set of buttons, or to do the coding gymnastics needed to make those built-in buttons behave properly, will depend on things like how easily your users take on and learn new things, which browsers you need to support, the emphasis you place on accessibility, and your tolerance for having browser-specific hacks in your code.

# Search App Enhancements

This search application is a nice start, but we could implement a few enhancements that would make it much nicer to use.

## Paging

Currently, the application returns only the first page of results at the default page size set by the selected web service.

Most of the web services allow you to specify within your query how many records you want per page, and how many pages you want to have in the results set. This allows you to create the same kind of pagination you'd see on Google, Amazon, eBay, and any number of other sites that allow searching.

## History Menu

It would be fairly easy to extend the history code to include a history menu that would give the user easier access to previous searches. For instance, you could maintain a list of previous searches in a drop-down list or a `div`.

# Further Reading

Here are some online resources for learning more about the techniques and concepts we've discussed in this chapter.

## Apache2 and OpenSSL on Linux

http://www.devside.net/web/server/linux
This is a step-by-step instruction guide to building a web server.

http://www.debian-administration.org/articles/357
These documents explain setting up a LAMP server on Debian Sarge with Apache2, PHP5, MySQL5, phpMyAdmin, Smarty, and ADODB. The information covers installation and just enough sample code to let you test everything.

http://www.tc.umn.edu/~brams006/selfsign.html
This is a step-by-step guide to creating a self-signed server certificate with OpenSSL on Linux.

http://czarism.com/debian-ubuntu-apache2-and-openssl-https
This document explains the steps involved in enabling OpenSSL encryption using the available Apache2 package in the apt-get repositories (for Debian and Ubuntu Linux).

## Apache2 and OpenSSL on Windows

http://www.devside.net/web/server/windows
This provides step-by-step instructions for building a web server.

http://raibledesigns.com/wiki/Wiki.jsp?page=ApacheSSL
This document describes the installation of the Win32 version of Apache with the `mod_ssl` extension.

## WSDL

http://www.w3schools.com/wsdl/default.asp
This is the WSDL tutorial at the W3 Schools.

**http://www.ibm.com/developerworks/library/ws-soap/index.html**

This tutorial explains the ins and outs of using WSDL in SOAP applications—it's a solid introduction to WSDL for SOAP programmers.

**http://www.w3.org/TR/wsdl**

This is a note published by the World Wide Web Consortium (for discussion purposes only). This draft represents the current thinking within Ariba, IBM, and Microsoft.

# Summary

In this chapter, we built an accessible "Web 2.0"-style application that searches multiple web services and displays the results in a single search interface. This app provides a good example of how AJAX makes things more convenient for the end user by reducing the need for page refreshes, but it also fails to meet user expectations about the way their browsers' navigation should work. This issue, known as the Back button problem, can be fixed either by implementing your own history navigation within the application, or—if you're willing to tolerate some hackishness in your code, and don't want the app to be accessible to screen readers—you can hack the browser's Back button to work as users think it should.

# 8

## Drag and Drop with AJAX Chess

*I'm following your orders, Captain. Queen to queen's level three.*
—Scott, *Star Trek*, The Original Series Episode 71: *Whom Gods Destroy*

One of the biggest benefits that AJAX has brought to browser-based programming is that it gives us the ability to achieve within the user interface tasks that previously could only be done in a traditional installed desktop application. This is where a lot of the hype around AJAX comes from: the idea that a web-based application can mimic—and sometimes even replace—an application that you would previously have had to install on your computer.

One of the user interface features that's very popular in both desktop and AJAX apps is drag-and-drop—the ability to click on UI elements and drag them around the screen. Drag-and-drop has been possible for some time in browsers that support plain DHTML. However, marrying that functionality with the asynchronous connections that AJAX makes possible gives developers some very powerful possibilities in terms of the new features we can build into web applications.

## AJAX Chess

Games development has always been a forum that encouraged the creation of new functionality and features within the computer world. And though we won't see browser-based versions of Unreal Tournament any time soon, a game is still a very appropriate way to demonstrate what's possible when you combine drag-and-drop with AJAX.

In this chapter, we're going to develop a multi-player-capable AJAX chess game. Figure 8.1 shows what the finished product will look like.

## Figure 8.1. AJAX Chess in action

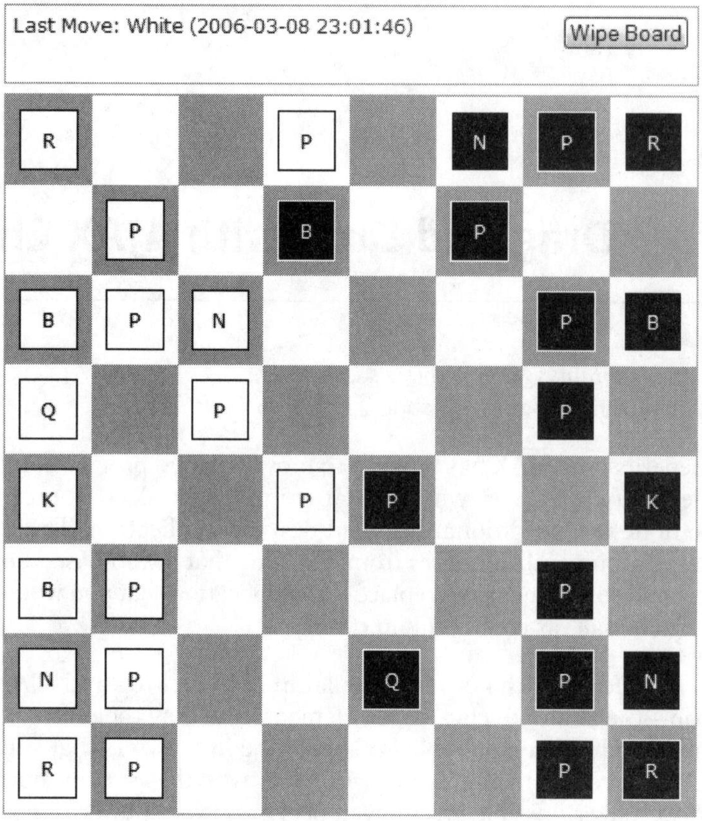

## Problems to Solve

The chess game will be the most sophisticated application in this book, and provides the chance to apply a lot of the techniques you've learned in previous chapters. It will also demonstrate real solutions to some of the thorniest problems that face AJAX application developers as their apps become more and more complicated. Here's a brief list of the functionality we'll be building into this application:

☐ placing interface elements relative to browser window size while using absolute positioning

☐ allowing users to interact with lots of elements on the page without cluttering up your code with loads of event handlers

☐ implementing drag-and-drop capabilities within the boundaries of the chess board (i.e., users won't be able to drag pieces off the board)

☐ aborting drag-and-drop functionality on error (i.e., putting the pieces back when something goes awry)

☐ using AJAX polling to synchronize the game state between multiple machines that are running the application

The interface elements for the game are fairly minimal—the board and all of the pieces in the chess game are absolutely positioned div elements; a bit of CSS sets the colors of board squares and pieces. Each piece is associated with a single letter that indicates its type: R for rook, P for pawn, and so on.

### Chess Convention

Note that the knight piece uses an N, because the letter K is already taken by the king.

# The Chess Class

We'll start off as we have in every other chapter, by setting up a main, singleton class around which we'll organize our code. Here's the code that sets up the class, with some initial properties and a constant:

File: **chess.js (excerpt)**

```
var REFRESH_INTERVAL = 5;

var Chess = new function() {
  this.ajax = null;
  this.boardDiv = null;
  this.leftPos = 0;
  this.topPos = 0;
  this.squareSize = 56;
```

```
  this.boardSize = this.squareSize * 8;
  this.pieceOffset = 10;
  this.pieceSize = this.squareSize - (this.pieceOffset * 2);
  this.panelHeight = 56;
  this.pieceList = null;
  this.selectPiece = null;
  this.dragPiece = null;
  this.lastMove = null;
  this.pollInterval = null;
  this.xPos = 0;
  this.yPos = 0;
};
```

This is a long list of properties, but most of them have to do with the maths of positioning the chess pieces during the execution of drag-and-drop functionality. There's quite a bit of math involved in calculating the sizes and positions of our game elements, so put on your thinking cap and be prepared to do some math in this chapter. The good news for you is that even though I'm terrible at math, I can do what's needed here. And if I can, anyone can!

# Starting the Application

We start the application with an `init` method tied to the `window.onload` event. This guarantees that the page is loaded before we start trying to use the elements in the page to build the user interface.

File: **chess.js (excerpt)**

```
window.onload = Chess.init;
```

Once again, the `init` method kicks everything off, positioning the game board and other UI elements, loading the game state, and placing all the pieces where they need to be located on the board. Here's the code:

File: **chess.js (excerpt)**

```
this.init = function() {
  var self = Chess;
  self.ajax = new Ajax();
  self.boardDiv = document.getElementById('boardDiv');
  self.placeBoard();
  self.placePanel();
  self.loadGame();
  self.doPollDelay();
};
```

The last thing this method does is start up the polling process, which hits the server every five seconds to update the game state. This allows multiple people to play or watch the game, and ensures that the display in each browser will be up to date within a few seconds.

# Setting Up the Board

Here's the first half of the code for `placeBoard`. `placeBoard` is the method that sets up the board on which the game will be played:

File: **chess.js (excerpt)**

```
this.placeBoard = function() {
  var self = Chess;
  var w = self.getWinWidth();
  var h = self.getWinHeight();
  var sq = null;
  var sqL = 0;
  var sqT = 0;
  var minDiff = 0;
  self.boardDiv.style.width = self.boardSize + 'px';
  self.boardDiv.style.height = self.boardSize + 'px';
  self.leftPos = (parseInt((w - self.boardSize) / 2));
  self.topPos = (parseInt((h - self.boardSize) / 2));
  minDiff = (self.topPos - this.panelHeight);
  if (minDiff < 0) {
    self.topPos = self.topPos - minDiff;
  }
  self.boardDiv.style.left = self.leftPos + 'px';
  self.boardDiv.style.top = self.topPos + 'px';
```

The `getWinWidth` and `getWinHeight` methods return the width and height of the browser's viewport. They include some cross-browser code that we need in order to get IE to give us the measurements we need.

File: **chess.js (excerpt)**

```
this.getWinHeight = function() {
  if (document.all) {
    return document.body.clientHeight;
  }
  else {
    return window.innerHeight;
  }
};
this.getWinWidth = function() {
```

```
if (document.all) {
    return document.body.clientWidth;
  }
  else {
    return window.innerWidth;
  }
};
```

We use these measurements along with the size of the board to position the game in the middle of the browser viewport. The main snippet of math used to determine the position of the board is this:

File: **chess.js (excerpt)**

```
self.leftPos = (parseInt((w - self.boardSize) / 2));
self.topPos = (parseInt((h - self.boardSize) / 2));
```

For those who want to keep track of the math, the top of the box should be positioned at the height of the browser viewport, minus the board's height, then divided by two. The left of the box should be positioned similarly, using the width of the viewport and the board's width (remember that the board is square, so its width and height are the same). There's also a check to ensure that there's enough space at the top of the viewport to allow the control panel to display. If there's not enough room, we move the board down just enough to make room.

The less mathematically inclined reader can just plug in the variables and know that they work.

Once we have the basic board in place, it's time to lay down the black and white squares:

File: **chess.js (excerpt)**

```
sqT = 0;
for (var i = 0; i < 8; i++) {
  sqL = 0;
  for (var j = 0; j < 8; j++) {
    sq = document.createElement('div');
    sq.id = 'square' + i + '_' + j;
    if ((j + 1) % 2 > 0) {
      sq.className = 'boardSquareWhite';
    }
    else {
      sq.className = 'boardSquareBlack';
    }
    sq.style.width = self.squareSize + 'px';
    sq.style.height = self.squareSize + 'px';
```

```
      sq.style.top = sqT + 'px';
      sq.style.left = sqL + 'px';
      self.boardDiv.appendChild(sq);
      sqL += self.squareSize;
    }
    sqT += self.squareSize;
  }
};
```

This code adds the squares to our board in two loops—an outer loop to create each row, and an inner loop to lay down the squares in that row. We create a div for each square, set its size to squareSize, then put it into place. We use sqT to keep track of the current square's position from the top of the board and sqL to keep track of its position from the left. Once we've added the square to the board, we increment sqL by squareSize, and return to the start of the loop to add the next square in the row. This way, all the squares in the row sit right next to each other. The same thing happens in the outer loop: we increment sqT by squareSize and set sqL to 0 to start the next row.

As it turns out, it's really easy to get the square colors to alternate. We simply add the inner and outer incrementers (i and j) within the inner loop to get alternating odd and even numbers. Checking the remainder of this number divided by two (i + j % 2 in the code above) is an easy way to see if a number is odd or even.

# The Status Panel

The user interface also includes a panel at its top, above the game board, as Figure 8.2 illustrates. We'll use this panel to display status information about the game and to show errors. A Wipe Board button is also displayed, to allow users to start over with a fresh game board that has all the pieces in their original positions. This panel is created and styled in the placePanel method.

## Figure 8.2. The status panel displaying an error message.

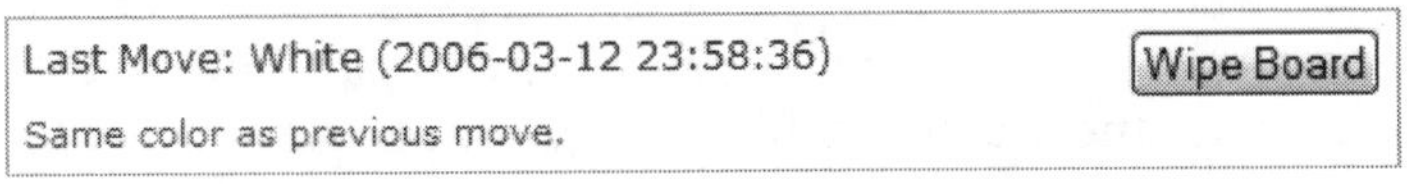

Last Move: White (2006-03-12 23:58:36)    [Wipe Board]
Same color as previous move.

File: **chess.js (excerpt)**

```
this.placePanel = function() {
  var self = Chess;
  var panelDiv = document.getElementById('panelDiv');
```

```
    panelDiv.style.width = this.boardSize + 'px';
    panelDiv.style.left = self.leftPos + 'px';
    panelDiv.style.top = (self.topPos - this.panelHeight) + 'px';
};
```

# Loading a Game

It's time to start talking to the server. We have the game board set up. Now, let's load a game and start playing. We load up a game using the `loadGame` method:

File: **chess.js (excerpt)**

```
this.loadGame = function() {
  var self = Chess;
  var str = '';
  var cmd = new Command('load');
  str = JSON.stringify(cmd);
  self.execCmd(str, self.handleLoadGame);
};
```

This method is pretty short, and really just sends a single command—`load`—to the server. It sends the command using the `execCmd` method, which is really just a wrapper around the `doPost` method of the `Ajax` object that we're using to talk to the server:

File: **chess.js (excerpt)**

```
this.execCmd = function(str, handlerFunc) {
  var self = Chess;
  self.ajax.doPost('chess.php', str, handlerFunc);
};
```

Since all our commands talk to the same processing page on the server in the same way, it makes sense to put this code in one place.

The command that's sent to the server is an instance of the very basic `Command` class, formatted using JavaScript Object Notation, or JSON, which we'll look at in just a moment. The `Command` class has two properties: `cmdName`, which identifies what we want the server to do, and `cmdData`, which we use to pass any data the server may need. Here's what the class looks like:

File: **chess.js (excerpt)**

```
function Command(cmdName, cmdData) {
  this.cmdName = cmdName || '';
```

```
  this.cmdData = cmdData || '';
};
```

The purpose of this class is to make it easy to send the data to the server as a JSON string.

# Using JSON

We're going to be passing these Command objects back and forth between the browser and the server using an extremely convenient format for data exchange called JSON.

JSON stands for JavaScript Object Notation, and it's basically a really easy and convenient way to translate a JavaScript object into a string. This makes JSON perfect for passing data back and forth between the browser and the server in an AJAX web application.

JSON has become increasingly popular because it's much more light-weight, and easier to work with in JavaScript, than XML. Note that JSON does not handle complex data types like dates, but this isn't a huge drawback for the kind of data interchange we're completing here.

## Encoding an Object with JSON

To use JSON in your browser-side JavaScript code, you need the json.js file, which you can download from the JSON web site.[1] Using JSON in JavaScript is as simple as taking an object and converting it into a string using the JSON stringify method, like so:

```
var cmd = new Command('load');
var str = JSON.stringify(cmd);
```

Voila! Now str contains cmd as a string, and you can pass it around very easily—you can even pass it back to your web server to use it there.

To decode a JSON string into an object, you can take one of two approaches. If you trust the source of the data, you can simply run eval on the string, which is very fast (eval executes JavaScript code stored in a string). This works because JSON-encoded data is actually valid JavaScript that will work just fine in all modern browsers.

---

[1] http://www.json.org/

On the other hand, if it's possible that a third party could be inserting malicious code into your data, you can use the JSON parse method, which is slower, but much, much safer than eval.

This is how we could make our JSON string into an object:

```
var cmd = eval(str);
```

We could also use this:

```
var cmd = JSON.parse(str);
```

# Decoding JSON Strings

Because JSON is so simple and so useful, you can find libraries in a huge variety of languages that will encode and decode JSON strings, which means it's easy to turn your JSON-encoded string back into an object for use with your back-end language of choice. The JSON web site[2] offers links to a large number of such libraries.

For our chess game's PHP back end, we're using Services_JSON, which, as I write this, is a proposed addition to PHP's PEAR repository. It's not a full PEAR release yet, but it's perfectly usable and is currently available for download from the proposal's page on the PEAR web site.[3]

Services_JSON is a single file, JSON.php, which you have to include in your PHP script to encode and decode JSON strings. Using it is as simple as this:

```
$cmd = $json->decode($str);
```

$cmd will be a PHP object that looks just as cmd did in JavaScript. We can translate that object back into a JSON string like this:

```
$str = $json->encode($cmd);
```

Again, you have a nice, portable string that you can pass back to the browser.

 **Tip**

## Understanding JSON Strings

In this book, we've used the following method of creating objects:

---

[2] http://www.json.org/
[3] http://pear.php.net/pepr/pepr-proposal-show.php?id=198

```
function Command() {
  this.cmdName = '';
  this.cmdData = '';
}
```

There is another way JavaScript objects can be represented: in **object literal notation**:

```
var Command = {
  'cmdName': '',
  'cmdData': ''
};
```

This is fairly easy to understand at a glance: it just declares a bunch of properties, followed by their values. JSON takes this representation of an object and makes it into one long string:

```
str = '{"cmdName":"","cmdData":""}';
```

# Displaying Game State

Once we've passed that JSON-encoded command to the back end in order to load the game, our PHP back end will send us another JSON string of the previously saved game state.

## The `handleLoadGame` Method

This string comes back to `handleLoadGame`, which we defined as the handler for the `Ajax doPost` call we used to talk to the server. Here's the code:

File: **chess.js (excerpt)**

```
this.handleLoadGame = function(str) {
  var self = Chess;
  var resp = JSON.parse(str);
  if (resp.respStatus == 'ok') {
    self.displayGame(resp.respData);
  }
  else {
    alert(resp.respDatastr);
  }
};
```

Here, you can see how truly easy it is to use JSON-encoded data. We simply call `JSON.parse` on the string that's passed in, and it magically gives us a nice JavaScript object with which to work. The response from the server is a JSON-encoded `Response` object. In PHP, the `Response` class's definition looks like this:

File: **chess.php (excerpt)**

```
class Response {
  function Response($respStatus = "", $respData = "") {
    $this->respStatus = $respStatus;
    $this->respData = $respData;
  }
}
```

When it's decoded by `JSON.parse` in your JavaScript code, it will be as if this class was declared in JavaScript—it will have `respStatus` and `respData` properties, just like it does on the server side. This `Response` class looks a lot like the `Command` class: it contains a property that communicates the status of the game, and a property for any data the server is sending back with the response.

After we send the PHP back end a `load` command, the server will return a `Response` object with `respStatus` set to `ok`, and `respData` set to an instance of a class called `GameState`, which looks like this:

File: **chess.php (excerpt)**

```
class GameState {
  function GameState($lastMove = null, $pieceList = null) {
    $this->lastMove = $lastMove;
    $this->pieceList = $pieceList;
  }
}
```

This object has the two important pieces of information that we'll need in order to build the game board:

❏ the most recent move

❏ the current positions of all the pieces on the board

With JSON, it's easy to encode and send this data back to the browser, and it's even easier to use the information once it gets there.

254

# The `displayGame` Method

In `handleLoadGame`, we receive an instance of `GameState` in the `respData` property of the response, and pass it along to the `displayGame` method like this:

File: **chess.js (excerpt)**

```
self.displayGame(resp.respData);
```

Here's the first chunk of the `displayGame` method:

File: **chess.js (excerpt)**

```
this.displayGame = function(gameState) {
  var self = Chess;
  var piece = null;
  var label = '';
  var pieceDiv = null;
  var colX = 0;
  var colY = 0;
  self.lastMove = gameState.lastMove;
  self.pieceList = gameState.pieceList;
  if (self.lastMove.moveTime) {
    self.setStatusMsg(self.lastMove.movePiece.color,
      self.lastMove.moveTime);
  }
  else {
    self.setStatusMsg('(New game)');
  }
```

After some initial variable setup, which includes setting `lastMove` and `pieceList` to their respective properties (as taken from the `GameState` object that was passed in), we display the status message using `setStatusMsg`, which tells users what's going on in the game. If there was a previous move, it displays some information about that move; otherwise it just says, "New game."

## The `pieceList` Array

Next, we do the hard work—putting all the pieces into the right spots on the board. We're stepping through the items in `pieceList`, an associative array that contains a JavaScript `Object` for each piece. In this array, the number five black pawn would look like this:

```
pieceList['black_p5'] = {
  'color': 'black',
  'id': 'black_p5',
```

```
  'pos': [6,4],
  'origPos': []
};
```

The first thing we need to do is to load all of this data into a series of `Piece` objects, which we will use to control the pieces on the board.

# The Piece Class

The `Piece` class offers methods for performing tasks such as informing users that their move is being processed after they move a chess piece, and determining if a piece has moved from its original location after it's been dropped:

File: **chess.js (excerpt)**

```
function Piece(color, id, pos) {
  this.color = color;
  this.id = id;
  this.pos = pos;
  this.origPos = [];

  this.backUpPos = function() {
    this.origPos = [this.pos[0], this.pos[1]];
  };

  this.updatePos = function(colX, colY) {
    this.pos = [colX, colY];
  };

  this.restore = function() {
    this.pos = [this.origPos[0], this.origPos[1]];
  };

  this.startProcessing = function() {
    var pieceDiv = document.getElementById(this.id);
    pieceDiv.style.background = '#bbe';
    pieceDiv.style.cursor = 'progress';
    pieceDiv.style.zIndex = 10;
  };

  this.endProcessing = function() {
    var pieceDiv = document.getElementById(this.id);
    if (this.id.indexOf('white') > -1) {
      pieceDiv.style.background = '#fff';
    }
    else {
```

```
      pieceDiv.style.background = '#000';
    }
    pieceDiv.style.cursor = 'move';
    pieceDiv.style.zIndex = 5;
  };

  this.wasMoved = function(colX, colY) {
    if (colX == this.pos[0] && colY == this.pos[1]) {
      return false;
    }
    else {
      return true;
    }
  };
}
```

You can see that we've defined this class with parameters, effectively giving ourselves a constructor method for this class. We use these parameters to initialize the properties of each `Piece` in the list. We do this in the next part of `displayGame`:

File: **chess.js (excerpt)**

```
for (var i in self.pieceList) {
  piece = self.pieceList[i];
  self.pieceList[i] = new Piece(piece.color, piece.id,
      [piece.pos[0], piece.pos[1]]);
  piece = self.pieceList[i];
  label = piece.id.split('_')[1];
  label = label.substr(0,1).toUpperCase();
  pieceDiv = document.createElement('div');
  pieceDiv.id = i;
  pieceDiv.className = piece.color + 'PieceDiv';
  pieceDiv.style.width = self.pieceSize + 'px';
  pieceDiv.style.height = self.pieceSize + 'px';
  pieceDiv.style.left = self.calcPosFromCol(piece.pos[0]) +
      'px';
  pieceDiv.style.top = self.calcPosFromCol(piece.pos[1]) + 'px';
  pieceDiv.style.lineHeight = self.pieceSize + 'px';
  pieceDiv.appendChild(document.createTextNode(label));
  self.boardDiv.appendChild(pieceDiv);
}
return true;
};
```

After adding a new `Piece` to the `pieceList` array, we get the letter that identifies the piece from the piece's `id`. Remember that when we first looked at the `pieceList` array that was returned from the server, we saw that each piece was identified with a string, such as `black_p5` for the number five black pawn, or `white_k` for the white king. The code above extracts the character just after the first underscore character, converts it to uppercase, and uses it as the label for this piece.

Finally, we use DOM methods to create the `div` element for this piece and place it on the board. Part of this code sets the element's `className` to `blackPieceDiv` or `whitePieceDiv`, both of which include the declaration `position: absolute` in `chess.css`. These styles also include the declaration `cursor: move`; this gives the pieces a "move" cursor so that, when users move their cursor over the pieces, the cursor changes to indicate that users can click on and drag those pieces.

Note that, to make a label align vertically in the middle of a `div` properly, we have to set the `lineHeight` property of its `style` to the same value as its vertical height. The other interesting part of this code is the calls to the `calcPosFromCol` method, which figures out the pixel position of the piece on the board. The method below shows more of that pixel-pushing math stuff you can ignore if you're not mathematically inclined:

File: **chess.js (excerpt)**

```
this.calcPosFromCol = function(col) {
  var self = Chess;
  return (col * self.squareSize) + (self.pieceOffset - 1);
};
```

### Pushing One More Pixel

Part of the process of calculating our pieces' positions is the subtraction of one pixel. This is due to the slightly screwy CSS specs, which say that a one-pixel border on a `div` will make its actual size on the page one pixel larger. However, despite this addition, the `width` and `height` properties of its `style` do not change.

# Global Event Handlers

Now that we've loaded a game, it's time to start dragging some pieces around and playing chess.

By now, you're very familiar with the concept of DOM events, and using JavaScript to attach handlers to the events supported by the various DOM elements in your page. Some examples of technique include the ubiquitous `window.onload` event we use to start up our applications, and `element.onclick`, which will handle a mouse click on just about any element.

Using DOM events like this makes it easy to have your browser-based UI respond to user input in lots of interesting ways. However, as web applications become more complicated, so do the user interfaces. The UI needs to do more to give users the responsive, interactive experience they expect from a modern web app.

And as the interface gets more complicated, it can become increasingly difficult to keep track of the event handlers you're using, and what actually happens in your app when you click, double-click, or mouse over certain parts of your application's user interface.

# Going Global

The solution to the handler tracking problems that arise from increased UI complexity is to use global event handlers. Rather than tying event handlers to individual elements all over the page, you can create global, top-level handlers for each type of event that you want your application to handle, then route all of those events through a single handler. This handler determines what to do with each event based on the `id` of the element that triggered it. This process of routing input to the proper handling code is sometimes called **event dispatch**.

By using global event handlers, you control the flow of each type of user input through a single channel. And in the asynchronous world of AJAX programming, this is hugely helpful in managing your app's complexity, and in debugging when things go wrong.

# Handling Mouse Clicks

Let's start with the most basic example of an event dispatch: dispatching mouse clicks.

To create a mouse click dispatcher, we create a global event handler for mouse clicks by attaching a handler to `document.onmousedown`, like so:

File: **chess.js (excerpt)**

```
document.onmousedown = Chess.mouseDownHandler;
```

Now, every click of the mouse anywhere in the browser window will call the mouseDownHandler method of our Chess class. Here's the code for that method:

File: **chess.js (excerpt)**

```
this.mouseDownHandler = function(e) {
  var self = Chess;
  var id = '';
  if (self.proc) {
    return false;
  }
  if (!e) {
    e = window.event;
  }
  id = self.getSrcElemId(e);
  pat = /^(white|black)_/;
  if (pat.test(id)) {
    self.selectPiece = self.pieceList[id];
    self.dragPiece = new Draggable(id);
  }
};
```

The very first thing this code does is check to see if a move is currently processing. If the application is processing a move, the return statement will prevent users from moving any of the other pieces on the board. This is another advantage of centralizing your event handling in the one place—you can disable certain inputs from users much more easily.

Next comes some code that allows IE to see the event. You might remember from Chapter 5 that IE doesn't pass the event details as a parameter like Firefox does. Instead, it gets the event from the window.event property. The code passes the event to a method called getSrcElemId, which returns the id of the element on which the user clicked:

File: **chess.js (excerpt)**

```
this.getSrcElemId = function(e) {
  var ret = null;
  if (e.srcElement) {
    ret = e.srcElement;
  }
  else if (e.target) {
    ret = e.target;
  }
  if (ret.nodeType == 3) {
    ret = ret.parentNode;
  }
```

```
  return ret.id
};
```

This is very similar to the `getSrcElem` method we saw in Chapter 5. The last `if` statement makes sure we're not dealing with a text node. If `ret` is a text node, `ret` is set to its own parent, which will always be an element.

Once we have the `id` of the element that the user clicked on, we can decide what action to take. We use a regular expression to determine whether the `id` in question refers to one of our chess pieces. The chess pieces' `ids` will always contain either `black` or `white`.

Once `mouseDownHandler` knows that a piece was actually clicked on, it sets the `selectPiece` property to point to the piece that's currently being moved, and creates a `Draggable` object to complete the drag-and-drop procedure.

When users click on a chess piece, we don't know for sure that they want to drag the piece. Yet, on each click, we instantiate a `Draggable` object so that if they do continue to hold down the mouse button and drag the piece, we'll be ready to complete the move. We store this `Draggable` object in the `dragPiece` property of the `Chess` class so that we can reference it from the global event handlers for `mousemove` and `mouseup`. Let's take a look at these now.

# Moving Pieces

Now it's time to make our pieces move around on the board. Figure 8.3 shows a piece being dragged to a new position.

## Figure 8.3. Dragging a chess piece

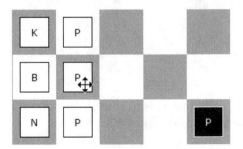

We use three events together to create our drag-and-drop functionality:

**mousedown**  As we've already seen, when a piece is clicked on, the handler for that event creates a `Draggable` object for the piece.

**mousemove**  If a `Draggable` object exists (i.e., the user has pressed the mouse button while hovering over the piece, but hasn't released it), this event's handler will move the piece's `div` around on the board to reflect the cursor's movement.

**mouseup**  If the handler for this event sees that a `Draggable` object exists, it will drop the piece into place, destroy the `Draggable` object, and save the move to the back end.

# The mousemove Handler

Every time the user moves the mouse, the `mousemove` event handler will check to see if a `Draggable` object has been created in response to a previous click. If there is a `Draggable` object in the `dragPiece` property, it knows to call the `move` method of `Draggable`, which will move the piece.

Here's the code for the `mouseMoveHandler` global event handler:

File: **chess.js (excerpt)**

```
this.mouseMoveHandler = function(e) {
  var self = Chess;
  if (e) {
    self.xPos = e.pageX;
    self.yPos = e.pageY;
  }
  else {
    self.xPos = window.event.x;
    self.yPos = window.event.y + document.body.scrollTop;
  }
  if (self.dragPiece) {
    self.dragPiece.move();
  }
};
```

The other thing we have to do when the mouse moves is to record the pointer's pixel position within the browser window in the `xPos` and `yPos` properties.

# The mouseup Handler

Here's the code for the `mouseUpHandler` global event handler:

File: **chess.js (excerpt)**

```
this.mouseUpHandler = function(e) {
  var self = Chess;
  var id = '';
  if (self.dragPiece) {
    self.dragPiece.drop();
    self.dragPiece = null;
  }
};
```

This code checks to see if a `Draggable` class has been created and, if so, does the `drop` of the piece, placing the piece in the center of the square over which it's being held. Finally, the move is saved to the back end.

After this code calls the `drop` method, it sets `dragPiece` to `null` so that the other handlers will know that we've finished dragging the piece.

# The Draggable Class

Here's the beginning of the code that creates our `Draggable` objects:

File: **chess.js (excerpt)**

```
function Draggable(divId) {
  this.div = document.getElementById(divId);
  this.clickOffsetX = (Chess.toBoardX(Chess.xPos) -
      this.div.offsetLeft);
  this.clickOffsetY = (Chess.toBoardY(Chess.yPos) -
      this.div.offsetTop);
  this.div.style.zIndex = 10;
```

Since we're going to be moving the piece's `div` around the board, we will, of course, need a reference to that `div`.

The last thing we need to do is to set that piece's `div`'s `zIndex` CSS property to a higher number than the other pieces. This makes the piece appear above all the others as you drag it around the board.

### Hyphens in CSS Properties

Some CSS properties, such as `z-index` and `font-family`, have hyphens in their names. When you're setting these properties in your JavaScript code, you must remember to change those hyphenated names to camel case. So `z-index` becomes `zIndex`, `font-family` becomes `fontFamily`, and so on.

# The Click Offset

The `clickOffsetX` and `clickOffsetY` properties are calculated when the `Draggable` object is first instantiated. They record the distance of the mouse pointer from the left and top edges of the piece when the user first clicks—a figure that's important for our pixel-pushing math. Figure 8.4 shows a graphical representation of the X and Y click offset values.

## Figure 8.4. The click offset from the left and top edges

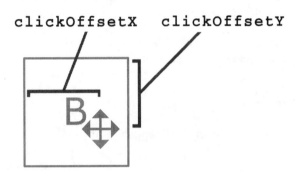

To move a piece to a new location on the screen, you set its `left` and `top` style properties, which, of course, set the position of the top-left corner of the piece's `div`. But if you set these properties to the position of the cursor, you'll find that the piece suddenly jumps so that its top left corner is positioned where the cursor is located.

To avoid this jumping effect, we add the `clickOffsetX` and `clickOffsetY` values to our positioning calculations so that, as the piece moves about, the cursor is located in the middle of it. This makes it look like your users are "grabbing" the element with the cursor and dragging it around.

# Viewport Positions and Board Positions

It's important to note that the `xPos` and `yPos` measurements are taken from the top-left corner of the browser viewport, whereas your pieces are positioned in relation to the top-left corner of the chess board `div`. Fortunately, it's very easy to calculate the mouse's position within the board based on the location of the mouse and the location of the board—we just subtract the left position of the board from the mouse's x-axis position, and the top position of the board from the mouse's y-axis position. Here are the methods we use to do it:

File: **chess.js** (excerpt)

```
this.toBoardX = function(xPos) {
  return xPos - Chess.leftPos;
};

this.toBoardY = function(yPos) {
  return yPos - Chess.topPos;
};
```

This allows us to take the values reported by the mouse as it moves, and translate them into the values we need in order to move the pieces around on the board div.

# The move Method

When users move the mouse, the global handler mouseMoveHandler checks to see if there's a Draggable object, and, if there is, it starts to move the div of the piece that's tied to the Draggable object using Draggable's move method.

Here's the move method of the Draggable class:

File: **chess.js** (excerpt)

```
this.move = function() {
  var calcX = 0;
  var calcY = 0;
  var xMin = 0;
  var xMax = 0;
  var yMin = 0;
  var yMax = 0;
  calcX = Chess.xPos - this.clickOffsetX;
  calcY = Chess.yPos - this.clickOffsetY;
  xMin = Chess.leftPos - 1;
  xMax = Chess.leftPos + Chess.boardSize - Chess.pieceSize - 1;
  yMin = Chess.topPos - 1;
  yMax = Chess.topPos + Chess.boardSize - Chess.pieceSize - 1;
  if (calcX < xMin) {
    calcX = xMin;
  }
  if (calcX > xMax) {
    calcX = xMax;
  }
```

```
  if (calcY < yMin) {
    calcY = yMin;
  }
  if (calcY > yMax) {
    calcY = yMax;
  }
  this.div.style.left = parseInt(Chess.toBoardX(calcX)) + 'px';
  this.div.style.top = parseInt(Chess.toBoardY(calcY)) + 'px';
};
```

At the start of this method, we add the offset value that keeps the piece in the right spot under the pointer as the user drags the piece around the board. If we didn't add this offset, the upper-left corner of the `div` would be sitting right under the cursor.

Next, we deal with the board constraints, and position the piece on the board. The left and top constraints are easy—they're the top and left-hand edges of the board. For the right-hand and bottom edges, we have to include the size of the piece as we figure the constraints, since we're setting the position of the piece using the left-hand and top of the game piece `div` elements. Figure 8.5 shows where the lines for the constraints are located on the board.

Once we set the minimum and maximum values for both the X and Y axes, we have to make sure the X and Y positions we're setting actually obey those constraints. We confirm this in a series of four `if` statements. Once we're sure that both `calcX` and `calcY` are within our constraints, we use those values to set the `left` and `top` properties of the `div` for the piece.

# The drop Method

The `mouseUpHandler` global handler fires whenever the user releases the mouse button. If there is a `Draggable` object, the handler calls the `drop` method of the `Draggable` class, then destroys the `Draggable` object.

The `drop` method takes care of two basic functions:

❏ the "snap-to" for the chess pieces when they're dropped on the board

❏ saving the data about the move to the back end

## Figure 8.5. Drag constraint lines on the game board

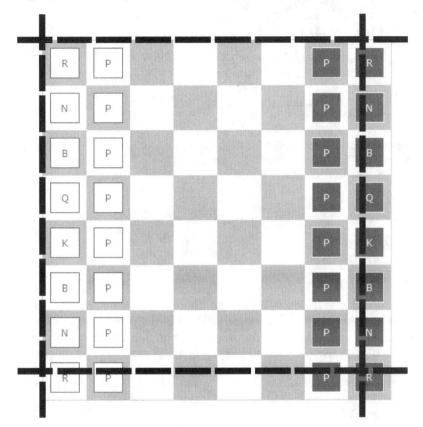

## Snap-to

You can see snap-to at work when the dragged chess piece "snaps" into place in the center of the square on which it was dropped. The snap-to happens in the drop method:

File: **chess.js (excerpt)**

```
this.drop = function() {
  var calcX = 0;
  var calcY = 0;
  var deltaX = 0;
  var deltaY = 0;
  var colX = 0;
  var colY = 0;
```

```
  calcX = this.div.offsetLeft;
  calcY = this.div.offsetTop;
  deltaX = calcX % Chess.squareSize;
  deltaY = calcY % Chess.squareSize;
  calcX = this.getSnap(deltaX, calcX);
  calcY = this.getSnap(deltaY, calcY);
  calcX = calcX + Chess.pieceOffset - 1;
  calcY = calcY + Chess.pieceOffset - 1;
  this.div.style.left = calcX + 'px';
  this.div.style.top = calcY + 'px';
  colX = Chess.calcColFromPos(calcX);
  colY = Chess.calcColFromPos(calcY);
  if (Chess.selectPiece.wasMoved(colX, colY)) {
    Chess.doMove(colX, colY);
  }
  else {
    this.div.style.zIndex = 5;
  }
  this.div = null;
};
```

The important variables to watch here are `deltaX` and `deltaY`. These are the remainders from calculations in which the X and Y mouse positions are divided by the size of a square (we get these remainders by using the modulo operator, `%`). `deltaX` and `deltaY` are the distances between the position at which the piece was dropped and the nearest edge of a square, along the X and Y axes respectively.

Once we have this number, we can figure which direction to "snap" the piece in by checking whether the number is bigger or smaller than half the height (or width) of the square. We do this using the `getSnap` method:

File: **chess.js (excerpt)**

```
this.getSnap = function(delta, pos) {
  if (delta > (Chess.squareSize / 2)) {
    pos += (Chess.squareSize - delta);
  }
  else {
    pos -= delta;
  }
  return pos;
};
```

This makes good sense if you think about it—we can work out which way the piece should jump by seeing whether it covers another square by more than half.

Once we've got the piece snapping into place, it's time to save this move to the back end in `drop`. We save our piece positions as row and column coordinates — not pixel positions — inside `Piece` objects, so we have to translate the piece's position into row and column numbers with the `calcColFromPos` method. Despite its name, this method calculates both row and column coordinates—the math involved is exactly the same regardless of whether we're talking about rows or columns. This is a short method that just divides the piece's pixel position by the size of a board square:

File: **chess.js (excerpt)**

```
this.calcColFromPos = function(pos) {
  var self = Chess;
  return parseInt(pos / self.squareSize);
};
```

Once we know the column numbers for the new piece's position, we perform a final check to make sure the player didn't drag the piece around the board and drop it right back in its original position. We perform this check with the `wasMoved` method of the `Piece` class.

The column number for each `Piece` is stored in the `pos` property. That property is a two-item array that stores the piece's coordinates on the board. The `wasMoved` method checks to make sure the values in the `pos` array have changed, like this:

File: **chess.js (excerpt)**

```
this.wasMoved = function(colX, colY) {
  if (colX == this.pos[0] && colY == this.pos[1]) {
    return false;
  }
  else {
    return true;
  }
};
```

If we can verify that yes, the piece is actually in a new spot, then it's time to go ahead and save that change to the back end. We do this with the `doMove` method in the main `Chess` class.

# The doMove Method

The `doMove` method actually takes care of updating the `pos` property of the `Piece` object that the user is moving, looks for captured pieces, then saves the changes to the back end.

Here's the first chunk of the method:

File: **chess.js (excerpt)**

```
this.doMove = function(colX, colY) {
  var self = Chess;
  var occPieceId = '';
  var cmd = null;
  var move = null;
  var err = '';
  self.selectPiece.backUpPos();
  self.selectPiece.updatePos(colX, colY);
```

# Making a Backup

Always back up your data. That's a lesson many of us have had to learn the hard way!

Before we save the move, we need to make a backup snapshot of the moved piece's original position data. We'll use this backup to put the piece back where it originally started if there's some kind of error. We use the `backupPos` method of the `Piece` to make the backup:

File: **chess.js (excerpt)**

```
this.backUpPos = function() {
  this.origPos = [this.pos[0], this.pos[1]];
};
```

That method just sets the `origPos` property to the same array values that were originally in the `pos` property.

Once we have a backup of the original position info, it's time to update the `pos` property of the `Piece` so that we can send it along to the back end to be saved. The `updatePos` method of the `Piece` class does this:

File: **chess.js (excerpt)**

```
this.updatePos = function(colX, colY) {
  this.pos = [colX, colY];
};
```

# Error Checking

The next section in the `doMove` method checks for errors, to make sure that users can't do something goofy, like capture their own pieces:

File: **chess.js** (excerpt)

```
if ((!self.lastMove.moveTime) &&
    (self.selectPiece.color == 'black')) {
  err = 'White has to go first.';
}
else if ((self.lastMove.moveTime) &&
    (self.selectPiece.color == self.lastMove.movePiece.color)) {
  err = 'Same color as previous move.';
}
else {
  occPieceId = self.getOccupyingPieceId();
  if (occPieceId.indexOf(self.selectPiece.color) > -1) {
    err = 'Cannot capture a piece of your own color.';
  }
}
```

The last section in the error-checking code also looks to see if any piece was captured. It uses the `getOccupyingPieceId` method to put the `id` of any captured piece in `Chess`'s `occPieceId` property. Here's the code for that method:

File: **chess.js** (excerpt)

```
this.getOccupyingPieceId = function() {
  var self = Chess;
  var p = null;
  for (var i in self.pieceList) {
    p = self.pieceList[i];
    if ((self.selectPiece.pos[0] == p.pos[0] &&
        self.selectPiece.pos[1] == p.pos[1]) &&
        (self.selectPiece.id != p.id)) {
      return p.id;
    }
  }
  return '';
};
```

If the square is unoccupied, the method just returns an empty string, which tells us that no piece has been captured.

# Aborting the Move on Error

If there is an error, we alert the user and put the piece back where it was. This is what happens in the next bit of `doMove`:

File: **chess.js (excerpt)**

```
if (err) {
  self.setErrMsg(err);
  self.abortMove();
}
```

The abortMove method puts the div for the piece back where it was, and restores the X and Y column data to the pos property for the piece from its origPos backup:

File: **chess.js (excerpt)**

```
this.abortMove = function() {
  var self = Chess;
  var pieceDiv = document.getElementById(self.selectPiece.id);
  pieceDiv.style.left = self.calcPosFromCol(
    self.selectPiece.origPos[0]) + 'px';
  pieceDiv.style.top = self.calcPosFromCol(
    self.selectPiece.origPos[1]) + 'px';
  self.selectPiece.restore();
};
```

It's always good to have a backup of your data. The restore method of the Piece class restores the pos property values from the backup copy stored in origPos:

File: **chess.js (excerpt)**

```
this.restore = function() {
  this.pos = [this.origPos[0], this.origPos[1]];
};
```

You can see this abortMove action at work if you try to capture one of your own pieces, or try to move out of turn.

# Saving the Move

If there are no errors, we can proceed to save the move to the app's back end. This makes up the remainder of doMove:

File: **chess.js (excerpt)**

```
  else {
    clearTimeout(self.pollInterval);
    self.ajax.abort();
    self.setErrMsg('');
    move = new Move(self.selectPiece, occPieceId);
    cmd = new Command('move', move);
```

```
    var str = JSON.stringify(cmd);
    self.execCmd(str, self.handleMove);
    self.proc = true;
    self.selectPiece.startProcessing();
  }
};
```

In the next section, we'll be talking about the polling process that keeps the game state displayed in the browser in sync with the back end. It's a process that runs continuously, hitting the server every five seconds and looking for the other player's moves. We don't want to be checking for those moves while processing our own move, so the first step in the process of saving the changes is to turn that polling process off, using `clearTimeout` on the `pollInterval` property that has the ID for that process.

Then, after clearing out any error messages that might be showing, we can go ahead and package up the move data to send to the server. Given JSON's ability to send objects back and forth between the app and the server easily, it makes sense to package up the data in a class called `Move`:

File: **chess.js (excerpt)**

```
function Move(movePiece, takePieceId, moveTime) {
  this.movePiece = movePiece || null;
  this.takePieceId = takePieceId || '';
  this.moveTime = moveTime || '';
}
```

The `movePiece` property is the `Piece` object for the moved piece, while `takePieceId` is the `id` of any captured piece. If there's no captured piece, the value is an empty string. We leave the `moveTime` property empty right now. That property is going to be set by the server, then passed back in another JSON string. It really is amazing how easy JSON makes it to pass objects back and forth between the browser and the server.

Once the `Move` object is all set up, we set it as the `cmdData` property of the `Command` object we're sending back to the server. It's then time to encode the `Command` object as a JSON string and pass it to the server.

The last thing we need to do is set the `proc` property of the `Chess` object to `true` so that we know to disable all user input while the move is processing, and to give the piece an appearance that indicates that it's in a "processing" state. We do that with the `startProcessing` method of the `Piece` object that's being moved:

File: **chess.js (excerpt)**

```
this.startProcessing = function() {
  var pieceDiv = document.getElementById(this.id);
  pieceDiv.style.background = '#bbe';
  pieceDiv.style.cursor = 'progress';
  pieceDiv.style.zIndex = 10;
};
```

The "progress" cursor style lends a very nice effect to the move: when the user drops a piece onto the board, the cursor turns into the "Just a moment please" cursor that makes it very obvious that something's happening to the piece. Figure 8.6 shows what this cursor looks like.

### Figure 8.6. Processing a move with the "progress" cursor

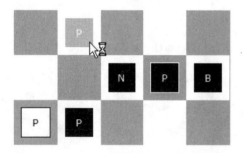

# The handleMove Method

The handler for the server response that's returned after a piece is moved is the handleMove method. If the server sends back a response with ok in its respStatus property, the code will look into respData for the updated lastMove object that the server has passed back.

This is a Move object exactly like the one we just passed to the server; however, the server has added the moveTime property so that we know when the last move actually happened. We're setting moveTime over on the server side so that people in multiple timezones can play AJAX Chess and all the move times will be correct. If we let the browser set moveTime, moves made by a girl on the west coast of the US would appear to have occurred four hours previously to a guy playing on the east coast.

Here's the code for handleMove:

File: **chess.js** (excerpt)

```
this.handleMove = function(str) {
  var self = Chess;
  var take = '';
  var takeDiv = null;
  var resp = JSON.parse(str);
  if (resp.respStatus == 'ok') {
    self.lastMove = resp.respData.lastMove;
    self.setStatusMsg(self.lastMove.movePiece.color,
        self.lastMove.moveTime);
    take = self.lastMove.takePieceId;
    if (take) {
      takeDiv = document.getElementById(take);
      self.boardDiv.removeChild(takeDiv);
      delete self.pieceList[take];
    }
  }
  else {
    alert(resp.respDatastr);
    self.abortMove();
  }
  self.selectPiece.endProcessing();
  self.proc = false;
  self.doPollDelay();
};
```

The handleMove method takes the updated Move object that's sent from the server, and uses it to set the status message in the panel above the board; this way, users know when the last move was made, and which color (or player) took the last turn.

Next, the code takes care of removing the captured piece (if there was one). We have to remove both the div that represents the piece on the board, and the Piece object in the pieceList.

The rest of the code deals with what to do in an error condition—if the server couldn't save the move for some reason, for example—and the cleanup that occurs after the move finishes. Once the move has been successfully saved on the server, we have to put the appearance of the piece back to normal using the Piece's endProcessing method:

File: **chess.js** (excerpt)

```
this.endProcessing = function() {
  var pieceDiv = document.getElementById(this.id);
  if (this.id.indexOf('white') > -1) {
```

```
     pieceDiv.style.background = '#fff';
  }
  else {
    pieceDiv.style.background = '#000';
  }
  pieceDiv.style.cursor = 'move';
  pieceDiv.style.zIndex = 5;
};
```

It also sets the proc property of the Chess object to false so that the global event handler for mouse clicks knows to start accepting user input again.

Lastly, the handleMove method starts up the polling process to keep the game state on the browser in sync with what's happening on the server. When the other player makes a move, the board will update so that we can see the new move.

# Polling for Server State

Playing chess all by yourself isn't that fun, and if you want to play with someone in the same location, you might as well dust off that old board in your closet and use real pieces. There's not much point having a web application if you don't take advantage of that fact that it's available over the Web.

AJAX Chess can be played by people in two different locations, as long as they're both pointing their browsers to the same server. (Actually, more than just two players can access the running game at any time, which means you can let your friends watch you play, or cheat by getting a friend who's good at chess to help you out!)

We keep all the browsers that are talking to the game in sync using a doPoll method that is called on a timer to poll the server and get the updated game state. The init method in the Chess class sets up this timer by calling the doPollDelay method.

Just like in the monitoring applications we built in Chapter 2 and Chapter 3, we only want a polling request to start when the current one completes. We achieve this by chaining the requests together with setTimeout—when a request finishes, it calls another setTimeout to perform another request after a short pause.

Here's the code for doPollDelay:

File: **chess.js (excerpt)**

```
this.doPollDelay = function() {
  var self = Chess;
  self.pollInterval = setTimeout(self.doPoll,
      REFRESH_INTERVAL * 1000);
};
```

The `setTimeout` call uses the `REFRESH_INTERVAL` constant to set the wait time that will elapse before the `doPoll` method that polls the server is run. We store the interval ID for the `setTimeout` process in the `pollInterval` property—as we saw earlier in the discussion of the `doMove` method, we pass this value to `clearTimeout` in order to stop the polling process while we save a move, so that the browser isn't trying to sync the game state at the same time as it's saving a move.

Here's the `doPoll` method:

File: **chess.js (excerpt)**

```
this.doPoll = function() {
  var self = Chess;
  var str = '';
  var cmd = new Command();
  cmd.cmdName = 'poll';
  cmd.cmdData = self.lastMove;
  str = JSON.stringify(cmd);
  self.execCmd(str, self.handlePoll);
};
```

The `doPoll` method sends a `poll` `Command` object to the server, along with the `Move` stored in the `lastMove` property, which the server compares with the most recent move.

The `handlePoll` method deals with the response from the server:

File: **chess.js (excerpt)**

```
this.handlePoll = function(str) {
  var self = Chess;
  var resp = JSON.parse(str);
  if (resp.respStatus == 'update') {
    self.clearPieces();
    self.displayGame(resp.respData);
  }
  self.doPollDelay();
};
```

If the `respStatus` property of the server's response is `update`, we know to clear the board with the `clearPieces` method, then update the board using the updated game state in the `respData` property of the server's response. This data is stored in the format we used in the application's initial load via the `loadGame` and `handleLoadGame` methods, and we display the updated game state the same way—with the `displayGame` method.

Otherwise, if there's been no change to the state of the game since our last move, the code does nothing.

The last thing that the handler does here is call the `doPollDelay` method again; this will set up another call to this method once the polling interval has passed.

# Wiping the Board

If you're finished with a game—or maybe you're just losing really badly—you may want to wipe the board and start over. Figure 8.7 shows the board after it's been wiped.

If you click that shiny Wipe Board button at the top of the app, you'll call the `wipeBoard` method that clears the board and resets it for a new game.

Here's the code for `wipeBoard`:

File: **chess.js (excerpt)**

```
this.wipeBoard = function() {
  var self = Chess;
  var str = '';
  var cmd = new Command('wipe');
  str = JSON.stringify(cmd);
  self.execCmd(str, self.handleWipeBoard);
};
```

`wipeBoard` sends back to the server a `Command` object with the `cmdName` of `wipe`, and sets the handler for the server response to be `handleWipeBoard`:

File: **chess.js (excerpt)**

```
this.handleWipeBoard = function(str) {
  var self = Chess;
  var resp = JSON.parse(str);
  if (resp.respStatus == 'ok') {
    self.clearPieces();
    self.displayGame(resp.respData);
```

## Figure 8.7. A fresh game on the board after wiping

```
  }
  else {
    alert(resp.respDatastr);
  }
};
```

The server responds with a JSON-encoded string of a clean game board. The code for handleWipeBoard parses it into the list of pieces and positions and we display it with the displayGame method, just as we do after a move or on initial application load.

# AJAX Chess Back End

The back-end processing page included in the code archive is a PHP page, called `chess.php`, which stores the game state in a flat text file, `chessboard.txt`. To allow the application to save the game state to the text file, you'll need to make sure your web server has write permissions for the `chessboard.txt` file. You'll also need the "proposed" PHP PEAR package Services_JSON, which, as of this writing, is downloadable from the PEAR web site.[4] All you'll need to do is make the `JSON.php` file available to your application.

As with all the examples in this book, you could implement a back end for this chess game in any language for which a JSON library is available—PHP, Ruby, Perl, Python, Java, or even Lisp. The beauty of using JSON is that your JavaScript code doesn't have to know anything about how the back end is implemented—it just hands off JavaScript objects to the server, and gets JavaScript objects right back.

The processing page is fairly straightforward PHP, but you might want to have a look at it if you're interested to see how you can use JSON to apply the same objects on both the front and back ends of your web application.

# Future Enhancements

If you've played around with the code archive, you can see that AJAX Chess is far from being fully-featured. There are many things that you could do to make this game more playable:

❏ You could add some pretty graphics to replace the boring letter shortcuts I used to show which piece is which.

❏ Right now, the app doesn't care if you jump your bishop over all the pieces on the board and take your opponent's king. Error-checking for moves that are legal for the piece in question, and moves that are blocked on the board, would be really helpful.

❏ You could have the app keep a record of each move so observers could replay the game, and you could optimize the synchronization process so that it doesn't have to re-send the entire board each time a move is made.

---

[4] http://pear.php.net/pepr/pepr-proposal-show.php?id=198

❑ You could add an "undo move" feature (although we always played by the rule that once you took your hand off the moved piece, there was no going back on it).

❑ You could connect the app's back end to a chess engine like GNU chess.

❑ You could add a chat feature to allow taunting of your opponents!

# Summary

This AJAX Chess game provides a good example of how we can create and place a complex set of user interface elements in the browser window. The global event handlers we used to implement the drag-and-drop functionality are a smart way to manage the more complicated interactivity that is inherent in more sophisticated web UIs. We also got a small taste of what it's like to deal with shared, browser-based access to data via the AJAX Chess game board, and saw a simple way of synchronizing your clients using polling, so they can all see the same thing at roughly the same time.

With the basic techniques you've learned here, you'll be well-equipped to begin taking your web applications to the next level—creating super-responsive, super-interactive AJAX apps that push the boundaries of what's possible on the Web.

# Appendix A: AJAX Toolkits

Although AJAX is only in its infancy, there are already many useful and stable JavaScript libraries that can help your AJAX development. This appendix is a list of some of the best libraries available at the time of writing, but, as with any new technology, new libraries are bound to appear. To stay up to date with latest developments, be sure to subscribe to SitePoint's *Tech Times* email newsletter[1] and *Stylish Scripting*,[2] SitePoint's DHTML and CSS blog.

## AjaxTK[3]

AjaxTK is an AJAX-toolkit component library that features a very large and comprehensive widget set. AjaxTK is used in Zimbra, a recently released client/server open-source email system.

## Dojo[4]

Dojo lets you build prototype versions of interactive widgets quickly, animate transitions, and make AJAX requests with powerful and easy-to-use abstractions. These capabilities are built on top of a lightweight packaging system and optional build tools that help you develop quickly and optimize transparently.

## JSON-RPC[5]

JSON-RPC is a remote procedure call protocol that's encoded in JSON. It's a very simple protocol, with only a handful of data types and commands.

## MochiKit[6]

"MochiKit makes JavaScript suck less"—so says the MochiKit web site. MochiKit is a highly documented and well-tested suite of JavaScript libraries that helps developers get their work done fast. MochiKit incorporates the best ideas from Python, Objective-C, and others, and adapts them for use in JavaScript.

---

[1] http://www.sitepoint.com/newsletter/
[2] http://www.sitepoint.com/blogs/category/dhtml-css/
[3] http://www.zimbra.com/
[4] http://dojotoolkit.org/
[5] http://json-rpc.org/
[6] http://www.mochikit.com/

## Moo.fx[7]
## Moo.ajax[8]

Moo.fx is a super-lightweight, ultra-tiny, mega-small JavaScript effects library written with Prototype. Moo.ajax is a very simple AJAX class designed for use with Prototype.lite from moo.fx.

## Prototype[9]

Prototype is a JavaScript framework that aims to ease the development of dynamic web applications. It includes a unique, easy-to-use toolkit for class-driven development and an AJAX library. Its development is driven heavily by the Ruby on Rails framework, but it can be used in any environment.

## Rico[10]

Rico is an open-source JavaScript library for creating rich Internet applications. Rico provides full AJAX support, drag-and-drop management, and a cinematic effects library. Sabre Airline Solutions is a corporate contributor.

## Sajax[11]

Sajax is an open-source toolkit that aims to make programming web sites using AJAX as easy as possible. Sajax makes it easy to call PHP, Perl, or Python functions from your web pages using AJAX.

## Sarissa[12]

Sarissa is a JavaScript library that acts as a cross-browser wrapper for native XML APIs. It offers various XML-related goodies like document instantiation, XML loading from URLs or strings, XSLT transformations, XPath queries, and so on.

## Script.aculo.us[13]

Script.aculo.us is a set of JavaScript libraries, built on top of the Prototype framework, that provide "Web 2.0"-style interactivity such as visual effects, auto-completion, drag-and-drop, and in-place editing. A lot of the more advanced AJAX support in Ruby on Rails uses this library.

---

[7] http://moofx.mad4milk.net/
[8] http://www.mad4milk.net/entry/moo.ajax
[9] http://prototype.conio.net/
[10] http://openrico.org/
[11] http://www.modernmethod.com/sajax/
[12] http://sarissa.sourceforge.net/
[13] http://script.aculo.us/

### Spry[14]

Coming from Adobe Systems' labs, Spry is a JavaScript AJAX framework targeted to users of web development tools like Dreamweaver. Even by the standards of AJAX—which is only just over a year old—Spry is a new player in the field of AJAX toolkits, but with the backing of a huge corporation in Adobe it should become a major player in the field.

### Yahoo! UI Library[15]

The Yahoo! UI (YUI) Library is a set of open-source JavaScript widgets you can use to build AJAX-style web applications. This library comes with some excellent documentation, and is used extensively in Yahoo!'s Design Pattern Library, a series of documents that explain how to build highly dynamic user interfaces.

---

[14] http://labs.adobe.com/technologies/spry/
[15] http://developer.yahoo.com/yui/

# Index

## H

handleErr property, XMLHttpRequest object, 26
handleLoadGame method, Chess class, 253, 278
handleLoginResp method, 109
handleMove method, Chess class, 274
handlePoll method, Chess class, 277
handleResp method
    Client class, 184, 187
    Search class, 218, 226–227, 229
handleSave method, Blog class, 156
handleTimeout method, 54–55, 57
handleWipeBoard method, Chess class, 278
hash, web addresses, 235, 237
hidden iframes, 4, 13, 129, 237
history menu, multi web service search, 240
HTML and AJAX, 33
HTTP
    (*see also* GET requests; POST requests)
    case-sensitivity of requests, 18
    proxy scripts and, 178
    REST protocol and, 169
    status codes, 24
HTTP_Request module, 179, 209, 211
hyphens, 263

## I

IBM Home Page Reader, 118, 120, 125
id attributes
    dangers of changing, 162
    global event handlers, 259
    locating div elements, 139
If-Modified-Since headers, 34
iframe elements, 10, 193, 236
    hidden iframes, 4, 13, 129, 237
IIS web servers, 31
images, positioning, 188

inheritance model, JavaScript, 38
init methods
    Ajax class, 16
    Blog class, 134, 136
    Chess class, 246
    Client class, 176
    Login class, 95, 121
    Monitor class, 48
    Search class, 202, 235
    XMLHttpRequest object, 16
innerHTML property
    blog page example, 141, 143, 148
    DOM method alternative, 10, 36
    multi web service search, 222–223
    single web service search, 187
    when to use, 208, 222
insertBefore method, Blog class, 160
insertEntryDiv method, Blog class, 159
Internet Explorer
    browser Back button fix, 235–237
    event handling, 138, 260
    GET request caching, 34, 182
    IBM Home Page Reader and, 120
    memory leaks, 71, 95
    opacity setting, 73

## J

JavaScript
    Date objects, 97
    debugging tools, 195
    DOM API, 10
    hyphen conversion, 263
    object creation, 14, 253, 257
    object model, 38
    objects from XML, 186, 219
    role in AJAX, 12
    screen readers and, 117
    separating code from markup, 37
    toolkits, 193, 234, 283
    users without, 97, 223, 233
    YAML parsing in, 155

## O

object literal notation, 253
object orientation, 14, 38, 44
onbeforeunload event listener, 192
onkeyup event, 100–101, 125, 206
online resources (*see* resources)
onreadystate event handler, 28
onreadystatechange event handler, 19, 23, 26
opacity setting, 72
open method, XMLHttpRequest class, 18, 87
OpenSSL encryption, 241
overrideMimeType method, XMLHttpRequest class, 25, 184

## P

page partials, 60, 97
pagination, 164, 240
parse method, JSON, 252, 254
parseYamlResult method, Blog class, 155
parsing XML, 186–187
PEAR repository
    HTTP_Request module, 179, 209
    Services_JSON library, 252, 280
    SOAP module, 212–213
PHP code
    blog-process.php, 152, 154
    chess.php, 280
    login page example, 105
    Services_JSON and, 252
    simulating response delays, 31
    use within this book, 32
    webservices2_proxy.php, 209–210, 212, 216
PHP Extension and Application Repository (*see* PEAR repository)
Piece class, chess example, 256
pixel-based positioning, 258
placeBoard method, Chess class, 247

placeholder IDs, 152, 158, 160, 162
placeholder pages, 237
placePanel method, Chess class, 249
pollArray property, Monitor class, 58
polling process, 273
    application monitor example, 48
    chess game example, 247, 276–278
    processing animation, 80
pollServerStart method, 53, 66
pollServerStop method, 66
pop method, 59
pop-up blocking, 27
positioning images, 188
positioning pieces, chess game, 258, 264, 267
POST requests, 85
    formData2QueryString library, 89
    login page example, 103
    SOAP and, 208
    when to use, 86
    XMLHttpRequest send method and, 21
    XML-RPC and, 170, 208
postData property, 87
printResult method, 35, 59–60
processing animations (*see* status notification)
progressive enhancement, 90, 201
promptInterval property, 108
prompts, editable text, 135
properties, adding, 14
properties, CSS, 263
protocols
    (*see also* HTTP)
    network-centric and app-centric, 171
    web services and, 169–172, 199
prototype-based inheritance, 38
proxy scripts, 178, 207–208, 217
pulsing status animation, 68

# Books for Web Developers
# from SitePoint

Visit http://www.sitepoint.com/books/
for sample chapters or to order!

sitepoint

*Build Your Own*

# Database Driven Website

## Using PHP & MySQL

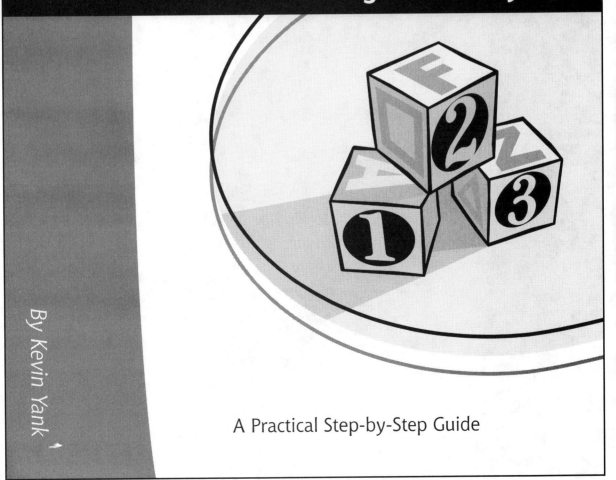

By Kevin Yank

A Practical Step-by-Step Guide

# The *PHP* Anthology

# *Object Oriented PHP Solutions*

## *Volume I*

By Harry Fuecks

Practical Solutions to Common Problems

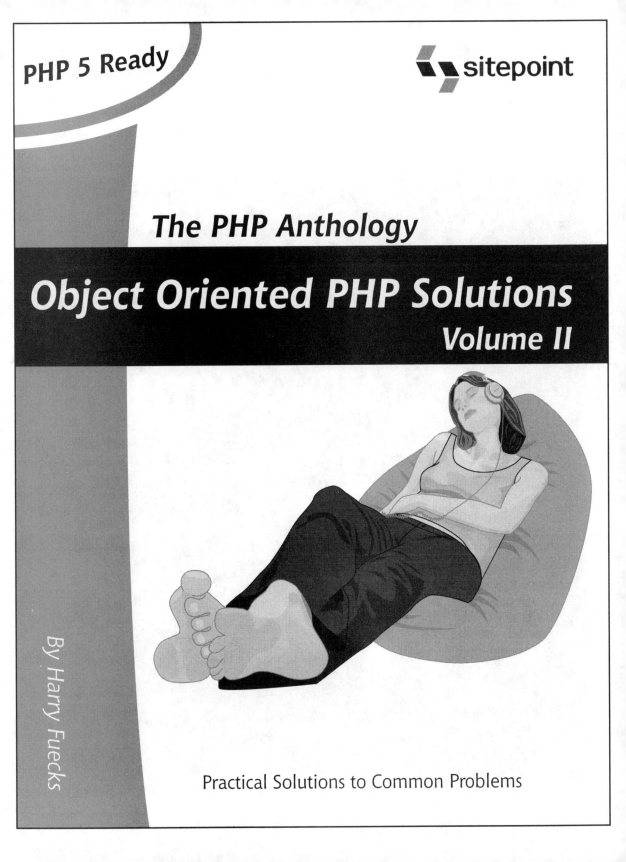

# NO NONSENSE
# XML WEB
# DEVELOPMENT
## WITH PHP

### BY THOMAS MYER

MASTER PHP 5'S POWERFUL NEW XML FUNCTIONALITY

# RUN YOUR OWN
# WEB SERVER
## USING
## LINUX & APACHE

### BY STUART LANGRIDGE
### & TONY STEIDLER-DENNISON

GET STARTED WITH LINUX AND APACHE — THE EASY WAY!

# BUILD YOUR OWN
# ASP.NET
# WEBSITE
# USING
# C# & VB.NET

## BY ZAK RUVALCABA

THE ULTIMATE ASP.NET BEGINNER'S GUIDE

sitepoint®

# HTML UTOPIA:
# DESIGNING
# WITHOUT
# TABLES
# USING CSS

BY **RACHEL ANDREW**
**& DAN SHAFER**

THE ULTIMATE BEGINNER'S GUIDE TO CSS

# THE CSS ANTHOLOGY

## 101 ESSENTIAL TIPS, TRICKS & HACKS

### BY RACHEL ANDREW

THE MOST COMPLETE QUESTION AND ANSWER BOOK ON CSS

# DHTML UTOPIA:
# MODERN
# WEB DESIGN
# USING
# JAVASCRIPT & DOM

## BY STUART LANGRIDGE

# THE JAVASCRIPT ANTHOLOGY

## 101 ESSENTIAL TIPS, TRICKS & HACKS

BY **JAMES EDWARDS**
**& CAMERON ADAMS**

THE MOST COMPLETE QUESTION AND ANSWER BOOK ON JAVASCRIPT

# BUILD YOUR OWN
# STANDARDS COMPLIANT WEBSITE
# USING DREAMWEAVER 8

## BY RACHEL ANDREW

A PRACTICAL STEP-BY-STEP GUIDE TO MASTERING DREAMWEAVER 8

Flash
MX 2004

sitepoint

## The Flash Anthology

# Cool Effects &
# Practical ActionScript

By Steven Grosvenor

Practical Solutions to Common Problems